What they are saying about Grandpa's Diary

Grandpa's Diary, the story of Schreuder's life journey from a small farm in Montana to the urban landscapes of cities and his experiences as a noted FBI Special Agent is framed with humor, fascinating stories and characters of both farm and FBI life. It is told with compassion, humor, and unflinching honesty. It's truly a memoir that begs the reader to savor each and every page. *Roberta Williams, Carson City, Nevada*

Adam Jacob Schreuder exposes his Grandfather's diary. I knew the "grandpa" when he was a kid, as we grew up and went to school together; so I could tell some good tales not included in Grandpa's Diary. He always was, and still is an adventuresome soul. A spirited guy, he got into and out of mischief on a regular basis, always using humor to get himself through the rough times. We are fortunate to have the diary opened for all to read. *Judy Rhoads, Cody, WY.*

I found Grandpa's Diary very hard to put down. The history, humor and sadness were presented in detail but with respect to his associates and the citizens he served in his career. *Dan Monica, Englewood, Florida.*

I met Dory ("Grandpa"), in San Diego where we were both working for the FBI. He was an Agent, dictating reports to me, a steno. During a break, we discovered we were family cousins. We had a mutual uncle, a cattle broker, affectionately referred to as "Horse thief Harry" who lived in Billings Montana. Conversation led us to realize we previously met at a family reunion when I was five years old. I was proud to read "Grandpa's

Diary." His grandson's decision to write this book was so right because everyone deserves to know Dory. He was what the FBI stands for...Fidelity, Bravery, and Integrity. *Vicki L. (Hemping) Hudak, Sykesville, Maryland*

Awesome! From the first page, I was immediately drawn into this interesting journey through Schreuder"s life. The book is full of wonderful and humorous stories from his life on a Montana farm, to his exciting career as an FBI Agent. I was completely drawn into the places, surroundings, and incidents. These stories are sure to stay with readers long after putting the book down. *Helen P. Owens, Columbia Maryland.*

Grandpa's Diary

Grandpa's Diary

From Country Boy to Counter Spy

ADAM J. SCHREUDER

This book is a work of non-fiction. Most of it is taken verbatim from the diary and scrap books of my Grandfather Dorwin Schreuder. Grandpa wrote about his life only to inform his descendants of "What it was like to be me." Many of the names have been changed to protect the innocent and at times to deny notoriety to the vile. His respected friends are often referred to with their rightful name. All character judgments, criticisms and opinions are the opinions of my Grandfather only, and should not be interpreted as substantiated fact. I have published these stories with his permission, because they, his ancestors, and he, are part of American History, and should be shared by more than my cousins and me.

To all of Grandpa's friends.
May you endure in life as you have in his memories.

Contents

Preface

What kind of a person would publish his grandfather's diary? What kind of a grandfather would write a diary he expected others to read?

In the introduction of part one my Grandfather, Dorwin Schreuder explains why he wrote the diary. But he had no plan to ever publish it. I, being his oldest grandchild was the first to discover his writing and believed his stories were too great to remain buried in his journals.

Grandpa's writing was discovered in a unique way that is a story in itself. It is not as he might say, "A two beer story", but is quite relevant to its publication.

In late 2009, I left California for Montana to start my college education. To save money, it was decided that I would move in with Grandpa Dory and Grandma Patty for at least my freshman year. I got my first job as a McDonald's cashier, working nights after class. My schedule didn't allow for much free time, so instead of going out after work, I often went back to my Grandparents house to study for the next day.

As every student knows, as soon as it's time to study, it's time to start looking for distractions. Luckily for me, my

Grandfather's house was unexplored territory, and thus full of distractions. One evening I decided to rummage through some old boxes in the spare bedroom. In truth, I was vainly in search of some old baby pictures of myself, hoping to take a stroll down nostalgia lane. What I found instead was much more captivating. Aged scrap books bulging with old newspaper clippings, blaring ominous yet fascinating headlines like "FBI Arrests 'Most Wanted' Fugitive On Jail Visit" and "Neo-Nazi Says Group Planned to Kill Prominent Men", hid in the boxes. I completely forgot about studying and baby pictures, and dove into reading about my Grandfathers more notable cases in the FBI. The more I read, the more I wanted to know.

The next night, my studies were neglected again as I got home from work and went straight for another box of memorabilia. This time, I knew what I was looking for, and tore through the boxes like a little kid who can't wait to get to the Cracker Jack prize at the bottom. This time I found more newspaper articles and a picture of my Grandfather in his early thirties, donning a full red beard. I couldn't believe it! I'd never seen so much as a five 'o clock shadow on his face, let alone a—

"Find anything good?" My Grandfather suddenly asked, breaking the silence that I had been sitting in for an hour or so.

I must have appeared to jump clear out of my skin, because he immediately laughed at my reaction (Grandpa and I still fall over laughing when we startle each other, it never gets old). I could feel my face blush with embarrassment and shame… after all; I had been caught red-handed snooping through his stuff. As I was mentally composing my apology, his tired expression turned into one of exhilaration.

"You know, I've got a box of old projection slides, and probably some other articles in the shop basement. I'd have to comb through them first though, to make sure there's nothing gruesome or incriminating." He opened another box, and pulled out a stack of black notebooks, something that I probably would have looked past had I continued snooping alone. "I also used to keep my own journal off and on for a number of years, but it's just personal stuff that probably wouldn't interest you much."

He couldn't have been more wrong. I was already hooked on his past after reading a handful of articles, but to read the first-hand account of these events would be the real deal. Over the next few weeks, my Grandfather combed through his old writings, making sure, out of respect, to keep the names of the innocent protected. When it was finally my turn to read them after weeks of anticipation, I did very little else until I completed the last notebook.

Although I knew I was reading my Grandfather's personal accounts, I read each notebook as if it were a part of a series of novels. The stories were fascinating, composed with humor and passion. I felt I had stumbled upon the undiscovered holy grail of my surname, and grew prouder of my kinship with each turned page. The man who slept in the room above mine my freshman year in college became the hero in my new favorite collection of short stories.

I could tell my Grandfather was flattered that I had taken such an interest in his past, and I was grateful he agreed to share it with me. However, it raised a solemn question in my mind. Would my little cousins ever get to know the type of man their grandfather is? What about my own father and two uncles, would they ever know about the events that essentially shaped their father? My concerns quickly escalated outside the familial wall as I thought, "Shouldn't everybody read about the incredible things that this man has done?" The answer to this question ultimately brought this book into being.

It is important to present my Grandfather's writing in its original form, without editing. You will get to know him as you read his history. But I must share my admiration with a few personal ramblings.

The man who wrote this diary was also an electrician, a plumber, a carpenter and cabinet maker, a building contractor, a businessman, an international athlete, a security consultant and I can even remember a time where Grandpa left for work, only to have Grandma point him out on television as a security agent for the Portland Trail Blazers. For fun he played electric bass in a Rock and Roll Band and an accordion in a Polka Band. He was known for his problem solving abilities, within the family and throughout his many friends. Even now, we still favor Grandpa's advice when it comes to tough life decisions.

Working with him, I have learned enough to warrant a whole new book. Presented here are the grass roots historical stories recalling Dorwin Schreuder's life, from ages zero to seventy, or what we can hopefully refer to as the 'first half' of his life. For those readers who reach the end of this book wanting more, as I'm sure most of you will, worry not; there's more to tell perhaps in the second half.

Let us begin.

Introduction by Grandpa Dorwin Schreuder

My father, Jake Schreuder, died in 2006 at age 94. After he was gone, it was as if we had burned a library. He was known all over Yellowstone County for his knowledge and recollection of local history. When the descendants of Montana pioneers would inquire in the local town of Worden, Montana, concerning geography and locations of where their ancestors resided, they would usually be sent to my Dad for information. He would often take the family tree builders to the places where their ancestors once lived, and frequently gave them a description of "the old folks"; complete with personal stories of their activities. He claimed to know almost everyone in the area when he was young, and with the help of his father, often had business and personal contact with them.

Dad detested writing about anything, and was too humble to cooperate in recording his stories. Thankfully he repeated many of them until I recall his words. But who will remember his stories and mine after my earthly departure? At the insistence of my children and of a few close friends, I considered putting some of these historical memories on paper with a little more detail than contained in my daily journal notes. After attending my 50th class reunion, I decided to write a more complete diary; something I could pass on to my surviving family.

I began to write about simple childhood events and a few unusual work stories. I should explain that for many years, agents of the FBI were required to maintain a daily log, on which every event, interview, and travel were hand recorded. They were not recorded in detail, but served as a reminder of the events of that day. I saved almost 30 years of these logs, and other similar appointment calendars. The logs became a fool proof memory bank. I even preserved them so that someday I might entertain myself by looking up what I did on some specific day in 19??

When I really got into the project, I intended to emphasize the family history, because the diary was meant for my descendants. But eventually I could not resist regressing to stories from my work. The diary became a mixture of both.

Samuel Clemens (Mark Twain) wrote in his autobiography that "anyone who says he didn't lie in writing his autobiography is a damn liar." After writing his own autobiography he insisted that it not be published until 100 years after he died. He opined the delay would allow him to tell the truth without either being embarrassed, ashamed, or hurting others. I understand his dilemma. He also wrote, "You never know how much enjoyment you have lost until you get to dictating your autobiography." I began this diary as a hobby. In its current form, it is definitely abridged. Perhaps as I get older, I will have the fortitude to tell "the rest of the story."

The stories are told just as they are remembered. I have tried to be accurate in all aspects, however out of respect to my friends, and some people who would prefer to remain un-named; I have renamed many of the participants. Good friends have retained their names. Friends whom I have lost track of, casual acquaintances, and villains have been renamed. Wherever my memory has been fuzzy, I have consulted with associates to fill in the gaps. Unfortunately I find that most of them have forgotten more than I have. By the time these pages are worn and soiled, no one but the diary will remember. Most importantly, I assure all who have the patience to plod here, this is not a diary of fiction. It is in a few parts, as I have been told, and in others as I have lived it.

THE BEGINNING

My early days spring out of my memory with quick visual and auditory glimpses of the past that place me with remarkable reality back in the beginning of my life. Some scenes are still vivid enough to allow me to step back into "Technicolor" re-enactment. At times I have doubted the accuracy of some of those recollections but have reviewed old photos, inspected old clothing, and even returned to the places of their origin. I have also consulted others to test my memories and have often found that the places have been changed more by time than the memories. I no longer doubt these images. Satisfied that memories are not yet being replaced by hallucinations, I now accept remembering detail as just something that I am able to do. I don't mean to imply that I have extraordinary talent for remembering, because I cannot remember the number of my own cell phone, much less the phone numbers of my children. However I am able to re-insert myself into past scenes. Like faded flowers, the visions drop fragile petals, but their color and fragrance still lingers.

How do I remember color? I don't know, but it's always an important part of how I see events of the past. I remember a day in March 1960 when four of my high school friends and I traveled in my 1949 Oldsmobile to the High School Basketball tournament in Billings Montana. On that day the girl who sat next to me as I drove wore a light blue sweater approximately the same color of my car. One of the other girls wore dark red. Although I remember conversations from that day, I have lost the details of the sports contest. My first grade teacher, on my first day of school, wore a short sleeved pink dress with black piping around the neck and sleeve openings. I also remember my interaction with her on that day. I strode into the room alone, in great fear of my life. She asked my name, looked me over and said, "Well you're a nice big boy, I think you will fit into one of these desks toward the back of the room." I tried the desk on for size, and got her approval. After I put my new pencils in the desk, she said I should go outside and play with the other kids until I heard "the bell ring." I shrank in the direction of the playground.

As I write this I am two months from being 69 years old. I met my first grade teacher, Miss Davidson, later known as Mrs. Bartley, about 9 months ago. If she was 20 years old during our first encounter, she is now 82. She remembered me, but not the dress. It was her first day of school as a teacher and my first day as a student. She was unable to confirm my still vivid views. I wish that she could have.

I don't know how old I was when I got out of the yard. My mother said I was three years old or less. She was often sick, and on that day was resting in the only bedroom of the cottonwood log house we knew as home. I was confined with our collie dog, in a large fenced yard. The yard was a grassy enclosure bordered by huge cottonwood trees. The fence was of course a Montana sheep fence of "woven wire" supported by irregular cedar posts scavenged from the hills across the river. The fence was designed to keep little kids in while keeping sheep, cows, chickens and river animals out. The yard and my mother's flowers were kept green through controlled flooding from a small irrigation ditch that terminated in the back of the yard. I remember how exciting it was when my dad irrigated the yard. It was great fun to play in a small water filled depression that was created from the refill of an old root cellar at the base of one of the giant trees. For a kid of three, water was a special attraction.

Our farm gasoline tanks were of course maintained in the farm yard outside of the kid fence. My dad's childhood friend Ralph "Toots" Dierenfield was the "gas man." Ralph often had help with deliveries from an employee, Dewayne. On that day in the summer of 1944 Dewayne delivered gas to the barrels, put the delivery ticket on the house door, and on his return to the truck, apparently left the wooden picket gate to the yard unlatched.

I have no remembrance of the great escape. I don't remember what "Goldie" the near human collie dog must have been trying to tell me. She was an intelligent herding dog, proficient with the cattle, but apparently unable to handle a little human youngster. Somehow my short little legs took me about ¼ mile across a grass pasture bordered by a steep banked irrigation ditch. I faintly remember trying to catch water skippers (a spider like bug that travels on the water surface) at the edge of the ditch. Water skippers are hard to catch, and in my serious effort, I tumbled into the ditch. I had no idea what swimming was, but it sure would have been handy right then. I do remember holding onto the grass at the edge of the ditch, but nothing else until later.

Goldie ran the ¼ mile back to the house. My mother, still in bed, heard Goldie persistently barking and scratching at the door. She got up to determine what was causing the dog's excitement, and saw that she was soaking wet. The dog ran through the open gate, out of the yard, and continued to bark at my mother. Mom of course followed her. They ran across the pasture to where I was still floating in the ditch and hanging onto the grass.

My most vivid remembrance of the incident was after being safely extracted from the ditch. I remember walking with water in my shoes. I thought that the squishing water was the water skippers which in my mind had now gotten into my shoes. I can also hear my mother scolding me, but it is just as well that I have forgotten the exact words used. From that day on, for 12 years, Goldie had a special place in our home. She was recognized as being responsible for my continued existence. Whenever I performed well and brought pride into the home, Goldie shared the praise. When I screwed up, both Goldie and I were banished to the dog house.

• • •

My parents were poor famers in a community where most survived and were happy with the bare necessities. I say poor, only by today's standards. They actually were better off than many in the area. But at that time material things were not given the importance that they are in our modern society. They worked hard, and entertained themselves with other friends by hosting or attending Sunday "dinners" which were the noon meal, and in the winter had friends over for "supper" in the evening. Those winter evenings usually consisted of playing cards and farm conversations. Sometimes there were other kids my age to play with, until we were put to sleep on some-one's bed, and covered with parents coats. I nostalgically re-member nights with my parents when they would return home from a winter card playing session. I was usually blanketed in the back seat, but awoke during the ride. I would often pre-tend to still be asleep, so that my dad would carry me into the house. I remember riding in his arms and looking up into the winter night sky. That is my first vision of remembering stars in the heavens. I remember breathing and my nostrils sticking together from the clear cold air. I remember the crunch of my dad's overshoes on the cold crisp snow. And I remember the phases of the moon. When the moon was full sometimes it was encircled by a glowing ring. I remember one time when we paused on the path to view the "Northern Lights." And always above it all, there were the stars. It was a wonderful combination.

On special occasions our parents attended country dances, held either in the Ballantine Community Hall, the Pompey's Pillar dance hall, or the Osborn (Agriculture Station) Hall. Most were held in the Ballantine Hall, because it was the larg-est. Many families could not afford baby sitters and brought their kids with them. Kids were allowed into the hall, but were admonished to sit on a bench in the front of the dance floor at the foot of the stage beneath the band. If not, parents never hesitated to discipline any kid regardless of their lineage, and we learned to "stay in our place". Older kids were encouraged to participate in the dancing while younger ones were eventu-ally "put to bed."

In that part of the Yellowstone Valley in the 1940's and 50's social rules were usually a simple consensus of local commu-nity agreement. Laws outside of the community were not as important as local custom. I remember when one of my Dad's sisters was married. I was 5 years old. After the wedding my grandfather sponsored the usual party. A "wedding dance" was held in Ballantine. There was a dance band, with the all-important accordion, and a couple of other instruments. Beer was served...and served....and served. Tradition called for the bride to dance with all men who signed the wedding register and pinned a dollar onto her gown. And beer was served. The groom remained attentive, and danced with the wife of the paying registered friend. And beer was served. The keg was kept in the back of the hall where it was easily accessible. During the early part of the evening, glasses (real glass because paper cups were not available, and would have cost money) of beer were served to guests who were sitting on benches at the perimeter of the hall. Glasses of beer were served to all, even to the children on the benches in front of the band. I remember sitting with several kids, preschoolers through junior high, and my grandmother passing by us with a tray of beer. We were encouraged to grab a glass full from the tray and "drink up". Most did. It was considered just part of our food, and no one objected. After a glass of beer, our eyes usually got heavy, and we were taken to the car by our parents. We were put to bed on the car seat under a pile of blankets. Our parents would check on us now and then to assure that we were still there and asleep. All of the community abided by those rules, and all knew that children were asleep in the cars. Any disturbance around the mobile nursery was taboo. I doubt that many locked the car doors. There was no need to.

The community hall was large, and a "good dance" meant an attendance of about 100 couples. The entry fee was always one dollar per couple, or fifty cents for the "stags." An interesting aspect was there were no bathrooms in the hall, and there were no toilets "outhouses" outside of the building. A simple country dance rule was; women went in the weeds and trees to the south side of the hall, and men went to the north. Any serious physical problem was postponed or in an emergency handled by visiting residential outhouses about a block in either direction. Deviations from the rule were met with a severe admonishment, and a fight would result from any errant male venturing into female territory where he might observe another man's wife attending to her duties. The cars were parked side by side, on the roadway both to the north and to the south of the hall. I remember that my brother and I thought it was far more exciting to be parked on the south side. We learned through perceptive little ears what went on in the dark to the south, but could only imagine what the night shadows hid. Diligent observation never paid off, but our failure seldom dampened our interest during the early minutes of our banishment to slumber.

• • •

My childhood house by the river was well kept by my mother. She did the best she could with what she had to work with. We always mowed the lawn and she attended to a garden and flowers. When I was age 12 and entering Junior High School, my Dad built a new house. It was a very conservative effort, with two bedrooms, a large kitchen and a bathroom without a shower. However it is the original log house that deserves recognition. My grandfather bought the river house and 40 acres on road 13 outside of Worden, Montana sometime in the early 1930's. Prior to its purchase my parents lived in a house at the intersection of "the township road" and N 12th road. Both houses were the original homestead houses that were constructed by the first people to settle in the area. The first house my parents occupied later served as a sugar beet labor house until it was destroyed in about 1970. After my grandfather bought the river house, my dad negotiated a deal with him whereby Dad could live in the house and rent the ground. In doing so, he could eventually buy the land, and make progress toward being "on his own." According to my mother, the structure was a complete mess. It was built in about 1911 from cottonwood logs transported from the river bank of the Yellowstone, about ¼ mile to the north of the house. The walls were bare logs, with very poor chinking. The windows were loosely framed had single pane glass and breezes blew through all three rooms. The house consisted of three small rooms; a kitchen, a bedroom, and a living room. It was crude, but it was the only habitable building in the area.

She began fixing the house by mixing flour and water to make a paste. She soaked discarded rags, scrounged from friends, in the paste and filled the voids between the logs with the pasted rags. She somehow got the walls smooth enough to cover two rooms with wall paper. The ceiling was a flat fiber board that was also covered with wall paper. She eventually saved enough money to cover the floor with linoleum. The house had neither plumbing nor electricity; but then neither did any of the other houses in the community.

When my older brother was born, his cradle occupied a space at the foot of the master bed. About the time I was born, my dad built a small enclosed porch onto the east side of the house, and had the entire outside covered with cement stucco.

The miracle of electricity was added and each individual room glowed with a single light bulb in the center of the ceiling. The kitchen and the living room each had one electrical outlet. The log gables were covered with cedar shingles and all shame of living in "an old log house" was completely hidden. There was a combination wood and coal stove in the kitchen and another one in the living room. The largest, in the kitchen, was known as the cook stove. During the winter these boxy menaces glowed red hot in the Montana subzero weather. In the summer my mother labored over the same glowing iron to cook for the family and the farm crew. I learned restraint by playing at the side of these stoves without touching them.

The stoves were the only source of heat, and had to be "banked" in the evening. Banking the stove consisted of putting wood or coal into it in large quantities and partially closing the air vent so that the fuel burned slowly. If it was done correctly, the fire would burn until sometime after midnight. At forty degrees below zero, it was not freezing in the house until about four AM.

The cook stove had a water tank at its side that was referred to as the reservoir. The reservoir was our source of hot water. Of course the water had to be dipped into a pan, used, and "thrown out" because there was no plumbing or sink to use as a drain. Usually there was a container referred to as the "slop bucket" behind the stove. A limited amount of wash water could be discarded into the bucket along with food trimmings and waste, before it had to be emptied. Of course the water in the reservoir had to be replenished daily…a wonderful chore for a kid. The chore was accomplished by taking a bucket out to a hand operated pump over a shallow well at the edge of the yard. The same pump also serviced the stock tank where the farm animals drank; another job for kids. Water did not come easy. The iron pump handle was much taller than I stood in those days. It had to repeatedly be lifted and pulled down until the bucket held the limit that little arms could carry. The water had to be carried back to the house, traversing on a board walk, consisting of 2x10 inch boards, one board wide, laid end to end. When returning to the kitchen through the door in the porch, it was difficult as a child to keep from bumping your leg on the bucket, thus spilling some of the water. However in the winter, if water was spilled on the porch linoleum it would freeze solid within a minute. Skating on the porch floor was sternly frowned on by my mother, and was gruffly addressed by my dad.

I must give you a few more details about the old pump and well. Living so near the river, and in a farm area where crops were flood irrigated, the water table was quite high. A well need not be very deep when the water is only 4 or 5 feet below the surface. Our well was hand dug, to a depth of about 10 feet. It was then lined with boards to prevent the sides from caving in. The open hole was covered with more wooden planks, and a large cast iron pump, bearing a long metal handle was bolted to the flat wooden surface. Of course a pipe extended from the pump base into the water below. It was great water....most of the time. However water had to be pumped for the cattle from the same pump. The corral was 50 yards from the house, 'cause Mom wouldn't have the cows "right by the kitchen window." The solution to watering the cows, was that Dad built a cement water trough, that I thought was larger than a river backwater pond, and placed it 10 feet away from the pump. Another one of those sheep fences was built between the pump and the stock tank. Our job as kids was to hand pump water into a home fashioned bowl attached to a pipe that carried the water to the stock tank. Although it may sound humorous, it worked. When my brother and I went off to grade school, an electric motor was attached to a "pump jack" and the chore was reduced to remembering to turn off the pump after the tank was full. But I must get back to describing the well.

The cows were watered by letting them out of the corral three times a day to allow them to walk to the stock tank. They always lingered there, and created a depression in the ground around the tank. The depression filled with rain and snow runoff, mixed with cattle dung, and in the spring became a soupy bog. Dad always kept his corrals dry and full of fresh straw, but was not able to apply straw around the stock tank, because he would then, according to mom, be building another corral "right by the kitchen window." The cattle tainted water runoff remained around the tank until it soaked into the ground. Remember, I pointed out that the well was only 10 feet away from the tank. In spring the well water, turned to a light brown for several days. Dad always shrugged it off by quoting some hard to find scientific study that claimed water was purified by running through no more than six feet of gravel. Perhaps he was right. We were rarely sick, we grew taller than most of the neighborhood kids, and had strong bones and teeth. I often smile when I see modern day "health nuts" sipping bottled water and coughing into their elbow. I wonder how they would survive with a bottle of that light brown stuff.

Years later when my father was in the process of selling the old home place, I returned and worked for more than a week cleaning up the reserve of treasures to make it respectable for one of the Balzer family who had purchased it. I removed that old pump from its rotten footings and carted it to my home in

Bozeman. I mounted it onto another aged wooden platform where it proudly stands between the house and barn. It has pumped its last water, but every time I mow the lawn, I raise the handle, and recall what it was like to labor at the end of that old rusty piece of iron. Remembering the old farm in the presence of that old pump can still bring tears to my eyes.

Fresh...in most instances... drinking water was kept in an enamel covered pail that rested on top of the wash stand in the kitchen. An enamel "dipper" (a large cup with a long attached handle) was kept inside of the pail. Anyone wanting a drink of water simply took hold of the handle, dipped some water from the pail, and drank directly from the dipper. All who thirsted drank from the same dipper. I guess rural Montana never had germs before about 1954. Much more important than considering germs, was the danger of freezing the dipper. In the evening before bedtime, the last one to use the dipper had to remember to remove it from the pail and lay it out on top of the wash stand. Otherwise the dipper would sometimes freeze into the water forming a large circular sludge hammer within the pail. This would cause serious stress in the family because with only one dipper, all morning progress was delayed until the utensil could be freed from the imprisoning ice block. Freeing the dipper was not a simple task because if the pail or dipper were banged or abused, the enamel would chip off from the metal container. Chipped enamel meant the utensil would soon begin to rust. Folk lore dictated that drinking from rusty objects was sure to cause quick death. It was better to drink from a cow track than drink from a rusty container. Even Goldie knew that the dipper had to be removed from the water pail at night.

I must be cautious not to create the impression that our lives were lived in an unclean environment; by today's standards, surely, but not in relation to the rest of society in those times. My mother struggled for hours each week to keep things clean. She often said, "It doesn't cost anything to be clean." I can still hear her chastising my Dad, "Jake those pants are filthy. Put them in the dirty clothes, and I'll wash them Monday." Monday was wash day.

Washing clothes was no easy undertaking for mom. In the "milk house", where the dairy milk was carried to be separated into skim milk and cream, was a large old wood stove. The stove was used to keep the milk from freezing until it was picked up by the creamery truck, and was also used to heat water for clothes washing. Mom would heat a large tub of water on the stove top, and then pour it into a mechanical washing machine that was also kept in the milk house. The machine was a round tub on legs with an agitator in it. It also had two rollers suspended above the tub to "wring", (squeeze), the water out of the clothes. After washing the clothes, she took them into the house yard and hung them onto the "clothesline" to dry. Sometimes I got the job of hanging socks onto the sheep fence. In summer, they dried. In winter they froze until the ice evaporated. If they didn't dry after being on the line all day, they were stacked behind the kitchen stove. A stormy Monday that prevented wash day and hanging out the clothes, upset her greatly, and complicated her entire week.

Another part of her war against dirt involved her brutal efficiency with a wash cloth. As a child I dreaded even the sight of a "wash rag." (They were never called wash cloths only wash rags.) Mom would dunk a wash rag into a fresh pan of cold water, and with the rag in one hand, and grabbing me with the other, she would slap the rag my face with deadly accuracy. Modern day "waterboarding" could not have been more brutal. The cold water took my breath away. The strong scrubbing motion distorted my mouth, I couldn't open my eyes, and if I would have yelped, the rag would have gagged me. A few revolving swipes and the rag was retracted for face inspection. If there was a speck of dirt anywhere on my puckered face, a second round was unavoidable. The rag was then hung menacingly on a nail at the side of the wash stand to dry. If the face was again blemished before the rag dried, it was used without the induction of fresh water. Within a complete day of face punishment, the rag sometimes began to smell sour. That made no difference to the applicator. As long as the face came clean, she saw no need to freshen the smell of the scrubbing tool.

Whenever we went into town...Worden...Mom donned a clean dress, and I was made to put on a clean shirt and pants. My hair was dampened with water, and combed, and my shoes were inspected. I was sometimes admonished to sit in a chair until she was ready to have me take my place in the car. I remember thinking how awful it must be to be a town kid. I thought that any kid that lived in town would be required to have clean clothes all the time, and never have any fun. In my case, I could get as dirty as I wanted, and play unrestricted, as long as I stayed away from the house.

My brother and I slept in the porch. It was enclosed, but there was no stove in the room. The heat from the kitchen stove came through the open door and furnished whatever warmth that dared to venture into the enclosure. My mother covered the bed with mounds of layered blankets. We entered the bed like a finger into a glove, careful not to disturb the blankets tucked under the edges of the mattress. When we had submerged to our chin she pinned the blankets to the outside edges of our pillow. In this fashion we were tightly locked into bed. Even with all those preparations, the initial entry under the covers was shockingly cold. I learned to lay dead still in one place until my skinny little body gave off enough heat to warm a little comfort zone. Moving around freely was not an option. Any change in position and I would be shocked from the hostile temperature, or crushed under the load of blankets.

Dad was never good at fixing things. Oh, he could repair machinery very well, and understood how equipment was supposed to work. Anything he worked with was usually in good repair. However it was only the practical stuff that received his attention. If a gate closed, and acted as a barrier, then it was adequate. If a tractor seat held your butt, it was kept as is until it no longer functioned. Appearance was not a concern. The door between the kitchen and the living room had endured many closings. It was a four paneled wood door that had been painted so many times its surface resembled the top of a flat dish of scalloped potatoes. But my mother coated over the mosaic with yet another coat of pure white enamel. The door was kept open by placing an object in front of it which held it against the wall. When closed, it remained so only because it bound against the door frame. A sophisticated quiet friction fit kept it closed and negated the need to fix the door knob. I say door knob only out of expectation for what might have been in the open hole where hands were supposed to direct its movement. The conventional was replaced with something more inventive and of course less expensive. A black piece of leather from the reins of a worn out horse harness was inserted through the hole. A knot was tied on each side of the leather strap to keep it from being pulled back out of the hole, and thus a not so decorative handle was improvised.

A small toy shelf stood in the southeast corner of our bed-room/porch. One day when my mother was dusting behind the shelf she slid it away from the wall and stepped on the floor boards near the corner. Her foot fell through the rotten boards and onto the damp earth a few inches below. I under-stand now, many years later, that the space under the floor had no ventilation, and the wood floor rotted. My grandfather who still owned the house was summoned. I should explain that the only person other than my dad who was less interested in fixing things around a house was my grandfather. Dad brought him to the house, and I remember sitting on the bed while they viewed the gaping hole. My mother perhaps should have anticipated the results and removed me from the scene. Some of it came out in Dutch, some in German, and even a little in English. I couldn't speak the foreign languages, but even by then I knew the meaning of the words that were spoken when the cow stepped on your foot, when the tractor wouldn't start, or when the wrench slipped off the bolt. Much was said in loud tones. The result of it all was my mother threatened to leave if the hole wasn't repaired, and my grandfather stormed out of the house; but the crisis was stalled when a remedy was found. An old piece of metal used as a safety fire barrier under a stove was found. (Nothing was ever thrown away lest it might be reused at a later time.) The metal was placed over the hole, the toy shelf was put back into the corner, and we were admon-ished to not walk on the floor near the wall. And so it was until the end of my residence there.

It was several years later that Dad bought the farm from my grandfather, and a new house was built. The old house has never been demolished. The cottonwood logs still stand. It was made into a "bunkhouse" where I slept in the summertime, and hid out in the old living room that I made into a hobby room. The old leather strap still hangs from the living room door. The kitchen was made into a garage, the porch and only bedroom became a store room, for the endlessly accumulated worn out objects that were kept "in case they may be needed again someday." My dad should have demolished the house years before he sold the place, but he was too emotionally attached to it. Instead, when he was in his 80's, he had a new metal roof installed on it to keep his treasures within it dry.

There is no order to the events that pop into my mind concerning those days of growing up in a rural community. I briefly mentioned my grandfather. I will comment on my grandfather and my dad's history in Montana later, however I can only place an incident told to me by a long time neighbor here because it relates to my grandfather and his regard for modern houses. I have listened to Ronnie Balzer tell this story about my grandfather several times, and it is worth sharing. But it would be unfair to the first Schreuder in Montana to repeat the story without drawing the character in his own cloth and time.

To capture the pathos of the moment, we need to know that my Grandfather, John Schreuder was born in Holland. He was one of several kids in a family whose father died around age 37 from "bum legs." His mother was unable to support him, so he left home at age thirteen. He did not see her ever again. He told me many times that the last thing his mother said to him was "Boy, save your money." We need to know that he worked as an indentured servant to a Dutch dairy farm owner where the policy was to furnish only room and board for his services for one year. If he, the servant, remained in service for a second year, he was to be paid a small allowance. The scheme of many landlords was to work the servants so hard the first year, they left before earning wages the second. When he immigrated to America, his first residence was in Hardin. After a short time of manual labor there, he moved to Billings Montana because he heard there would be farmable homestead land near the Yellowstone River. Again he worked shoveling coal in Billings to earn little more than money for food. Somehow he saved enough cash after several months of coal shoveling to buy a pair of boots, which enabled him to get a better job laying cobblestone on a new street called Montana Avenue, in Billings. The land he sought became available to the east of Billings; and he walked downriver from Billings as far as he could in one day. He claimed land there because he thought he should not be more than a day from a town. It's important to know that saving his money served him well enough, that in time, he owned much of the land for several miles in the valley along the river.....but here I must stop and tell the story. In the early 1950's at the insistence of my dark eyed fiery tempered German grandmother, my grandfather gave in to her demands of remodeling the old farmhouse where they had lived and raised 8 kids. Most important on the renovation list was the addition of a modern bathroom with "indoor plumbing." The Schreuders and Balzers shared many fences within their patchwork of farm land. Ron Balzer was considerably younger than John Schreuder, and spoke of him with cautious respect. He fondly recalls that shortly after the construction had begun, an over the fence, or perhaps roadside conversation between Ron and John progressed to Ron inquiring, "Well John, it looks like you're adding onto your house?" To which John responded,

"Ya! Gott verdammt." "Daht oldt voman iss schpending all daht money jhust so she can shit in da house."

• • •

My first experience of going to school was before I entered the first grade. Some sort of orientation was held in the spring before the fall session began. What I remember most from that day was the bus ride into town. Our neighbor, Elmer Walker, who lived even closer to the river than we did, was the bus driver. Elmer had been driving school buses for years. My dad had ridden Elmer's horse drawn buses when he was in Junior High School. My first trip to the Worden School house was on Elmer's bus. The bus was a long wooden box like structure mounted on a truck body. It appeared to be made of something resembling plywood, or fiber board with wooden boards covering the joints. It had spoke wheels, was painted orange, and made a loud rattling puttering noise when it shook down the gravel road. We sat not in forward facing seats as bus riders do now, but instead sat on canvas covered benches mounted to the sidewalls of the big wooden box. The riders faced each other from the side mounted seats, and there was a partial bench mounted in the center which also ran the entire length of the box. The windows looked very much like windows in a house. I have no idea if they even contained safety glass. The long exhaust pipe entered the passenger compartment through the center of the floor and served as the heater for the occupants. Passengers could warm their feet on the pipe where it was exposed on the floor under the center bench. I remember that entire ride, to and from the school.

Adam J. Schreuder

Unfortunately that was the last year of operation for that old bus. The year I actually began school, we boarded a brand new 1948 Ford black and yellow school bus. Mr. Walker still drove his bus occasionally when he and his wife went to town for groceries. One other wooden bus was still operational that year, but was replaced in 1949.

The Worden Grade School building of 1948 was less modern than Elmer Walker's school bus. It was located on the north side of Worden approximately 1/8th of a mile from the present fire station. Only sage brush fields separated it from Kraske's Locker Plant at the edge of town. The school yard was bordered on the south by a gravel road and on the other three sides by farm pasture. The school yard was a huge 3 acre gumbo patch of dirt with only a tennis court sized plot of graveled play area between two sidewalks near the entry road. Except on very muddy days, the fields were ours to roam. To the east of the school yard was the farm house where lived the owner of the surrounding pasture. Mr. Cheneworth, the farmer, raised Hereford cattle. The cattle, including several large Hereford Bulls, prowled in the pasture next to the school yard. To keep the cattle and school kids separated Cheneworth maintained a fence constructed with woven sheep wire on the bottom, and an electric wire tensioned on top of the fence posts. The electric wire was head high to a 6th grader and well within reach of even the smallest elementary kid.

The electric wire was effective with the Hereford Bulls, but of little value with the kids. Our baseball diamond and soccer field were in the northeast corner of the schoolyard, which was also the favorite pasture of the bulls. The only thing that made the area a soccer field is that we had a soccer ball to kick there. A goal post had to be imagined. Consensus was that to score

20

a goal, the ball had to be kicked over the sheep fence into the bull pasture. After a successful kick, whoever was on the defending team would venture through the electrified fence, scamper among the bulls, and retrieve the ball. If the bulls were too close, we threw dirt clods and rocks at them until they moved a safe distance away. On the other end of the soccer field there was only a small irrigation ditch between the school yard and a gravel road. To score a goal on that end of the field required that the ball had to be kicked out into the road. Most of us thought the road was more dangerous that the bulls, but it was rarely a concern. When we chose sides (picked teams by having the team "bosses" alternately choose from the group until the last and usually the least athletic kids were selected) we assigned the worst team to kick toward that goal. In that manner goals were rarely scored into the road.

The electric fence was merely an entertaining function of the playground. All who were afraid to grab onto it to demonstrate their toughness were "chicken." We often joined hands and the "leader" grabbed the fence. It's an old wives tale that the kid on the far end from the fence gets the hardest shock. We ran the experiment many times. The brave idiot who grabs the fence gets the most out of the effort. We also learned that certain kids seemed to be "denser" than others, because they "filtered" the shock, absorbing more than others. Being on the downside of "Big George" was much better than standing in line between little Harriet and the fence. To my knowledge no parent ever complained about the fence. Farm kids grew up with the idea; if you didn't like getting shocked, stay away from the fence. Teachers never ventured out into our soccer field. They assumed we knew how to handle ourselves around the Herefords and showed no concern.

The playground equipment consisted of three tall swings, and three "teeter-totters." We had two soft balls; one for the "little kids" and one for the "big kids." The class distinction usually stuck until the "little" ones were able to keep from crying while being thumped by the "big" ones. There were four ball bats. We used those four bats from first grade through the sixth, however about once a year our teachers were able to requisition from somewhere a new soft ball whenever the cover was worn off the old one..I faintly remember we had a basketball too, but we never had an adequate basket rim or pole, and surely not a level rock free place to play the game. The winter recesses were spent building snow forts, having snow ball fights and playing "fox and goose" in the new snow fields.

The snowball fights were brutal. There were no rules other than "no rocks allowed." We chose sides (teams) for the battles, but any organization always disintegrated in the frenzy of the free-for-all. Best friends ganged up on unpopular enemies and yet clobbered each other in the melee. Mittens became soaked, faces grew red and ice scraped. An occasional nose bleed left red spots in the snow. The war was never stopped to care for the wounded. They just dropped out and disappeared until the ammunition was re-stocked and the survivors vowed new destruction of their foes. I'm proud to say that I was among the toughest of the fighters; mostly due to a wonderful fully hooded coat that was a hand-me-down from my brother.

The teachers were quite competent in the classroom. However, prior to the 6th grade when we had a male teacher, I do not remember, ever, a teacher venturing past the hot lunch room toward the playground during recess. They were oblivious to any activity on the playground. We handled most discipline ourselves. There were instances when one of the "tattle tales" would report some conflict or infraction of the rules to a teacher; but it was then addressed in class after the recess. Serious disagreements were settled by crowding around in a circle enclosing two combatants while they fought out their differences.

Disagreements on the Worden playground were not settled by who was right, but by who was the toughest. It was a time when slower learners were held back and were made to repeat a grade. In 1950's school language they "flunked" the (whatever) grade. They flunked because they were "dumb." As children we had little charity for other's defects. The result was that the "dumbest" kids were always the toughest because they were the oldest. They were granted the right to be superior on the playground by evolution. If "Big Raymond" didn't think that he was put out at second base, in spite of close scrutiny by the less mature players, then "Big Raymond" was safe. A would be umpire who had the foolish spunk to seriously challenge the play, caused a short intermission in the game for a boxing decision directly related to the accuracy of his observations. Unless most of the class joined at the elbows of the truth seeker "Big Raymond" was always right. And so it went in most games. There was no concern for bullying because it was inevitable. One was either a "dumb bully" or a talented glib negotiator. Within the first month of school, one learned that if you wanted to avoid getting the crap beat out of you, avoidance, and alliances were part of survival. Whining to a teacher didn't work long term. Tattling to higher authority would surely renew your faith in Hell.

There were other games that grew out of complete imagination. One of the most popular through the second and third grade was "horses." It seemed almost genetic that all of

the girls loved horses. Therefore they thrived on pretending
to be, and acting as a horse. Of course all horses were known
to run...apparently all the time. The boys, most of us being
less fleet of foot were never the horses, but always the riders.
Now don't let your adult mind carry you away here, because
to be a rider only required that you could run almost as fast
as your horse when hanging onto its reins. The rein that attached the horse to its rider was always a belt removed from
whichever member of the horse/rider duo who could keep
his or her pants up while running beltless at full speed. In my
case I often wore my older brother's pants well before they fit
me, so I preferred grasping the belt removed from the pants
of the horse running in front of me. The game was played
endlessly in good weather. Although I participated whole-
heartedly, I have never faintly understood the object of the
game. The physical profile of the horse was simply a young
lady with a belt trailing from the back loop of her jeans. The
rider could be identified as a young man hanging desperately
to the trailing belt. The essentials were to have, or to be, a
horse that could do a great deal of whinnying, chomping, and
running. Most of all it was necessary to be a fast runner. The
fastest girls were the most popular.....the sociology of which
I am still considering. Many of the girls were quite difficult
to keep up with, and the boys were severely attacked if they
tired and began to fall behind. A slow rider couldn't keep
from pulling on the rein, a most serious defect in the world
of fast horses. The most apparent derived satisfaction was to
be the lead horse and rider, running out in front of the pack;
running to nowhere, only to reach the end of the field and
rerun the return.

We often morphed similar games into Cowboys and Indians. Participants had to first serve as Indians and were defeated through many games and contests before they were granted the status of becoming a Cowboy. During the shoot-m-up contests the Cowboys always won. That's how it was. The cowboys through their age and grade level were tougher, had better guns, (sticks purloined from the lunch room cook stove supply) and ruled the game. The game was always dictated by a "Boss." In order to play with a group, a would-be participant had to be approved by the "Boss." Protocol was that if you wanted in on the game, you approached the group and asked, "Who's the boss?" After being directed to one of the more socially adept of the group, you respectfully asked, "Can I play?" If you had learned your place in the miniature society you were usually accepted providing you knew how to remain subservient to the "Boss". You then loosely followed the rules of the game which were made up by the "Boss" as the game developed. However if you free lanced, or failed to "charge" with the other Indians while attacking, you risked being "kicked out" of the game. Banishment was usually short lived because with everyone wanting to be a Cowboy, Indians were in short supply. However if the non-compliant derelict was a repeat offender, banishment could be long lasting. It is not surprising that lifelong team players and outcasts were molded on the dirt of that schoolyard.

There were games reserved for rainy muddy days...days when no kid in his right mind would venture out onto the clay baseball/soccer field. Mud out there would stick to the bottom of your "overshoes" and become heavy shoe weights. You could grow two to three inches taller walking in it, but few had the strength to move in it very long. The worst thing imaginable was falling down into the glue. With schoolyard gumbo on your clothes, you were out of commission for the day.

To solve the muddy day dilemma, the school janitor provided an inexpensive solution. The furnace was coal fired. Cinders from the burned coal needed to be disposed of. The cinders were spread all around the sides of the building to cover the mud. The tramping, running feet of scores of kids ground the coal "clinkers" into a finely granulated black firm base. Cinders were formed into a path from the school to the outhouse. Cinders formed a walkway to the hot lunch building. Cinders paved the way to the road out front where the busses parked. And cinders were spread in a large area around the school building to keep the mud from sticking to our shoes. Of course, if you fell while running on the cinders, the result was black scrapes and embedded black pulverized cinders under the skin. It was just part of the day.

A rainy day game, played next to the school house was termed "five hundred". My thoughts were that the game was devised by idiots for idiots, but it was something to do. The game was simply to throw a ball, usually an old baseball, up against the brick wall of the building, and catch it on the rebound. Anyone catching the ball received one hundred points. The game continued until some player with good hands, accumulated 500 points, whereupon he then became the thrower of the ball. The thrower could easily control the game by carefully bouncing the ball in the direction of his chosen friends, and therefore the game was rife with cronyism and squabbles. Also a good elbow frequently used, kept competitors from crowding in on a good catch.

On a spring day, when we were in the fourth grade, Bill Kraske, a classmate then, and an old time friend to this day, and

I were playing five hundred but had tired of the routine. Bill discovered that rocks would also bounce when thrown against the building, but were harder to catch on the rebound. He also discovered that with a little more effort, he could throw them completely over the building. I remember saying "Bill you better not throw them clear over the top of the school, 'cause we can't see where they are landing. However to maintain a little more interest in the game, he threw about every third one over the top just so I couldn't catch it on the rebound. After about five minutes of this new sport, Bob Mitzel, a second grader came bawling round the side of the building with blood streaming from his scalp. He ran to his teacher, and apparently reported that the sky was falling. Of course the mystery was quickly solved by scores of observant tattle tales, who reported that Bill and I were throwing rocks over the building. Now the sky was sure to fall.

Bob's second grade teacher, Mrs. Lewis, was the Principal at that time, and quite protective of her brood. She took a rather dim view of the activity, and during her punishing lecture to us, delivered in the nurse's room, disclosed that she would be writing a letter to our parents, describing our wanton disregard for proper deportment. The poor lady underestimated both of us. Since I had not performed the act, and in fact had not thrown even a single missile over the building, I explained the entire incident to my mother. I carefully detailed the part where I had warned Bill that "over the building" was not a good idea. My performance was well received, and the letter from the Principal was regarded by my parents as an administrative mistake, to be forgotten among the many more important life stresses. Bill had a more difficult problem. He knew that even though I had kept my mouth shut during our school punishment, I had copped out with the truth at home. I unmercifully left him with no defense. Bill discreetly ran a twice daily reconnaissance mission around the family post office box in the Worden Post Office. One day after I disclosed that my mother had received the principal's letter, Bill confided that he had intercepted one intended for his parents. I thought at the time, that he was now making small trouble, into big trouble; although I couldn't help but admire his bold effort to control his ultimate demise. "What did you do with it?" I asked. "I read it, and then burned it", he whispered. It was our darkest secret for several years.

Bill and I have laughed about the incident many times in the years since then. Bob Mitzel was not seriously hurt. They taped his head shut and he was out with the rest of us by the next recess. Bob was another "river kid" who lived only ½ mile downriver. We were swimming together again by late spring. Our mothers were all social friends. No one can explain why my mother never mentioned to Mrs. Kraske the letter she received from the principal.

There were naturally two "outhouses" on the playground. They were multi-service facilities. In addition to serving nature, the girls "bathroom" was a refuge where they could run to escape pursuing boys during recesses. It was a place where girls could hide and gossip about the boys standing on the other side of the thin wooden walls. The boys building was both a place for necessary body functions and a chamber of enduring torment. Many are the hats that were thrown down the "toilet hole" by the "big kids." Once down the hole, there was no head that would ever again claim it. When entering the bathroom, a "playground wise" kid would always check to see who was in or lurking around the structure. If occupied by one of the tormentors, the choice was either to "hold it" or risk getting roughed up.

In that grey painted pathetic structure, during mid-winter, I learned a valuable lesson in aggressive bluffing. The outhouse was built in an L shape with a long concrete urinal (trough) that rested on the floor. Two toilet holes destitute of privacy were secluded in the back of the structure. The urinal always froze in mid-winter, thus cradling an expanding ice/urine block. By January the ice expanded to the floor. The floor in front of the trough became a slushy urine creek that flowed to the side of the entry. One cold day while I was carefully navigating the entry, I was ambushed by one of the worst of the "big kids." He grabbed me, snatched my hat from my head, and threw me across the humiliating tainted stream. I was only concerned about the hat. He immediately faked a pass of the hat into the toilet. I knew that he would torment me until I cried or was foolish enough to attempt to physically retrieve the hat. I also knew that I needed that hat. My parents would have little sympathy for any circumstances of its loss. Yes, I needed that hat back. I also had to relieve my bladder....very badly. The combination of both needs presented me with an idea. Any idea needed to be bad, really ugly. This kid wouldn't budge at anything less. As he made another farce at throwing the hat into the pit, I mustered all of my internal strength and said, "If you throw away my hat I am going to piss in your coat." A modern mortal has no idea how great a blasphemy that was. In my home, one was only allowed to describe the need of relieving one's self in hushed tones using the word "potty." The other "P" word was the vocabulary of only the lowest degenerates of the valley. But I needed something dark and terrible with which to threaten. It got his attention.

He whirled around and said, "You what?"

My hastily formed plan was either working or I was about to smother with my head in the bottom of the pit.

"I said if you throw my hat in the toilet I am going to piss in your coat."

"You can't do that. I'll beat your face flat."

"Maybe so, but I'll still piss all over your coat."

By now my hat was not the focus of attention. He held it away from the toilet pit.

"Not if you're dead" he said.

He was still way too confident. I said, "If you don't give me my hat back, I am going to wait until you hang up your coat in the hall, and during class I am going to take it out here and piss in the pockets and all over the collar." "You won't even know it until it rubs all over your skin."

He got red in the face, and if he still didn't have my hat, I would have run away, leaving my bladder somewhere in the outhouse entry.

Then he got a funny questioning look and said "You wouldn't dare!"

I began to think I was going to live through this, and gave it one last effort. "You can't stop me from pissin, so give me my hat or your coat is really gonna get pissed on."

He looked at me, and briskly flipped my hat at my feet as he walked out, his big boots slopping through the mire. It took a few moments to quit hyperventilating, and then as a little 3rd grade kid, I realized, I had won. I didn't cry, run or swing a fist, and I had won.

The old school building wore the scars of many decades of service. Generations grew their minds and stocked their moral medicine chests within its red brick sanctuary. The reputations of teachers were born there too. My lasting love for the place is anchored in its stark simplicity.

It was a sturdy red brick structure that both my mother and father and almost the entire community had attended. It had four classrooms, to contain 6 grades, and a "nurse's room." Two classrooms were on the ground floor, as was the furnace room. The upper floor consisted of two more classrooms and the nurse's room. In six years of abiding there, I only saw a nurse (from the county) visit the school on two occasions. The nurse's room was usually used for an administrative room. It was most famous for being the place where discipline was administered in the form of a large paddle.

The wooden stairs at each end of the building were well worn. Each step was ground down into a shallow saucer. A wide banister bordered the side of the stairs. The banister cap was wide enough to allow a battalion of little butts quick passage by sliding from top to bottom. Bannister sliding was a taboo act frequently practiced by all. The rooms were to one side of the Building to allow the presence of a full length hall which doubled as a coat hanging room. Each hall had one drinking fountain and one small sink. All floors were wooden, worn by the feet of thousands. Some of the bricks had been loosened by little hands bearing sticks. The mortar had been removed from two bricks on the outside wall of the closet under the stairway. It was always an adventure to stuff foreign objects through the wall into the closet. A stray snake, frog, jump rope or rock was not an usual discovery in the storage closet.

The sanitation practices of those times were quite remarkable. None of the children washed before lunch. None washed after using the outdoor rest rooms. There wasn't a convenient place to do so, and in addition it would have been wasting water. The single drinking fountain was used by all. The water was hauled to the school cistern in an old galvanized tank mounted on an older truck. The water came from a tile drain near the adjoining town of Ballantine. The cistern was a concrete box shaped container in the ground, covered only by a tin lid. It held about two week's supply of water if the kids were admonished not to waste it. Except in the best of weather the wooden floors were dusty, dirty or wet. They contained samples of the school yard, from the clay of the distant soccer field to the ice melt of the boy's latrine. We didn't worry about germs in the 1950's.

One square wooden building separate from the school, served as the hot lunch room. Later when the school population expanded, another similar building was moved in and served as a classroom for the first grade. The entire school population of about 120 was served in the hot lunch building by one cook laboring at a wood burning stove. The cost was three dollars per month per child. Costs were kept minimal and so were the delicacies. I was not alone in my dislike for the unimaginative menu. Each day you had two choices. (1) Take it or (2) leave it. On most days the food content would rot the innards of a cast iron dog. Depending on the attitude of the teacher, we were not allowed to completely decline the lunch. So if we were served a bowl of soup, we needed to find something acceptable about it. For a time some of us were able to occasionally get by with eating bread and a cup of milk. Then we poured the soup into the cup which was held to our side or back while passing by the teacher watching for "wasted food." Because of the quality of the food, we always fought over the raisin bread.

Each child was responsible for bussing their own plate. Waste was scraped into an unlined large metal garbage can located at the end of the serving counter. In unpleasant weather, the can was emptied, but not washed. All of the dishes were washed in one sink of warm water and rinsed with a light spray to flush off the soap. Occasionally when the cook was not feeling well, a couple of the older boys were recruited to assist the cook with the dish washing. It was promoted as an honor to be selected to work in the kitchen. It was a hard sell, and I never bought it. Sanitation was not a priority and it neither improved nor degraded the food.

Through it all, the Worden Grade School was a happy place. It was a life style that will never be repeated or simulated. We were educated in the classroom and were expected to take care of ourselves outside. An incident to illustrate our independence occurred in the 5th grade. A group of us were playing at the southeast corner of the school yard, where a row of cottonwood trees bordered the school yard. We had a rope, intended for a "jump rope" with which we were practicing "cowboy roping." We soon became bored with roping each other, and progressed to tying kids together. Near the end of recess, we tied Jimmy Ruland to one of the cottonwood trees. We did a good job, and Jimmy couldn't move. While enjoying his plight, the end of recess bell rang. We all ran into the building, leaving Jimmy tied to the tree. Midway through the period, (about 45 minutes) the teacher noticed that Jimmy was not present. She asked the class if anyone knew what had happened to Jimmy, or where he was. Only about four of us knew he was outside tied to a tree, and none seemed to be able to assemble enough vocabulary to explain the circumstances. It was probably the quietest any of us had been all day. No one "squealed." The teacher having no answers, proceeded with class for the remainder of the period. During the next and final recess of the day, we returned to the tree to assure that Jimmy was still alive and securely bound. By then, he no longer saw the humor of it all, and effectively cursed his way into receiving some sympathy. We gave him his freedom, which didn't include an explanation for the teacher. Jim provided the truth for his absence, and we were all prepared to at least receive a stern lecture in the nurse's room. However the teacher seemed to find more humor in the incident than we did. We were punished by having the jump rope impounded for a week.

Not every day was unrestricted play in the schoolyard. On some days we were assigned special chores. Yes, can you imagine chores at school? On certain days, particularly after a strong wind, we were assigned clean up duty. Fifty kids picking up trash could clean up three acres of ground in less than five minutes. Another enjoyable chore was getting bread for the hot lunch room. The cook did not have time to bake, so the bread was purchased on account at the local grocery story in Worden. Each day two kids were dispatched to walk the ¼ mile from the school to the store. There we picked up the bread from the owner who knew exactly what and how much we were to take. We learned that the order was prearranged because one day when we attempted to obtain an extra loaf of raisin bread…..we had good intentions of eating it on the way back to the school…..we were sternly rebuked for our attempt.

While working the bread run with a designated "partner" another classmate whose father owned one of the three bars in town, decided he would come with us. He had not obtained the approval of anyone at school to do so, but that was not a serious matter. Kids often snuck uptown to spend a nickel that had been found somewhere on their country safaris. Danny did not go with us to the grocery store. Instead he went to his dad's tavern. He joined us on our return to the school, and proudly disclosed his amazing acquisition. He had taken a pack of cigarettes from the bar. Neither of my parents smoked, I was not familiar with the vice, and in great curiosity thought that it might be even better than raisin bread.

During the noon recess, Danny broke out the cigarettes and about five of us who very quickly had become Danny's best friends gathered in a deep, dry, irrigation ditch at the edge of the playground. There were not of course enough cigarettes for everyone on the playground, so some vindictive losers were left out. Because of these deprived many, word soon got back to the teachers. When class resumed, we were rounded up like convicts and escorted to the nurse's room. The nurse's office was an appropriate place for a couple of the gang because they had partaken of the forbidden fruit much more than I, and were beginning to show signs of illness. However we all knew that the medicine to be applied was not going to come from a bottle. I honestly don't remember how many individual swats with the big paddle we got that day, but it was adequate to cause me to believe that smoking was not worth the trouble. From that day on, I thought smoking was rather stupid, and it was something I could definitely do without. I don't know why, but for some reason the incident was never reported to our parents. For that small favor, I was for years grateful.

There are so many great memories hidden within the image of that old school that it would take volumes more to include them. But times pass, people and buildings change, and the school finally outlived its purpose. When I had been a graduate of the old grade school for two years, the Huntley Project School system consolidated four old school houses into one elementary school system. They built a new elementary school in Worden, behind the Junior High School. I remember spending my noon hour on several occasions watching workers lay bricks, forming the walls of the new long, low, sleek school. I was a "grown up" eighth grader by then, but I recall thinking, "This is never going to be the same."

THE ORDINARY

Growing up in Montana, there were many trivial incidents that do not rate as exciting literary material. But when I put the right focus on them, they become important occurrences. A complete picture of a kid's life in rural Montana should include more than just the showy experiences. Episodes dealing with common folks vastly outnumber the celebrity incidents, but could be similar or familiar to all who finger these pages. I will share those that I best recall.

It would be easy to assume that in my childhood, my family lived in poverty. That was not the situation. We just didn't have money. Our lives were as rich as any in the valley at the time. In summer we had a large vegetable garden. My mother canned the produce from most of the garden, along with "store bought" fruit such as peaches, flathead cherries and raspberries which filled a great root cellar in the fall. We grew and processed our own meat and stored it in a locker plant in town. We had our own chickens, eggs, made our own butter, ice cream and lard, and sold raw dairy products. I wore my older brother's clothes because that's just what little brothers were supposed to do. We ate well, and lived happy. I had no idea we were financially deficient. We had more than most within our acquaintance.

I was a small child tucked into my bed one evening when I overheard my parents conversing about money. My dad never kept a check register, but mentally monitored his bank account. On this occasion in about early winter my mother was planning a trip into town the next day, and he asked her to stop into the bank and determine the size of their bank balance. I noted some concern in their voices, and for the first time in my life I realized that money was important. It was so important that my parents wondered if they had enough to get through the winter. What if they didn't? As I contemplated it, the worry became much greater for me, than it ever could have been for them.

The next day, I accompanied my mother to town. I sat quietly in the car while she went into the bank. When she exited, I watched for signs of distress, or even happiness. She ran flat. I got not a clue as to our financial ability to survive. That night again tucked into my bed, but wide awake from anxiety, I heard the parental conversation returned to money. My dad inquired "How much do we have in the bank?" Mom replied, "We have three hundred and sixty dollars." I stiffened wondering how much that was. How much did we need? Why was dad quiet? He seemed to be figuring. Finally he said, "Well, that's real good! That should take us clear through until spring." I knew nothing of money, but I felt rich. Our family was apparently well off, we had no money worries. But from that day forward, I was aware of the concerns of other families in the valley. Some had more money, some had less, but we were all rich with the wealth of community and good life.

The Yellowstone River washed a path that guided much of my youth. It was always there, just a mere 500 yards from the house. I could hear it where I slept. When I was outdoors, whether working or playing it was present in every conscious moment. In the spring, it roared, bank full, and overflowed, lapping at the banks of the irrigation ditch only 200 yards from the house. In winter, it groaned and grumbled, sometimes throwing automobile sized ice cakes up on its bank. When at rest in mild seasons, it whispered softy, revealing secrets of fragile life living in the curtains of its edges, and on its dancing surface. In summer and fall, it held a wonderland maze of pathways to secret hideouts, forts, and to places never visited by men....places only known to little boys. In winter it created a random pattern of ice ponds, perfectly personalized for young skaters. There were beaver ponds, slough ponds, backwater ponds from gorged ice jams, and road side ponds big enough to be cleaned by farmer's tractors. There were ponds disclosed to "town kids", and ponds kept secret because they were in sheltered areas and frozen too perfectly smooth to expose them to excess skate scars. There were trees – so many trees. Some cottonwoods still stood where they were markers for my grandfather. Others reached down to lift the venturous high into their arms. From the tops of their lofty masts, I could see completely across the river, reconnoiter the islands below, and watch for approaching "enemies." There were trees felled by beavers – bridges across the sloughs, and fortresses among their massive horizontal trunks. Willows provided spears, fishing poles, lashings for fort roofs, and multiple use poles for rafts, stream jumping, and imaginary track and field pole vaulting. Cedar and Juniper trees, were located and staked out for Holiday use, providing Christmas Trees, wreathes and decorative boughs.

The river also provided refuge for runaways with dampened spirits and hurt feelings, perceived slaves escaping from chores, and swimming holes for the naked. It was a clinic for the mind, a conscience for the soul, and an amusement park and zoo for the local privileged. It was a science and biology class where I learned of the complexity and fragility of life. It was a cathedral where I contemplated how, why, and the meaning of it all. It was a powerful place, humbling to visit, moody in its own ways. It entertained only the appreciative, was unselfish with its possessions, shared its charm only in real time, and gave up scores of memories. For those who learn to trespass with benevolence its mystique rests in their hearts eternally. It was my back yard...a place I shall never forget.

I was allowed to explore the river at will. I guess my parents thought that since I almost drowned by falling into an irrigation ditch when I was very young, I had learned the danger of water, and would refrain from falling into something even bigger. They were right. I had a lot of respect for the river bank, and visions of being sucked under by the revolving current were frightening. But the lure of its magic pursued me like a disease. A full day off, all to myself meant I could stuff some simple sustaining morsel into my pocket, inform my mother I would not be home for lunch, (we called it dinner, and the evening meal was referred to as supper), and head for the river. My companion was always my collie dog. I should mention that the dog (Goldie) who saved me from drowning lived until I was 12 years old. She succumbed to age, and another working collie was raised to fill the void. (Notice I did not use the word replace....it was not possible to replace Goldie.) But the new collie, Penny, fulfilled all the needs of a dairy farm and a boy. We were one. Her language I could not understand, but her thoughts I could read instantly.

Penny and I became inseparable in those days. She was smart, but only in Collie ways. She was not a hunting dog, unless it was finding a calf in high grass. She walked beside me when I hunted pheasants, as opposed to flushing out game in advance of the hunter. When a pheasant jumped up in front of me, it usually scared me so bad that I jumped and flinched and by the time I regained control was late getting the gun up to shoot. Penny was no different, because she would also become startled, spin around toward the rear and jump in retreat until she was several feet closer toward home. But other than hunting, I was able to teach her all the usual dog tricks. I knew nothing about good dog health and dog diets. She ate what I ate. With a batch of bad tasting cookies made by my mom from an experimental recipe, I taught Penny to "speak", sit, roll over, lie down, play dead and shake hands. She knew that the sound of the cream separator being picked up out of the utility wash basin meant it was time to bring in the cows. I thought then that she must be able to read because she sometimes stood in the milk house and stared at the Farmer's Almanac Calendar and, retreated to her dog house just before it rained. We could never speak the word cows aloud or conversationally in her presence. It had to be spelled "C – O – W – S" otherwise she would bolt from the yard and herd the poor beasts into the corral. However in spite of all her talents, she was a lousy poker player. She always wagged her tail when she had a good hand.

Choices Penny and I had about what we would do at the river were many. She usually let me decide. She did not prefer fishing, nor did I. Exploring was the most exciting, and fishing was reserved for days where clouds of mosquitoes prevented us from tramping through the tall river grass. While fishing,

Penny usually became bored, and napped on the sand in the shade of some beached flotsam. I usually cast my line, and waited, dreaming of someday crossing the river to explore the cliffs and caves on the other side.

Fishing in that area of the Yellowstone was not a vigorous pursuit. Any prey was acceptable, but the usual victims were carp, red horse, suckers, shad, and occasionally cat fish or ling. Only the latter two were edible. My devised fishing method was as crude and simple as my equipment. For a pole, I used a long willow cut from the river bank. Line was most often from a ball of string, much like woven carpenter string that was purchased from the local hardware store. Hooks, usually BIG hooks, also from the hardware store were crudely tied to the string. The hooks had to be big enough to accommodate the plump healthy earthworms dug from the garden. An old tin can containing a little dirt kept them fresh if I didn't forget to stash the can out of the sun. The part of the assembly most unique was at the very end of the line. The object dictating the style of fishing was the "sinker." For a sinker, I took from my dad's farm machine shop, a hand full of threaded "nuts" that were made to be screwed onto machine bolts. Tied onto the end of the line, they provided a sturdy anchor to hold the whole mess firmly onto the rocky river bottom, in the swiftest current. Casting the line was a simple art within the capabilities of any farm boy. I unrolled the string from the wound up wad at the end of the willow pole. With the string in a loose pile at my feet, I grasped the end of the line, and twirled the weighted string around like a windmill in a mild hurricane. When I released the string at just the right time, the nuts flew like a missile out over the water. Bad timing resulted in cutting the nuts and string out of the grass and willows…..an activity Penny never fully understood. She always assumed that we were looking for grasshoppers or more bait, and confounded the problem by getting entangled in the string. Her long hair protected her from getting hooked, but she thought the entire operation was very humanesque and stupid. She found the flopping fish curious, but thought they smelled bad, and would never touch one to her mouth. But as I was saying, once the line was twirled out into the river, fishing only required patience. Dreaming contributed to the patience, and had to be practiced. For years I dreamed of what I might discover in the cave predominantly wedged in the sandstone cliff across the river. It teased and taunted me for years. I was in high school before I finally conquered that challenge, but that's another story.

If we chose exploring, we had to decide in which direction to proceed...up river, or down. We were limited in distance, only by time. Both the dog and I knew that we had to be home by cow milking time. We could only travel a distance which we would be able to return over an equal or lesser time. As I got older that distance expanded, but my record distance, although it seemed like an astronomical measurement exceeded only by Lewis and Clark, was only about two miles in either direction. Most often, any distance attempt was interrupted by beaver dam construction, muskrat ramblings, or deer tracking. On occasion my fright factor was tested in the tall grass. I preferred narrow game trails through the willows and tall grass, which were also the favorites of deer and raccoons. Penny was not a leader, nor a hunting dog, and usually chose to walk behind me. On more than one occasion, I met head on with a deer, who was no less startled than I. A deer bolting in any direction, at close range, always caused us both to retreat into the brambles in schizophrenic panic. Luck was always with us and the critters ran in opposite directions, allowing us to realize that we weren't being consumed by Big Foot, and that we were still king of the jungle.

An activity that forever frustrated Penny was tree house building. Her useful participation was limited, and she probably recognized that it was an unnatural function, creating a good way to get injured. I never understood her language, but knew exactly what she was thinking. She usually pouted at being ignored and observed from a safe distance. But she was tolerant and never told my parents. It began when I discovered a stash of old bridge spikes at the base of an abandoned irrigation bridge. I reasoned that they had to be used for something…to waste them would be unthinkable. I fashioned some ladder steps from discarded fence boards, and carried them down to the river. My intent was to nail these steps on the side of a tree near the river, and use the tree as an observation tower. It worked, but sitting in the tree soon became uncomfortable. In successive trips to the location I smuggled from my dad's shop, a wood saw, hammer, extra nails, and baling wire. I fashioned a floor platform for a tree house. It still felt incomplete. Sitting on the platform 20 feet above ground left me extremely exposed to the weather, and in full view of any "enemy" that might pursue me into the woods. Building walls was a new unpracticed skill. Penny soon learned not to loiter under the tree, because it often took me more than one attempt to get materials up to the construction level. By the time I had three walls around the platform, the base of the tree looked like a well exercised football field. Alas, it finally developed into an elevated fort, the likes of which were so secret and bizarre in architecture that even river birds avoided its silhouette. Through several successive years, friends were initiated into my secret river fort society. In a solemn private ceremony they were given an oath to never disclose its location and were taken to the tree house by a circuitous route the likes of which would have confused Christopher Columbus. Many years later, as an adult, I returned to the area, and found that the floor of the tree house, still hung tiredly in the same, but very much older cottonwood.

Summer was for bike riding and swimming. Riding a bicycle on those country gravel roads was a feat of pure strength. The bicycles owned by me and my friends were heavy steel indestructible lunkers, with wide balloon tires and mud fenders, equipped with imitation leather seats wide enough to support any grandma's behind. They were low geared, one speed monsters driven by a sprocket and chain that would snatch your pant leg from your ankle and gobble it into a bunched up wad that would take upwards of a half hour laying on your side in the thick thistly gutter to extract. Riding into the Montana wind could only be accomplished by standing on and pushing down on the pedals with all your weight while at the same time pulling up on the handle bars, to exert extra pressure on the feet. Boys were molded into mighty men on those bikes.

A onetime venture involved my building a sail to capture the wind and forever after make bike riding an effortless pleasure engaged in by only the most brilliant of my kind. According to my imagination it would propel me wondrously down the road. I had read how good sailors could even rig the sail so they could sail back against the wind. I had time, I would figure it out. I located a canvas irrigation dam, but it turned out to be too rotten to withstand the wind. I dug around in the attic and came up with an old blanket. The milk house yielded a shovel handle and an old broom handle (broomstick) was cut from a worn out barn broom. I tied the blanket, a green flannel treasure, to the makeshift shovel mast and wired on the broomstick as a cross mast. The entire contraption was secured to the handlebars. Fortunately I put together the invention out on the road, because in the inspiring wind, I was immediately propelled downwind on the gravel path. The wind was at my back. The sail was furled out in front of me. It was exhilarating until I entered a rougher part of the road. Suddenly I found myself thinking religiously. "Holy crap", I am going down this road at 25 mph and can't see beyond my handle bars!" Each second, and with every new puff of wind I coasted faster. I was totally blinded by the wide blanket in front of me. I moved toward the smoother edge, and realized that I was unable to tell even vaguely where the road transitioned to gutter. The front wheel soon defined the difference between the two. It ran off the road and I catapulted over the handlebars into the gutter. My fall was mercifully smoothed by the blinding blanket, but I skinned my knees, my chest, and much of what lies in-between. The shovel handle threatened to remove parts yet to reach maturity, but I was still breathing. I slowly rolled up the sail in deep thought. Bicycle sailing was eliminated from my activity list.

Roads were pot holed mine fields that demanded concentration and agile reactions. At certain times in the summer, they became rather smoothly packed dirt. These were the times young residents would turn into country vagabonds, traveling the several miles to visit our neighbor friends. Parents rarely took us anywhere purely for social reasons. If we wanted to go somewhere we rode our bikes. If the event was too distant to get there by bicycle, we just didn't go. My mother did not set specific limits to my travel, but generally I was not expected to venture further east than Worden, about 4 miles from home. Sojourns to the west were about the same distance. The river to the north was a natural barrier, and US Highway 10 & 12 four miles to the south was an asphalt ribbon no sane rider would venture across. I figure I routinely roamed about 18 square miles on a bicycle until I was old enough to solo in an automobile.

In the spring I rode to bible school each day for two weeks. The trip became routine and boring, to the extent that if the sessions had lasted one extra day, I may have been among the missing. But Saturday night trips into town to the "show" (the local word for movies) were never routine.

It should be understood that the Yellowstone valley did not become exposed to television until approximately 1955. We did not have television in our home until 1957. Worden had a vibrant movie house, run by the Kraske family. The theater was open only on weekends. Bill Kraske was a friend and school mate. He and his brother were assigned the job of sweeping the floor, wiping the seats, and making popcorn before the theater opened. They also sold the popcorn as the customers entered. Bill's sister sold tickets at the outside window, and his dad ran the projector. Admission was twenty five cents for kids, and popcorn cost ten cents. If I arrived early, Bill would sneak me into the theater through the side window, and I would assist with the chores. I was quite willing to help sweep the floor for the free admission.

The bicycle journey to the theater in town was a major undertaking. We began the trip in the daylight, but had to return in the dark. I was about seven years old, in the second grade when I was first allowed to attend the evening show via bicycle. My older brother, Jerry, had done so several times, but made the journey in the company of a couple of older neighbor kids. When I was old enough to ride the distance, my brother was strongly opposed to my presence which would inhibit his social indiscretions in town. He was commanded to chaperone me on the journey and to assure my safe return home. His responsibility charade lasted only until we were past the plum bushes 100 yards from the house. He rode a bigger bicycle, was 4 ½ years older, and generally much faster. He wanted no part of taking care of a little brother. During the return trip in the dark, Jerry took great pleasure in riding ahead, off into the darkness, leaving me pedaling alone down the dirt road. We had no lights. It required concentration and full attention to stay in the smooth path, on the slightly lighter color of the packed road tracks. I was easy prey for my brother when he hid by the roadside. His favorite trick was lying in ambush, waiting for my arrival. Just as I was passing him, he would jump out and scare the night's popcorn nearly completely through my bowels. But I had to be brave about it, or the torments would become more frequent.

One night I devised a plan that I hoped would discourage his Dracula theatrics. An old abandoned house we referred to as the ghost house lurked along the side of road 14, near the Novotney house, about two miles from town. Jerry always rode as fast as possible past the house, because it was made of crumbling stone, was bordered by huge cottonwood trees, and was always darker than anything on the route. I knew he was afraid of that place. So on this wonderful summer night, I lagged behind as we were approaching the old stone house. He rode off into the night, and I am sure passed quickly by the ghost house. When I approached the house and drew near the darkest area next to the trees, I got off my bike, and pushed it into the gutter. I waited there. I knew that even when Jerry did ride ahead, he would at some time, stop and wait for me. It was an established pattern that worked for him because it gave him the opportunity to rest until I got nearby, and he would ride on again. I was sure he would sprint by the house, and rest a safe distance down the road until I came along. I reasoned that if I did not come by, he would eventually turn back to determine why I hadn't arrived. I waited in the tall roadside weeds.

All of my thoughts were perfectly accurate. The results were beyond my best expectations. Because of his own fears, he did not believe I had the fortitude to dally anywhere near the ghost house. The big "Pig weeds" near the entrance gate cast horrible moonlight shadows of imaginary monsters. With these monsters at my side, I pulled several of the tall weeds, and fashioned them into a six foot long stalky broom. On his first pass, he rode by with great speed. But when he neared the place where I had lagged behind, Jerry realized that I must have disappeared somewhere near the dreaded ghost house. His return was cautious, fearful and halting. I waited until he was within arm's reach. Hiding in the deep blackness I said nothing; but swung the weed broom whacking him in the face. He yelled like a cat under a rocking chair. With arms flailing the weeds, he fell to the ground churning the dust into a moonlight cloud. Still silent, I smacked him a couple more times while he was trying to get up. He was grabbing for the bike, yelling like a squeezed pig, believing that he was about to die of something more than terrible.

I grew so delighted with my accomplishment I finally burst into laughter and collapsed in the weeds at the roadside. He finally gained his senses, and furiously tried to locate me in the weeds. I escaped his wrath, and from a safe distance in the depth of the weeds, negotiated a promise to not kill me on the remaining journey home. It was wonderful. The old ghost house was demolished years ago, but some of the trees still remain. A tour by the area always brings a quiet smile. I just love those trees.

Riding a bicycle at a good speed on a worn country road in the dark must be personally experienced to appreciate the full sensation. It is like being suspended in semi darkness, following a faint ribbon of lighter earth that wards off vertigo and quietly guides you through your daylight memory of the path. Only faith and instinct prevent disaster. I often rode during the early hours of summer darkness. If my dad gave me the chore of turning off the irrigation water in a field, I usually went by bicycle. The irrigation ditches were no more than a half mile from the house, and an evening ride was refreshing. However not all of the valley's inhabitants rode bicycles. Some walked.

Between our house and one of the irrigation head gates, was a house that sheltered seasonal migrant workers. The workers were Mexican migrants who worked in the sugar beet fields. They got their wash water by dipping it out of the irrigation ditch several yards down the road from their house. When the buckets were full, they carried them home along the road. On a late spring evening I was speeding back home from a quick trip to the irrigation head gate, when poor timing and inattention nearly caused serious injury. As I was closely watching the road directly in front of me I sensed there was something immediately ahead. What I was unable to clearly see, was a Mexican lady in the path, carrying a bucket of water in each hand. I clobbered her from behind, rode the bike right up her back and flattened us both into the dirt. I wasn't sure what I had hit, but I knew it was "crackity damn big." It lay in the road with me, screaming and striking me. I envisioned it must be a dark river monster – some type of deep water creature living in the slough. I was sure they came up out of the river at night. The beast was also surprised by my unintended attack and began thumping me with its tail...in reality the bike was lying on the poor lady who was trying to kick free from it. The monster continued thrashing, kicking me with hooves as big as five gallon buckets. Water was all over both me and it/her. I was uncertain for a few moments whether I was bleeding profusely or if it was wet slime from the river monster. The monster was screaming at me in... what? ... Spanish? ... oh, oh, now I got it... I knew that the river didn't produce Mexican water monsters. I didn't understand her yelling, but I did recognize that she was madder than hell. I wasn't very old, but through local prejudices I figured this was really going to be worse than a deep water slough monster and I was probably going to be stabbed at any moment. I tried to assemble myself, and kept saying, "I'm sorry, I'm sorry", but it wasn't gaining me any favors. Had I not been so scared I would have volunteered to return to the ditch to get more water, but that didn't seem to be her biggest complaint. When I got my eyes focused and saw that she wasn't going to be a lifelong cripple, I reasoned that a good run was going to be better than a poor stand. I could already hear others approaching from the labor house. I thought that the longer I tried to make this better, the worse it was going to get. Once again I offered that I was sorry, and rode past her comrades on my retreat, with bent bike fender rubbing on the tire. I told my dad about the incident the next day. He broke out in laughter, the extent of which I could neither understand nor appreciate. When he returned to normal, he related a story from his childhood. It was almost exactly the same. Dad checked with the laborers the next day and found that my monster had only a few bruises. Time had allowed them to see the humor in it too. The lady apparently thought for a brief moment that she had been attacked by a mountain lion until the beasts claws became bicycle spokes.

Summer also was the time it became the swimming season. There were no swimming pools, only irrigation ditches. All ditches had "check stations" which were miniature concrete dams placed in the main ditches that held "check boards." The boards were inserted in the dams to hold or "check" the water back, raising the water level to the opening gates that directed water to adjacent ditches. Downstream from the check stations were miniature water falls. The swirling water from the falls usually formed a wide deep area in the ditch that created a natural swimming hole. Friends gathered at the swimming hole in the afternoons to play as long as allowed.

I say allowed because we were plagued by a disease labeled Infantile Paralysis or Polio. It was a horrible disease affecting mostly young people. It resulted in anything from complete paralysis and disfiguring of the limbs to sometimes death. Its cause was unknown at that time, but since it struck mostly in the summer months, many thought it was acquired from water and swimming. Parents were understandably paranoid, and fearful of excessive water exposure. We were usually admonished that we could not be in the water in excess of one hour per day. Where that value came from I don't know, but that was the consensus. My friends and I distorted that value as much as we could to our advantage by reasoning that we could surely swim for two hours if when we got cold, we climbed out onto the ditch bank and warmed up for a while out of the water. We also reasoned that we could swim in the morning, and again in the afternoon, if we only went for an hour each time. If we went home for lunch, we had to be sure that all clothing was dry, there could be no mud on the face, and hair was made to have the natural windblown look.

In spite of all of our devious precautions, we were still subject to, in our opinion, too much adult observation and supervision. If we met at the river, we could be free to swim unencumbered. It was always up to me to find the best and safest place to river swim. I usually chose the backwater channel, referred to as the slough. My dad swam there when he was a kid, swam with us there as little children, and perceived the area as being safe, even though the area extended for as far as one half mile. Our river swimming hole was perfect. It had both deep and shallow water, slow moving current, a sandy beach, and trees from which to dive. It had one other necessary feature. It was totally out of sight. Our caution came from first of all, the admonition that we were not supposed to be swimming so long and so frequently. Therefore if swim suits were left at home, we could not possibly be swimming. The second most important element was that we were all boys. Swim suits were not necessary at the river. In fact they were ridiculed and highly frowned upon. If you were going to be accepted as one of the boys, you swam in the nude, you sun bathed in the nude, you wrestled in the nude, and you kept it all secret within the gang. Members of that group were most often me, Frank Beltran, "Little Raymond" (Ray Beltran), "Big Raymond" (Raymond Devilla), James Kiel, Mike Mitzel, Bob Mitzel, Bert Mitzel, Phillip Fenwick, Jesse Bonilla, and Clifford Balzer. They were all farm kids, all living within two to three miles from the swimming hole. We got the word to each other in pony express fashion. Many of us did not have a telephone, nor would we have risked discussing the subject on a party line. If the water looked good, and the weather accommodating, I rode my bike in the direction of the nearest kid. The word was passed to him, who in turn rode to his nearest friend. The chain was repeated until the member at the farthest fringe was notified. We had a solid and secure underground message system.

Those summer moments were all too brief. As we grew older many of us were compelled by economics and farm life to spend much more time in the fields than gathering at the river. Sundays were sometimes accommodating but when we grew older, we often drove to the river to meet for an after supper swim when the day's labor could be washed from a sun burned skin. But life evolves. Eventually the secrets of childhood are poorly kept, loyalties are naturally dissolved, and sanctuaries like swimming holes are transformed by a new concept...co-ed. Thus another phase of life passes.

The river water was good for much more than swimming. The winter entertainment value far exceeded that of the fleeting summer months. The slow moving water in the channels north of our house became legendary for ice skating ponds. They were special because they were self-maintaining and always changing. The first strong freeze of the season created the fall ice. We tested it with a hole chopped in the new ice. Anything more than two inches thick, as long as it had airless water under it was termed safe. We skated the channels until the first snow. If necessary we pushed the snow off the ice with tractors or shovels, and continued until the first river gorge. Usually shortly after the first snowfall, the floating ice in the main river channel would build up in the shallow places, and eventually form an ice dam, or would "gorge." Often these ice dams were very strong and would cause water to back up for as much as two to three miles upstream from the dam.

The river ice gorges were at times quite spectacular. It was not unusual to see foot thick ice chunks, as large as a pickup truck, tossed up onto the bank by the surging water. On one occasion, my dog Penny and I had traveled across the frozen slough onto one of the many islands near mid river. As we neared the bank near the main river, I noticed something was different. I watched the swirling ice cakes and realized that the water and ice was flowing upstream. The ice had formed a dam downriver, and the backward flowing water was beginning to flood the lowland. I had to get off the island very quickly, or I would be marooned out in the flooding river. We ran across the frozen island, through the crusted snow drifts and arrived at the slough separating us from safe dry land just as the water began rushing over the ice. We crossed the ice with water surging up shin high. Penny was a collie with long winter hair. She was not a water dog or a good swimmer. She began having trouble keeping any traction on the ice with her feet. She too knew we were in trouble. I grabbed her neck hair with one hand, and pulled her behind me. By the time I got to the safe side of the river bank, the water was almost three feet deep, or midway between knee and thigh. I pushed her up into the bank, and pulled myself to safety. We still had about 100 yards to scramble to higher ground before we were completely out of danger of the rising water. When we finally reached the road, we were both hurting. Hurting because the temperature was zero, (I checked the barn thermometer when I got home), and the two pair of pants I wore were frozen solid. It was like walking with a plaster cast on each leg. My feet were freezing, and the clothing on one arm was also iced solid. Penny was limping and had ice hanging from her stomach. We walked the half mile home in silence. Neither could run because of the ice, and cold. It was a miserable walk home. We thawed by the stove with no ill effects, but had gained even a greater respect for the many moods of the river.

The fun part of the river gorges was that the back water would flood the low lands, and freeze at night. When it was very cold….cold enough to freeze the backwater several inches in one night, there was usually no wind. That caused the slow moving backwater to flood the lowlands and form a mirror smooth ice wonderland covering hundreds of acres. Usually, the shallow back water would freeze solid, clear to the supporting ground beneath it, thus remaining a solid pond even when the gorged river dam broke and the water subsided. The ponds remained until spring.

The results were fantastic. Residents would travel for miles to skate on the new ice. The area was usually so large there was little danger of wearing out the surface. In the daylight we played hockey with bent willows as sticks, and flat rocks as pucks. We skated through "long jumps", "high jumps", jumped tires, jumped barrels, had short races, long races, backward races, and played "crack the whip." There were sore elbows, sprained ankles, occasionally a lacerated head, and always endless fun and laughter. Nightfall brought renewed but more subdued energy. Fires were built on the ice with driftwood. Old tires were sometimes burned in spaced out intervals along the river bank. Five gallon cream cans were filled with milk from the local dairies, flavored with chocolate and served to skaters and observers. Even hot dogs were stuffed into frozen buns and consumed by skaters perched on fireside logs. Couples skated into the darkness, and held mittened hands. The bravest hugged in the moonlight shadows through thick coats, and embraced with cold wet noses. The joy was shared through the valley by 4-H clubs, FFA clubs, church clubs, school sponsored clubs, lodges, and just plain good old folks. Skating was part of my identity from grade one, throughout college until employment caused me to move south.

Church and Sunday school were a dreaded pleasure. Dreaded because I disliked the cleaning I had to undergo before I donned my "Sunday clothes" and joined my mother for the Sunday morning ritual. My dad and brother usually stayed home. Dad would attend on Christmas Eve, and Easter Sunday, but practiced his own respectable religion at other times. Because it was broken up by music and song, I didn't mind sitting in church for the hour long punishment of speeches and mystical talk I didn't really understand. I loved the hymnal, and became familiar with all of the old standards. However it was decided, not by me, that all children should attend Sunday school class in the far side of the building during regular services. There we were required to hold hands and perform what I thought were stupid little dances while singing little kids songs. Our Sunday teacher, Mrs. Johnson, was a very nice lady, intemperately religious, with a tireless sense of community duty. But I thought she was weird. She always made us pray at great length. She would lead the praying session and throughout her verbalizing she kept her eyes tightly squinted shut. The roof could have caved in during prayer and Mrs. Johnson would not have opened her eyes. I watched her often, and she was so diligent with her eye clinching that they quivered and blinked even while shut. She also lost credibility with me even at preschool age because she told what I thought were "tall tales." I was normally a fan of "tall tales" but if I had understood the word sacrilegious, I would have labeled her such for telling these tales in church. Her incredible stories were of things like all animals two by two into a large boat, then a big flood covering the entire world, a kid killing a giant with a rock, a lady turning into a salt pillar and other stuff perceived outrageous by a young practical mind. I wasn't getting it, and I gave her a lot of space.

Worse yet, the minister, a well-liked man, frightened me terribly. He always approached all of us in a very soft mannered knowing way. I felt I needed to avoid him at all cost. It was my power of reasoning that created such foreboding. Somehow I threw Santa Claus, God and Jesus into the same club of guys who always knew what you were thinking, and knew about everything you had done wrong. Wasn't that a reasonable conclusion from our early teaching? Then along comes this all knowing preacher who was the only one that I had ever heard talking with God. He had conversations with God loud enough for all of us to hear. I figured that if God and Santa Claus knew what I was thinking and doing, they were sure to cop out to this preacher guy who was always talking with them. I hoped that if I never got too close to him, he wouldn't know me well enough to compare notes and get the book on me. I even discouraged my mother from talking with him when I was around. For me this guy was neither to be trusted, nor confided in.

I outgrew my fears, but remained private in church. I abandoned the Sunday school in favor of the regular services. I looked forward to the weekly hour because it was a time when I could sit next to my mother, and receive her full attention. I doubt she was tuned too tightly with the sermons, but instead she watched and interpreted my reaction. She had a knowing way of controlling me. She always told her friends I was "such a good boy" that she took from me all other options. She was always so busy...I wish I could have known her better.

I got to know my dad when I grew old enough to work in the field. By the time I could walk, I wanted to drive the tractors. My dad would sometimes put me between his knees on the tractor seat and teach me to steer the tractor. It was just absolutely grown up grand. I remember an occasion that occurred before I was in grade school. I was pestering him to ride along while he rolled (broke the dirt crust around plants) sugar beets. Since he was babysitting me while my mother was either sick or in town (I don't remember exactly) he put me on the tractor with him. However it was a small tractor and we decided I would have a better time riding on the roller. After I had ridden for a time on the roller, he turned at the end of the field and the roller hit a high bump on a ditch bank. I flew into the air, lit on the ground, and the heavy steel roller passed over me. I apparently fell into a depression near the ditch and was only mildly hurt. I remember a strong pain in my pelvis and one leg. Dad placed me back onto the tractor seat, and we finished rolling the field.

By the time I was in the first grade, my tractor skills were put to use. Dad had piled the sugar beet tops in rows out in the fields. With the use of a pitch fork, he loaded them by hand onto a flat trailer and eventually hauled them into feed bunks for the cattle. He put the tractor into low gear and walked beside the trailer loading the tops. I told him that I could steer the tractor. He gave me the chance I was waiting for. I drove the tractor most of the rest of the day. I guided the rig in a straight line while he loaded at its side. When I came to the end of the row, I shut off the tractor, and got off while he restarted it and turned it around. Then we proceeded to the other end of the field to begin all over again. By the third grade I was driving our old pickup truck between farms. I have saved a separate part of this writing to describe a few of the now extinct methods of farming in that era.

REGRETTABLY ACCEPTABLE

My mother occasionally lectured me that we should never believe we were better than anyone else, and conversely no one was ever going to be any better than we were. She believed that we should conduct ourselves better than those who chose to disrespect authority and their community. She was firm in her belief that associating with persons of questionable behavior, and poor personal hygiene degraded our own personality. Most parents of my friends shared the same moral values. It all seemed valid and reasonable to them at the time, but unfortunately transcended into separation by different economic and education levels. The concept interpreted by the minds of adolescents had interesting results. As kids we didn't care about social levels. We were all immersed together and generally got along quite well. But whether it was from adult influence or by just natural selection, separation by social classes eventually occurred. It was with good feeling that I observed those in attendance at out 50th class reunion had grown away from those distorted and unfair judgments. Yet I don't doubt that some of those among the missing were absent for ancient unforgotten personal reasons.

My school years were a mixture of blindness and sharp awareness to social differences. My favorite memories are from the times of blindness. Other recollections convince me that we have aged into better people. A few memories make me wonder how I ever lived through it.

Danny's dad owned and operated a Tavern in town. I don't know what happened to Danny's mother, she existed somewhere, but she disappeared early in Danny's life and was never spoken of. Danny lived with his aged "Old Country" Dutch grandmother, and was generally ignored by his father. Sadly, Danny's dad spent an inordinate amount of time interacting with the local High School sports teams, and seldom spent even an afternoon with young Danny. His superstitious grandmother attempted to mold his behavior through the creation of witches and goblins and a deep fear that ghosts would pursue him for wrongdoing. In short, Danny got a rough start.

During the summer of Danny's 9th year, which was my 8th, his grandmother decided to return to Holland for a 3 to 4 month visit. His dad inquired into the community, searching for somewhere to "farm out" Danny for the summer. My mother saw an opportunity to make a small amount of money, and also thought she might be able to help out a child who already exhibited antisocial traits.

Danny moved in with us early in the spring. My brother moved to a bed in the unfinished attic of our cottonwood log house. Danny and I shared the bed in the porch of the ancient structure. Danny came to us with virtually nothing, and was even void of some essential items of clothing. It was explained to me that his residency was going to be a temporary situation, and that I should share almost everything with Danny. The summer was off to a tumultuous beginning.

Danny was one year older than me, but had been "put back" a grade in school. Among my peers there were no efforts made to cloak the dullness of the "just plain dumb." In my 2nd grade language and understanding, he had flunked the first grade, and was "dumb", with no other explanation needed. Danny couldn't yet read, was afraid of the dark, couldn't play baseball, and had trouble tying his shoes. I took advantage of that from the very beginning. I knew he could probably whip me in a fist fight, but I usually triumphed through deceit and trickery. Through it all, we were two boys, turned loose to struggle through the summer, and did so by becoming reasonably good friends. Danny was good for me. Through him I found empathy and what it was like for someone to be ignored, rejected and a failure in all eyes that were cast upon him.

My mother's struggle was of a different nature. She was having some early success in controlling Danny, but was unable to guide his father in any beneficial way. She had to badger the man for money to buy Danny shoes and other essential clothing.

While it didn't much concern me that Danny often had to run barefoot, it was essential that he have a bicycle to ride. I was vehement that he was not going to ride mine but to fit in with me and the other neighborhood kids, Danny needed a bike.

After some heated arguments with my mother, his dad (John) finally found a very used bike somewhere and dropped it off at our house. This bicycle was the biggest, heaviest, ugliest thing ever put to wheels. Danny and I had to take several farm tools to it to render it functional. We found a can of blue paint in the farm shop and painted it with a stiff paint brush. It was a gruesome sight. It's heavy pipe frame held onto two crumpled tin finders. The fenders shamefully shielded a pair of worn out tires which were barely kept round by rusty spoke wheels. But it was a bike, and now Danny needed to learn to ride it.

Unless you were there, you can't imagine how hard it was for a "not too quick" kid, to learn to ride a large, heavy rickety bike. When Danny fell, and it was often, he landed in a cloud of dust with a raucous clatter. His wounds were many and during the spring of 1950, road 13 was speckled with the blood of the frustrated beginner. I was of little help, other than to continually chide him for his faults. At times I would try to help him only to be another victim of the falling metal monster. I was impatient for him to get on and ride so we could see the countryside together. I understand now that his upbringing had conditioned him to failure. He often wanted to give up, but I would not let him rest, either physically or emotionally. I knew that Danny needed a success, and that bike was going to be a big boost to his self-esteem. At times I fastened playing cards on the fenders of my own bike so they would flutter in the spokes, imagining that it sounded like a motor bike. I would ride past Danny crying on the roadside just to inspire him to continue trying.

When Danny finally learned to keep the bike on its two wheels, we progressed into another problem. The bike was big and heavy, and Danny was not physically strong. As a rider, he was slow and couldn't keep up with the rest of us. With all the compassion of youthful cruelty, we just left him behind. But this part of the story doesn't end badly. Through the summer with Danny eating regular and good meals, and exercising to exhaustion, he developed into a healthy strong kid. The big blue pipes tortured him into being a tough country ruffian.

I can only now appreciate the culture shock that Danny must have embraced living with us. He went from social isolation, having little to no supervision from an Old World grandmother, to communal living within what must have appeared to be a children's boot camp run by my mother. He learned to sit straight at the dinner table, and to appear there at exactly the never changing designated time. While at the table, he had to speak softly, using only pre-approved words from the pages of mom's etiquette books. A clean face and hands were required at the table, and a shirt covered torso was law. Hats had to be removed indoors, and failure to remove head cover before sitting at the table was near fatal. Adults were referred to as Mr. or Mrs., and by their age alone were socially elevated to a position of respect.

Danny struggled to compete for my mother's attention. I give her credit for her understanding and patience. In spite of all his problems, she loved him and tried her best to be impartial....a condition that I selfishly didn't always appreciate. He found his way to recognition through chickens. Yes, I said chickens, the real barnyard thing ... filthy, feathered, stinking, pooping birds.

My mother grew and marketed "fryers", which were as you might guess, young chickens suitable for converting to fried chicken. The problem with them was the feathers had to be plucked from their lumpy little chicken skins, and then they were dismantled into pieces. I hated the process and rebelled every time I was directed to assist. Danny on the other hand, demonstrated ability for chicken plucking, and pretended he liked it. It worked for him, and these many years later I smile at the vision of Danny sitting on a bucket under the old cottonwood tree, next to my mom, both surrounded by stinking chickens in hot water, grasping feathers in both hands. She only wanted to supervise one person at a time, and God bless Danny for volunteering. Her "no nonsense" but friendly voice healed many of Danny's wounds while they sat under that tree among the stench of those headless chickens.

Danny almost met his demise that summer next to the chicken house in the shadow of the old cottonwood tree. My brother and I had a rope swing suspended from a branch on the tree. It lasted for several seasons, but the rope finally wore through on one side of the swing, and became more of a Tarzan vine than a regular swing. Its new function was simple. Climb onto the chicken house roof with the single rope in hand. Run down the roof and jump off. Swing out into space, but stop before you swung back and smack into the side of the building. The single rope gave freedom to much twirling, spectacular summersaults and showmanship.

But the rope soon wore through as did its paired partner, and we were grounded. We impatiently pestered my dad for several days to reattach the rope to the tree. Part of the delay was due to my dad being afraid of heights, and he was reluctance to somehow scale the tree to the level of the branch. Danny decided to remedy the problem on his own.

Danny climbed onto the chicken house roof with the frayed end of the rope draped over his arm. He twirled the rope over his head and flung the end toward the overhanging branch. After several attempts, the loose end caught on the rough bark and was partially draped over the limb. He gave it a slight tug and it held to the tree. He said, "I did it! I got it fastened to the tree!" From my view I knew it was fantasy. My response was, "No Danny, I don't think that will stay up there." The most respectful way to say this is not to say that Danny wasn't real smart, so I'll say he just didn't have a lot of luck thinking. He strode to the peak of the chicken house, ran in triumph to the edge and swung out into space gripping the rope as if it were tethered to a hook in the sky. He was suspended. . .well, not for long. He crashed at the foot of the tree, elbows first, chin next, and toes last. And I was youthfully cruel. I laughed. I rolled and kept laughing through his cries of pain and anguish. I laughed at his torn shirt. I laughed at the dirt on his tongue. I laughed at the blood on his forehead. But we were still friends.

The summer progressed, with Danny and me growing in different ways. He learned to sit at my mom's table, and eat with manners. He learned to respect older people and to get along with the other kids in the area. He was evetually thought of as an equal by his peers, and developed his own confidence. I no longer thought of him as an inferior intruder and sometimes even enjoyed his company. We rode the dirt paths along the river together. I shared the location of my most secret river hideouts. We played baseball in the pasture, and I even shared my old worn baseball mitt. Then the summer ended.

Danny's grandmother returned from Holland, his Dad was no longer forced to provide for his needs, and he fell into his old ways. Danny dropped out of school in about the 8th grade. He and another juvenile procured a car, a bottle of whiskey from his Dad's bar and joy rode themselves to a wheels up position in a roadside gutter. In the process, Danny scraped off one of his ears on the roadside gravel, and had other minor injuries. It was like the chicken house, he didn't have much luck with thinking. For me the lingering thought was that the moment Danny left for the summer, he was repainted by those old prejudices. He was again downgraded from normal, a community assessment that was regrettably acceptable.

Dan somehow survived his teen age years, and became a loyal dairy farm hand for his uncle. The last I heard he had become a truck driver.

My other close friends in the rural neighborhood were Mexicans. OK, now we say Mexican Americans, even though they are, and were just plain Americans. But in the Yellowstone Valley of Montana, many Mexicans at that time were decedents from Mexican citizens who came to the valley to provide hand labor in the sugar beet fields. Many stayed in Montana and built new lives throughout society. My grandparents also labored by hand in the sugar beet fields as did many of the Dutch, German and Russian immigrants who settled there. But the stigma of being different stuck with the Mexicans, and the settlers did not readily accept them into their society.

My Mexican friends were quite acceptable. Their father worked as an auto body repairman in Billings. They were a catholic family with several children, and were surviving within a very low economic scale. But they worked hard, were clean, respectable, and my very good friends.

My mother didn't see it that way. My friends didn't speak English at home; they ate different food, and only associated with other Mexicans. (Really?) But a humorous parallel emerges. The local Russian families also ate differently. They consumed a lot of watermelon and "that damn cabbage", and spoke German/Russian at home. She didn't approve of me dating Russian girls either. They lived differently and sometimes rearranged their grammar. It was strange, but regrettably acceptable.

In spite of it all, Raymond, Frank, and Little Raymond, were my close childhood friends. For years, they lived within ½ mile of our home. We shared the river and miles of bike trails. A few of our adventures together are worth sharing.

None of us had a lot of toys; at least not toys that were purchased from a store. We either made our own, or invented activities that needed no formal toys. We made our own high jump and pole vault standards out of river willows and hammered in finish nails as pegs to hold up the crossbars. We trimmed down a straight willow for a vaulting pole. Our landing pad was a pile of hay or straw that usually had to be replaced after each strong wind storm. We were all track stars – or so we thought. When we advanced to real competition in high school, we all had developed such bad habits and form, that we were initially far inferior to many of the kids with no experience.

The best times rose out of inventing new activities. One day while we were lying on our backs watching the clouds, we observed a large hawk descend to snatch a mouse from the tall roadside grass. Someone retold part of a comic book story modified from Greek Mythology. In the legend, a man and his son were imprisoned in a castle, and could only escape through a high tower bordered by the sea. The pair made wings from eagle feathers and wax, thus flying to freedom. However the boy flew too high and the sun melted the wax, resulting in his demise.

The story was a catalyst for great thought and speculation. Why couldn't we make a pair of wings and learn to fly? No one offered a reason to the contrary so we set out to construct at least one set of wings.

We quickly concluded that there were not enough eagle feathers in the entire valley to build a set of wings. In fact no one in the group had ever seen an eagle. The best material we had was some large pieces of cardboard from a mattress box. We cut the cardboard into two pieces about two feet wide and long enough to just clear the ground when attached at the shoulder. Attaching the wings to the body was a more difficult problem. Several experiments resulted in selecting the old standby of baler twine. We wrapped several strands through holes perforated in the cardboard at the arm pit region and at the hands. The "wings" could then be fastened to the shoulders and flapped by grasping the hand loops and gyrating the arms.

If we wore the wings, and faced into the wind, it was an exhilarating experience. Even a mild breeze would dump the test pilot onto his butt. Such force was great encouragement to the design staff.

By far, the largest problem was getting enough speed to launch our home grown version of Captain Marvel. Frank was assessed as being the strongest for his size, and was also the most enthusiastic about flying. He was chosen as the one who would be the first to fly. I knew full well that this would never work, but I gave my full hearted support to the experiment. This was going to be fun to watch.

The solution to the launch problem was daring. Flight would begin, not from the ground, but from altitude. The plan called for Frank to put on the wings, and launch himself from the high side of the cattle shed, gaining a 12 foot altitude advantage over a previously planned bicycle launch. Additional launch speed would be obtained by running up the sloped roof, and jumping off the high beam of the shed. Frantic wing flapping was planned, until a glide path could be established. As a safety precaution in case of wing failure, the landing would be in the soft cow manure at the base of the shed. Landing in the manure was an unpleasant thought, but optimism allowed that if the experiment was even mildly successful, Frank would be able to glide to the cleaner straw a few feet beyond the shed.

We climbed to the roof of the shed like an assembly of scientists. By now Little Raymond and I were snickering, certain that this was not going to end with valuable aerodynamic discoveries. My own failures with model airplanes kept me from stepping to the forefront of this venture. But we all strengthened our support, wanting to view the results.

The wings were fastened as secure as baler twine would allow. We all counted. "Get ready, one two three." On three, Frank sped up the roof as fast as his Keds would carry him. Shouts of encouragement were, "Flap hard." "Jump into the wind." He toed the edge at full speed, working his cardboard wings out from his body. He spread himself out horizontally like a giant Frisbee, and fell straight down like a box of rocks.

Someone said, "Oh shit!"

I added, "Yah, he landed in it."

Frank struggled to rise out of the thick manure. Brown juice ran in rivulets from his chin to his groin. He looked up at the roof beam, and saw that he landed a mere eight feet from the roof edge. He straightened up, pointed at the roof beam and shouted, "Look! I flew! I flew this far."

I sarcastically suggested he try it again, but this next time we should fashion him a tail for greater stability.

He countered with, "No, I've had my turn, now you guys can have yours."

True flight was never obtained, however the word mythology was better understood.

● ● ●

I was sharing my secret river tree house with Frank and Little Raymond when we found where someone had dumped parts of an old log building. There were several 15 foot logs in a pile that could be used for something. Oh yes, a log raft.

The beavers working the river bank provided several more that were salvageable, and a new adventure began.

We drug the logs to the edge of a slow moving side stream (slough) and contemplated a safe way to fasten them all together. "Safe" was a good concept, but available material was much more of an issue. We returned to our homes, and local cattle feed bunks to salvage discarded bailing wire, and twine. We traveled back to the slough with yards of rusty wire and rotting twine. We tied everything together, and from bank side willows, broke off a "twist stick" to tighten the strands and form the logs into a firm platform.

We cut long willow poles to "pole" the raft around in the slough and dreamed of imitating Huckleberry Fin by taking the makeshift raft out onto the main river. We fantasized poling across the river and exploring the taunting, ever so near, but out of reach cliff cave on the other side. Someone of our trio scrounged an old rope, and we launched the craft. It drifted wonderfully in three feet of water, and was easily maneuvered by the self-taught helmsmen. For some reason, every undertaking had to be secret to make it more exciting. Secrecy also avoided adult scrutiny. We now had a secret raft, owned by our own little co-operative. A pact was made that we were not to disclose its existence to anyone, and to only set it afloat when all three of us were present. We tied the raft to a cottonwood tree with our only rope, and departed, anticipating new river adventure.

Before this writing, the rest of this story has never been told in honest detail. It is a frightful account of my own youthful stupidity. Even at that time, the activity was contrary to my character and judgment. That poor judgment could have cost me my life and is to this day an embarrassment. The experience is barely believable. Those many thoughts account for never having told the entire story. Though it will never fade from my memory, it is time for an explanation.

When Frank, Little Raymond and I returned to where the raft had been tethered, it was gone. It had been two weeks since we roped it to a tree in the slough. During those two weeks, the spring runoff had swollen the river to the very edge and in some places over its banks. The annual muddy torrent ripped trees from the lowlands and pushed acres of topsoil downstream to form new islands. Willow clumps were washed away and new marshes were formed. It appeared obvious that the angry spring river had taken our raft.

We all agreed that the river was at fault, and only mourned the loss of the raft until we made plans to build another one. I had no enthusiasm for the new plan, which I let die through non participation.

OK...I knew exactly what had happened to the raft. I still know. I'll take you with me while I explain.

When we first tied the raft to the bankside tree the river was already beginning to swell with the spring runoff. I wasn't overly concerned because it was sheltered in the backwaters of what we called "the slough." The current there was almost non-existent. During the high water we often went there to spear carp in the slow moving backwater. The big fish migrated there during high water to loiter in leisure.

Five days after tying up the raft, I returned to examine our proud accomplishment in construction. My first shock was observing how the rising water had changed the upstream natural barriers, and caused the water to rush through the slough. The muddy torrent was tugging on the frayed makeshift rope, and would predictably soon pull the raft from its anchoring tree. I saw that the roiling current had made a new backwater pool just 10 yards downstream from the tree. The slow moving water in the pool would be a safe place to tie the raft until the high flood water subsided.

I thought about getting Frank or Little Raymond to help me move the raft, but had noticed earlier that they weren't home. In addition, we had agreed not to use the raft unless we were all together. I didn't want them to think I was violating their trust by stealing down to it alone. There was also the need for immediate action. By the looks of the rope, the raft may be torn away within the hour.

I tried tugging on the rope to see if I could stand on the shore and drag the raft to its new location. I was not strong enough, and the pull of the current nearly drug me from the shore. Three willow poles we had used to move and guide the raft around the shallow slough were still on the raft. I reasoned that I could take the longest pole, stand on the back of the logs and brace the pole against the rear of the raft. I thought I could push the back side around so that the current would assist me in pushing it into the backwater pool. From there I could easily throw the rope around the bankside willows and scamper back up the bank.

I had to step down onto the raft to accomplish all of this. It was a big step, but I was certain I could make it. As I moved close to the watery edge, my dog Penny looked at me as if to say, "Are you sure you know what you're doing?" Just to be sure I could span the distance, I backed away from the bank a few feet and reversed direction launching myself over the water gap with a running leap. I landed on the raft with ease. But I hadn't realized that the rope to the tree was frayed beyond providing any restraining strength. The extra force of my landing on the raft, separated the rope, and by the time I turned to look toward the river bank, I was drifting out into the current.

I grabbed the longest pole and punched it toward the muddy slough bottom. It was one of those times where experience gives you the test first, and the lesson is learned afterward. Of course with the high water, the raft was much further from the bottom. The pole was too short to allow me to get enough leverage to guide the raft. Within a few seconds, the pole did not even touch the bottom. I was in the middle of the slough, and the current was rapidly taking me to the main channel of the flooding Yellowstone River.

There was nothing I could do to guide the raft or slow my downstream progress. The longer I drifted the better grip the current had on the rough logs. As I got closer to the mouth of the slough, the current began making waves. The logs had been loosely bound with wire and twine. They started moving independently, bouncing side to side and at times elevating up on each other like pencils bound with a rubber band. I couldn't stand upright without dropping a foot down between the moving logs. I was thrust onto the main river squatting and half straddling three logs that had risen to form the center of the pile.

Fear began to paralyze me. I felt like vomiting and was so weak I could barely hold myself to the logs. I looked toward the bank and could see Penny running at the edge of the sugar beet field bordering the river. I wanted to cry out to her for help, but she was only a dog. Seeing her helped me regain my senses. I wondered if she would be the last living thing I would see. If I didn't make it to shore that dog would run all the way to Miles City, or at least until I sank out of sight. How would she tell my folks what happened?

I looked back down to see that two of the logs were leaving me. They broke loose from the side and were spiraling away from me in front of the raft, indicating the roiling muddy river current was moving a little faster than me and the rest of the flotsam. I grabbed two of the wires that had failed when the logs tore away, and wrapped them around the largest two of the remaining center logs. During the process I had to reach down through the logs, while they were grinding and banging against each other. My hand was smashed twice, but in the cold water, I barely felt any pain. By then, I and all of my supporting garbage was really bouncing. I concentrated on keeping the remaining logs together. One more was nearly free, and protruding out to the side. It continued in a slow twist, and then suddenly spun back parallel with the raft. It slid half way out the back side before catching a knot on one of the wires. I realized that my logs were probably striking submerged objects and were being wrenched free from the others. If this continued, I would soon be in the water hanging onto just one or two remaining sticks. I took what remained of the frayed mooring rope and lashed the back of the logs together. Some of the smaller logs were completely submerged. Moving about was very dangerous because it was impossible to gain any footing on the slick uneven pitching pile. My legs were like two green beans in a bowl desperately trying to evade a half dozen pairs of chop sticks.

I struggled to determine where I was. Penny was still in sight, running as fast as she could navigate the rough river bank, but she was falling behind. I was about to drift past the Mitzel farm which was about a mile downstream from where this all began. I was still far out toward the middle of nearly a ¼ mile wide river, traveling between 15 and 20 miles per hour.

All around me were swirling brown liquid vortexes, little whirl-pools that would appear and fade away into the depths of no return.

I knew that beyond Mitzels the river turned slightly to the south and pressed against the south bank farm land before racing north up against the sandstone cliffs of the dry-land hills. Beyond there, I was not familiar with the channel. I knew I wouldn't last 2 minutes swimming, and never heard of anyone with strength enough to survive falling into a flooding river. I had to find someplace where I could get near enough to grasp the bank. With the speed I was traveling, and the terrifying hopeless distance to the river bank, it didn't look promising.

As I drifted past some of the familiar landmarks, my fear settled enough to allow desperately needed problem solving. I gathered up more loose wire. There was plenty of it by now. I lashed the three push poles together in an attempt to make an oar. It actually worked to the point where I could rotate the raft. Then I discovered that if I kept rotating it in a clockwise direction the pressure of the water at the rear caused the raft to move to my right, which was toward the south bank.

I paddled furiously, but the raft turned very slowly, only moving in small increments. The movement gave me hope because I was progressing toward the south bank.

It was a green blob flopping in the distant muddy water when I first saw it. Soon it became all too clear. It was a partially submerged, uprooted tree; its branches bouncing in the current like an axe on a chopping block, operated by the river, daring anything to venture close. The fear returned to my stomach. I was only 12 years old, and I saw where I was going to die. The current was going to take me into that floating threshing tree. The raft would surely snag in the tree and rip apart. No one would ever find me. For a moment I was glad that Penny couldn't talk, so she couldn't tell anyone how foolish I was.

As I got closer, I saw the tree wasn't floating. It was snagged, and it was big....real big. The top branches were out into the river, but the trunk was wedged against a second tree that was still anchored to the bank.

I thought with a slightly sobbing breath, "Maybe it won't be so bad if the raft does hit the tree. If I can grab onto one of the branches that is above water and work my way over to the tree by the bank, I might make it out." The furiously surging current was shaking the branches of the huge tree like weeds in the wind. The chopping block branch was slapping the water like a giant whales' tail. "I have to try to get out! I may never have another chance. When the raft hits the tree, I will probably drown anyway. If not here it will probably be the next tree. No, it's too risky. Maybe I should wait until I drift all the way down to the Pompey's Pillar Bridge. Maybe I could somehow grab onto the bridge as I pass under it. No, that's stupid, like something you would see in a Superman comic book." I thought I saw the dog. "Is that you Penny?" "That's ridiculous, she can't hear me, and there's nothing she can do anyway. Dear God, the tree is getting closer and *I am* going to hit it low and get sucked right under it. Untie that little bit of rotten rope. I may be able to use it. If I can tie myself above water, I may be able to work my way toward the trunk near the bank."

The paralyzing fear seemed to leave as I thought, "Well this is it. If I don't make this work, the river wins." I calmly rode into the monster. Perhaps this was just another school yard bully.

The front side of the raft hit the tree broadside near the top third of its length. The logs immediately dove under the main spar of the strong cottonwood, while the back side of the logs tilted up as if to purposely flip me up into the branches. I grabbed an upright branch in time to see part of the tail end of the raft rise up almost vertically. Then the tree slowly bent downstream under the pressure of the dam being formed by the raft.. For a few seconds I thought the force would snap the top of the tree and I would drift away with it. More wires toward the center snapped and two logs catapulted up and over the main tree branch, while the others emerged on the downstream side. There was a standing wave on the downstream side of the tree, but it slowly regained it original position. The raft drifted away, torn into nothing more than disjointed wooden sticks.

I don't remember everything in detail for a few moments after grabbing the tree. There was a lot of cold water. The force of the current pushed water over the tree's center causing a water fall on the downstream side. My feet slipped sideways on the tree at least two times but I had part of the rope around my arms and the remaining part loosely wrapped around one of the branches. I furiously held to the rope and kept reattaching it to branches nearer the bank as I inched in that direction. My vision and memory remains rather blurred up to when I recall getting completely covered with mud as I climbed through the roots of the cotton wood still wedged against the bank. I had painful rope burns on my hands where I had used the old rope to keep from being washed off of the tree. It was quite a rope. It nearly got me killed with its initial break, and then it saved me from the flood.

I can still visualize sitting on the grassy bank shaking violently, not just from the cold, but from the totality of what had happened. I scraped most of the mud covering my body off onto the grass. I was too afraid of the water to go near it. It hurt to remove the mud, because both of my arms were scraped and skinned, as well as the side of my left leg. "I guess that marvelous old tree took off a little skin."

I sat there a few minutes, too weak to move, and too scared to cry. I could see that I was close to a farm that I knew to be near the end of road 16. That put me 3 ½ miles from where it all began. "That's fine, I'll walk back home, but I can't go back up to the road. I have to find Penny."

I started back up river, always keeping the river bank in sight. About ½ mile upstream I had to cross a drain ditch that emptied into the river. I found a shallow place to wade the ditch, and paused to wash the mud and all the other evidence of the excursion from my body. I heard movement in the weeds just above the ditch, and saw my partner, wagging her tail.

She never left me, she just couldn't keep up. She knew we'd had a serious experience, but it was not in her nature to scold me, deliver a lecture, find fault, or tattle to anyone. She stayed within a few inches of me during the entire three mile return. She and I shared that secret all of her remaining eleven years. She greeted me each time I returned from college though she never seemed to understand the cause for my long absences. We shared the summers of those college working days, even though the trips to the river, for her, became physically painful. Then came the day I left home with finality; on that day I packed my belongings and left for the Air Force, three hours after my departure, resting on the back porch, she quietly died.

Riding Shotgun Part One

S tagecoaches had shotgun riders. Modern battlefield ve-hicles have turrets on top with large bored weapons but for essentially the same purpose. The mental image emerging from the term "riding shotgun" is still of a protector ready to defend against the evil waiting in ambush; a fearless arms man, shotgun in hand, prepared, and expecting to puncture the ozone, to shred the bushes and eliminate all elements of prey. Well, sometimes.

The law enforcement profession soon taught me the many meanings of riding shotgun. Whenever asked by a colleague to "ride shotgun" it was foremost a compliment. It usually meant he needed a competent assistant to help with a pending task of some risk. At other times it meant as little as needing company during a coffee break. Neither request fades the honor of being asked. Hands on the reins or on the trigger, I've eaten mounds of dust in both seats.

In 1966 I was not yet an Agent of the FBI. I was a Lieutenant in the United States Air Force, but few knew it. Shortly after learning that minor physical problems (allergies) were going to prevent me from flying, I volunteered for a specialty that culminated in my becoming a Special Agent of the Air Force Office of Special Investigations. (OSI) In 1964 I attended a military (Spook) school in Washington D.C. and started a life of being different. My rank was classified Secret. I put my uniforms away under lock and key, only to be worn on special occasions and away from my geographic area of assignment. My job was to investigate serious crimes or security matters within the Air Force. As an officer I was by edict in charge of several lower ranked investigators. My associates like me wore modern business suits to blend with the masses, and as armor against all being investigated who outranked us. An OSI Agent was to be feared, and we answered to no one at our base; only to a commander at another headquarters miles to the east. It was a huge assignment and culture shock for a Montana boy from a small farming community where a part time farmer/deputy sheriff was the supreme law of the land. I was learning to be a man, in a job that required steel nerves and an emotionless disposition. I learned that if anything went wrong, the only acceptable answer was "No excuse Sir," and therefore it was damn important that nothing went wrong. When the inevitable happened, only the quickest wit and best ingenuity escaped closure by imposition of career damaging discipline. The architect of a stratagem trick became a hero in the eyes of the benefactors, and a promising supervisor to his superiors.

Paul was in his 30's. He was a sergeant and a good Special Agent. He was also a good Catholic, with five children under the age of eight. They were all at home with their mother the day the storm began. School had been cancelled. Blizzards were not unusual on the flat land around Ellsworth AFB, South Dakota. Personnel reported for duty, but stayed close to shelter. By 9:00 AM, the wind driven snow was racing by the barracks containing our office at an angle near full horizontal. We were contemplating putting our vehicles on the lee side of the building to keep them from being covered and snowbound. About then, Paul's wife, a calm dispositioned lady called him to report that through some shopping oversight, they were out of milk. The 4 month old would have to be fed before the day was over. If the blizzard continued, we could be snowed in and the child could be in danger.

"Taking care of the troops" was never something I had to ponder over. What little benevolence I could bestow, relieved my guilt for the harshness of the job in other venues. The plan quickly developed. Our assigned military vehicles were very benign unmarked cars with economic engines and "straight stick" transmissions. However my car was a Ford V-8, was the newest in the fleet and had new snow tires.

Paul lived on base, in staff housing, so I said, "Let's take my car. It'll get through the drifts best, and maybe we can get to the store and back before we lose visibility completely."

Paul insisted that he drive because he "knew the route blindfolded." We set out with him driving, and me riding shotgun. The road had been plowed to the store, but was nearly invisible in the whiteout. Two gallons of milk were purchased, and we began navigating toward enlisted housing as if it were a trek across the Pacific. The wind was blowing hard enough to force snow into the car cabin through the heater vent. We sighted a row of duplexes that Paul identified as his residence. However a drift, door handle high, covered the path to our destination. I ventured into the drift on foot and discovered it was only about a car length wide. We both decided that with enough speed straight on, we could break through it into the clear all the way up to his driveway. Paul said "Let's go for it, we can't turn around here anyway."

I've since learned that big snow drifts have different densities within their bulk. We hit the drift straight on, were catapulted up over the front portion, spun half around to the left and obliquely struck a very yellow fire hydrant that was hiding in the snow. It was a tough fire hydrant, sturdier than the car. It remained unaffected, but left a long yellow gash on the rear side of my new light blue government car.

Paul predicted our fate, "Oh oh, this is going to be trouble. We'll have to report the damage to headquarters in Omaha, and we'll both be cremated."

"Not yet," I said, not knowing how the hell I was going to get us out of this mess. "Let's just deliver the damn milk, and we'll figure this out later."

It was "The blizzard of 66." Ellsworth AFB had deep snow and sustained winds of 80 mph for three days and four nights. Those lucky enough to get to their homes (including myself and staff) were captured by the storm for three days. Anyone foolish enough to walk outside into the blinding wind and snow risked getting lost only feet from his front door. When it was over we had drifts from gable to gable in base housing. Thousands of cattle died on the prairie, and dozens of people died in their cars.

And my car...in theory it belonged to a frantically over reactive full Colonel at Offutt AFB, Omaha Nebraska. The Colonel was so "nutso" about vehicle safety that if any personnel within his command had a car accident, he ordered the poor soul to buy a bus ticket to headquarters and thereafter stand at attention before him to explain the accident. I spent three days marooned in my house, worrying about what to do with that garish yellow stripe.

When the wind died, and we finally dug our way back to the office, I was impressed by the huge drifts around our vehicles. The gigantic plows from the airfield had plowed around the cars, but still left a lot of hand work to be done before they were mobile. As I surveyed my blue beauty's scar, I was struck with a possible solution. The idea in itself was a little yellow, but with some careful negotiation it would be in the best interests of all involved. The snowplows were yellow! Everything on the base colored yellow was _that_ yellow; out of the same government paint barrel. Plows, airplane tugs, wheel blocks, curbs and fire hydrants, were all the same yellow. They plowed all around our cars in the poor visibility. The plows were so big, and the drifts so solid, they couldn't possibly tell what they were hitting......could they?

I rushed into my office, and looked up the number of the Base Motor Pool. I shook dice at the Officers Club one time with the Lieutenant in charge of the vehicles down there, and chances were he was also in charge of snow plows. I came up with his name, and gave him a call.

"Hey Wheels, this is Agent Schreuder up at OSI. How's things going? You lose any vehicles during the storm?" The Lieutenant of course needed more explanation.

"No, but even if I did, it wouldn't be a crime would it? You know, it would have been an accident, or an act of God or something."

"Well sure, but I have a little problem that I thought I should talk to you about first."

"Ahh, OK, what's up?"

I paused just enough to build the suspense and gave him the bad news. "Well I have a fairly new unmarked OSI car up here in the lot that got pretty well covered with snow. It's not quite the same as before the storm."

"What do you mean, like how?" asked Wheels.

"It just has a big yellow stripe carved into the back side of it. Now the way I look at these little accidents it's less important how they happened, than how they are fixed." Then I give him his escape route. "I would imagine that your unit is as crazy about vehicle accidents as mine and this could involve a hanger full of paper work which I would like to avoid. Don't you guys have a body shop down there that can fix minor dents and spray paint?"

He got the idea right away. I turned up the current. "I don't want to go through all the crap on this end just to get some airman in trouble for trying to do his job in a Blizzard."

It was a delicate venture in language. I needed to protect my associate; however I did not want to set an example of leadership by lying. I intended to put out just enough of the facts, all true, and let my concern for confidentiality stoke the Lieutenant's imagination.

Wheels saw where this needed to go. "Yeah we have a place we could fix that right up, but we'd have to do it on the quiet, like it was one of our cars…you know what I mean?"

"Well, do it any way you want, just so it comes out light, not dark blue, and without the damn yellow stripe."

"Sure, I got it, bring it down tonight after day shift."

Mission accomplished. Neither of us ever discussed how the accident did, or might have occurred.

The fire hydrant crash of 66 remained one of the highest classified secrets of our little organization. Paul has passed on, but perhaps during cold snowy days, his descendants retell stories about their Pa, and his shotgun rider.

Riding Shotgun Part two

The winter of sixty six also took me to places away from Ellsworth AFB. There was a "special" (an unusual investigation requiring high level attention) being worked in Iowa and Kansas. I was ordered to Iowa and found myself checking into a motel in Cedar Rapids Iowa during the end of a still very wintery season. There, I was to help another officer conduct several very difficult interviews and compose several reports "suitable for congressional review." That generally meant if the work and resulting report was good, your commanding officer got an award, and if it wasn't your ass was going to Viet Nam. I arrived determined to be the next Pulitzer candidate.

Jim was the officer assigned to the area. He was a monster of a man, although younger and less experienced than even I. He was a six foot five 250 pound specimen too big for pilot school. He was a mixture of fearful features; born with a stern jawed face, steel gray eyes, and with a personality that hid moments of pure hilarity. He could make the Devil laugh while his fire went out. But you had to know him to share the fun side. He was under a lot of stress when I arrived, and was quite happy to have a friend he could trust and share the burden of his assignment.

After a complete briefing and a strategy meeting we set out for our first interview. I was riding shotgun. The weather was cold, the streets were glazed ice, and the traffic was typical city, on a lousy weather day. I pulled my seat belt extra snug and was happy to be in the shotgun seat. Because we looked like civilians, traveled like civilians, and behaved like civilians, we thought it only civilian to stop at a local shop for coffee. It was going to be a long day.

We spotted a small diner ahead just across a large ice coated intersection. The traffic light was red, and Jim came to a cautious stop. In the bright icy glare of the morning sunlight, we could both see him approaching from the rear. A little, but fast approaching car was obviously out of control. BLAM! We absorbed a solid smack in the rear that made my ear bonk the headrest, leaving flesh on the cheap cloth covering. We stopped sliding somewhere near the edge of the intersection, and were happy to quickly assess that we were survivors with no serious problems.

Jim was about to get out of the car when a little shadow emerged from the striking car at the rear. Jim rose to the occasion, all six feet five of him, leaving the door open. The lone occupant of the ice missile was a small frail little middle aged fellow dressed in black. Looking closer, we realized that the black clothing had a purpose. Black shoes, black pants, black coat and black shirt. The only glint of white was visible on a small portion of his stiff circular shaped collar. The guy was some sort of a Priest.

The Priest halted next to Jim who rose before him like a giant before a horse jockey.

And then in an elevated tone he began to speak. "Oh, Lord forgive me! I don't know what was on my mind! Oh, well yes

I do know what was on my mind. I was distracted by thinking of the Lords work that has to be done today. I was so engulfed with God's plan that I was entranced by the goodness of what shall become of it. Oh, allow me to introduce myself. I am Father Agusta of Saint Mary's Parish."

Jim reached for his badge and official credentials, seizing his opportunity to emerge superior. He withdrew them from his coat, and with a glint of humor in his eye he said, "Please allow me to introduce myself. My name is Jim Browning (showing his credential and badge), and I'm from the U.S. Government Office of Special Investigations."

The little Priest sucked in his breath, slapped his forehead and said, "Ohhh, my fuckin' luck." A shotgun rider is never supposed to become incapacitated by laughter. If Geronimo had descended on our disabled stagecoach I could not have at that moment defended it. Realizing his spontaneous "heart felt" error, the little man attempted to recover but never regained his preferred stature. The Diocese paid for the repairs. The interviews were conducted an hour late after getting another car. Jim never had to report to Omaha to explain the accident. It too remained a secret because this time God was on his side.

RIDING SHOTGUN PART THREE

L et's get through the sad part of this story at the beginning. I worked with a lot of good people, both as the shotgun rider, and as the driver. When you have the same good shotgun rider along on several occasions, you get used to him. You learn to appreciate his methods and can anticipate actions without explanations. A shotgun rider is different than a partner, because he is only temporary while the partner is usually an arrangement with longevity and another whole chapter. It is very important that the participants understand each other quickly. Among the best who ever rode with me was Henry or "Hank" as we called him. We worked together in Tucson Arizona. Hank was always happy to be there whenever I anticipated needing help out in the desert. He had a successful career and retired from the FBI. Retirement for law enforcement personnel is graduating into the era of "Good Ole Boys" living to tell stories about "how great we were". Hank made it, but not for long. Shortly after retiring, Hank was preparing for Christmas by putting up lights on the roof of his house. He fell off the roof and died. After years of dodging trouble and injury, he met his death preparing for his own family celebration. Who could have prepared him for that? It is with great respect that I relate this story about one of the many times that Hank rode with me.

When I got to Tucson, it was my third geographic assignment with the FBI. I had previously been assigned to San Diego and Phoenix. In Tucson, I was one of two new additions, making us number seven and eight. It was about a year later that number nine and ten were added. One of the latter two was Henry. He was from Texas, and soon became known as Hank. Hank was a Mexican American and spoke both Spanish and English very well, but his English had that little south of the border rhythm that could identify him in a room of voices. His fame from the past included national recognition as an award winning football player from "UTEP" or University of Texas at El Paso. He was quick, tough, and loved a physical challenge.

Hank also had a sense of humor, and wasn't afraid to exercise it. In Tucson there were ten of us with desks crammed into a small office space. Outside of Kermit our supervisor, the oldest agent in attendance was Sam. Sam was a crotchety sort who seldom did his share of work, but was always present to criticize others, especially the younger ones. Hank loved the challenge of Sam's frequent put downs. One day Hank returned from our Phoenix Headquarters tired and hot from the tense 120 mile drive. As he often did, a couple of new jokes from up north were shared with the boys. One that Hank reported sharing with the ladies in the steno pool was particularly spicy and questionable for mixed company.

Sam rose to the occasion. "Don't tell me you told that joke to the steno pool!"

"Sure," Hank said. "They loved it."

Sam frowned even deeper. Slowly emphasizing every word he asked, "Would you tell that story to your wife?"

With a wide grin Hank replied, "No, but I'd tell it to yours."

One Thursday evening as we were about to leave the downtown office, we got a call from a local contractor. He had just been given an extortionate ultimatum. He was to have a cab driver deliver $50,000 in cash (no it's not a small amount - remember this was 1972) to a tavern, the "Horny Javelina" on the south side of Tucson. Failure to comply would cause one of his building projects to be blown up. There were additional instructions. The money was to be placed in a particular type of suitcase that was to be purchased at K Mart. He was to summon a cab driver the next day at 2:00 PM and pay him to deliver the suitcase to the Tavern. The Cabbie was to place the suitcase just inside the entry tavern door, return to his Cab and leave the area.

It all sounded too simple. How could anyone expect to get away with that? There had to be another development in the making that we were yet to discover.

On Friday morning, all agents were assembled. We purchased the exact described suit case. We filled it with a couple hundred dollars in twenties which were bound on the outside of precisely cut plain paper made to look like stacks of twenty dollar bills. A quick glance inside would lead one to think there was at least $50,000 present, and would act as temporary bait until we could "move in." If a life were threatened, there probably would have been real cash in the bait can, but crimes at this level rarely required real cash. We conducted a site survey of the Horny Javelina, and found it was a biker bar in the crappy part of town. (If I gave a damn about being politically correct, I would say it was in the lower social economic area, adversely influenced by industrial activity.) But to put it plainly the place was a real dive, in a shitty neighborhood. Just by appearance, only real low life characters would go there. At least we had a clue as to what type of people we would be dealing with.

As 2:00 PM approached, we organized into teams, two persons to a car. I was in my police pursuit Ford, with Hank riding shotgun. Most of us set up as near the tavern as we dared, given our contrasting appearance with the environment. One unit followed the Cab after he picked up the money from the victim. Another unit "had the eye" meaning they were in visual contact with the front of the tavern where the "package" was to be placed.

The operation began smoothly. The victim called the cab company, and soon placed the "package" into the care of a known reliable driver. (That too was set up before the call was made. We thought it best to use a real driver instead of an undercover agent in the event the subjects knew or were involved with the cab company.) The cabbie arrived at the Horny Javelina and parked in plain view as instructed. We fully expected someone to emerge from another vehicle and snatch away the package before it was placed into the tavern. But it didn't happen. The driver went inside, and emerged within 5 seconds. He got into his car and left. What now? We had the place surrounded, so the only thing to do was watch and wait for some type of development. Within two minutes, another taxi cab, from a competing company arrived, and the driver went into the Tavern. Obviously this was red alert, because no one in this neighborhood had the cash or class to hire a ride. The parking lot, and side streets were crammed with Harley "Hogs", Mexican customized pickups and abandoned trash.

The radio chattered relaying observations. "What the hell is a cab doing in…OK there he is coming out again."

"He has the suitcase in his hand."

"He's getting into his Cab. A black and white, with a checkered meter light on the roof."

"Who's got him?"

The two cars nearest the cab responded, while other assignments were made by the case agent. (The case agent is the one to whom the case is assigned and is responsible for its operation.) The radio crackled with new assignments; someone to get in touch with the Checker Company, a couple more cars to get ahead of the "package" so a rolling surveillance could be established, someone to cover the rear to watch for a tail or counter surveillance. That left Hank and me behind at the Tavern to watch for any residual movement.

"Hell!" I thought. "We got out maneuvered by the office studs in front, and won't get in on the arrest when the target picks up the package." We relocated so that we could have the "eye" on the tavern, and listened to the excitement develop.

The cab driver traveled to a shopping mall in mid-city Tucson. He had gotten out with the package and placed it in a men's room near the mall entrance. Then he left. The Surveillance crew peeled off one unit to detain the cabby while the others watched the suitcase in the men's room.

"Ha!" I mumbled sarcastically. "That must be fun! Serves them right."

As the boys in the potty surveyed the suitcase they began to think that perhaps it was not exactly the same as the one we provided.

"H-m-m imagine that, a switch."

All agents agreed that it was time to "blow this trick open." It was becoming likely that someone in the tavern was our target and had the original package.

Then came the message, "We will still have to continue here with this package. Can you guys at the Tavern I.D. (identify) everyone inside? We'll run records on them later to sort out who's the target. Get a description for a search warrant. Can you handle it, or do we need to wait and get you help?"

Hank and I were elated. Can you handle it? Do you need help?

"Over my bleeding ass," I hissed to Hank.

We were back into the good stuff now, and weren't going to give it away.

"Ten four, consider it done."

"We're ten 97", I transmitted, meaning we were at the scene and getting out of the car. We acted quickly before anyone could change our geography. But now we needed a plan, and had very little time to form one.

Hank spoke first. "OK Dutchman, how we gonna do this?"

I reverted to my military experience and said "We have to force our way into that hell hole and take complete control of the entire bar and all of the people."

Hank raised his eyebrows and offered, "Yeah sure, and when we are done we can fly back to the office with our angel wings! Are you f—ing kidding me? At least thirty bikers are in there, three hours into their Friday beer, and you think they are gonna bow down to a couple of suits like us?"

I insisted, "If we go in strong, and keep eye contact with the leaders, we can pull it off".

Hank breathed deep. "OK brother, I'm with you. But let's park the car so we can get our asses out of here before they roll it over."

We could hear the music loud from the bar as we planned. I continued, making up the plan as I spoke. "Hank, we'll go in together, tight, with jackets wide open so if they look close they can see our weapons. But they are gonna know we are cops right away. You go over to the juke box and pull the plug. Then we will announce who we are, and tell them all to line up along the wall away from the door. We will tell them that they have to pass between us one by one providing their identification. I will take it from them, read it, and you write it down. We'll tell them no one leaves until we have their ID information, and then they are free to go or move to the other side of the room. If anybody gives us any crap we will threaten to arrest them, but let's not be foolish enough to attempt to arrest anybody in there without a much bigger crew. If everything goes south, you know the rule. We don't pull guns unless we know we are for sure getting killed or killing somebody."

Hank gave me that grin again. "Just like the movies Dutchman, let's go. The light inside was dim, but as soon as we entered, I could see what turned out to be 27 pair of eyes glaring us down. Rough looking bastards, all of them.

The stench in the bar was a combination of marijuana smoke, old lager and urinal deodorant. Hank strode straight for the juke box, grabbed the cord and yanked it out of the wall. With a dramatic two fingered shrieking whistle he silenced the entire snake pit. I was impressed thinking, "Man Hank is really going for it." All eyes were on him.

Just as the suspense peaked he announced with a pointed finger toward me, "He wants to tell you something!" After that it was as if someone had pulled the plug on Hank.

Startled by the sudden transfer of responsibility, I had to catch my breath before I began my speech. I badged them and loudly dictated my instructions. When I was done, they all looked at me in hateful silence. Then the biggest degenerate in the collection moved forward.

The records show he was only 6 ft four, but at the time I thought he must be nearly seven feet. Three hundred pounds slid in front of me and snarled, "Do I really have to do this shit?"

I snarled back, "Do you think I'd be in here if you didn't?"

He came back with, "Well what if we just throw your ass out of here?"

I could see Hank in my peripheral vision moving to my right side, just like we were taught in the academy. Protect your partner's gun side, and keep your own free by angling toward the rear. Then I thought "Dammit Hank, I'm left-handed. My gun's on the left. Get the hell on the other side." But he stayed close. My mind went immediately searching in quiet panic for sharp words. They had to be quick, strong and nasty. All brains cells were on instant over drive. The big gent lumbered one step closer about to lay claim to his superiority. From somewhere I remembered a line from some old movie, maybe spat from Dirty Harry in combat.

Staring into Bubba's nostrils I said, "If you come one step closer, I'm going to jam this .357 up your ass and see if it fires in the dark."

I heard Hank suck up his breath, preparing for either fight or flight.

"Now hand over your driver's license and let's get this over with."

The big biker belched a sour breeze and reached for his chain suspended wallet. In silence he offered his drivers' license through greasy fingers. We wrote down his personal data, and returned the card. The others followed behind him without comment or objection. A few even joked about the process, and offered more than one identification.

We emerged victorious. When safe in the car, Hank reflected on the triumph. "Jesus Schreuder, those guys could have stomped our nuts into dust. I thought for a minute they were gonna do it."

"Na!" I said. "I knew they wouldn't."

From Hank came, "How the hell did you know they wouldn't?"

"Because I saw the tattoo on the big guys arm; it said 'Mom'."

The target turned out to be the bartender in the Horny Javelina. He had worked for the contractor in the past. We watched the place only a few more minutes until our co-workers showed up with a warrant to search the Tavern. The suitcase in the men's room at the mall turned out to be a decoy. The original was found in the store room next to the tequila. The bartender knew he was doomed when he found the ballast in the money, but didn't run for fear we would figure him out immediately. It was a great Friday afternoon.

The Horny Javelina served as a bond for Hank and me. It was forever an inside joke, and only we knew the meaning of asking for a shotgun that would fire in the dark. He was a good hand. I miss calling him.

The Downside

Part One

Some incidents that could make interesting stories will not make it to this collection. I see no value or purpose in descriptively recounting incidents for example when deceased victims of violence were recovered from desert mobile homes days after their demise. Nor can I recount the pain of informing the parents of a young would-be narcotics entrepreneur that his body has been located at the end of a remote desert landing strip. There is seldom little joy derived from arresting and removing a father from the home of an innocent wife and children, knowing they will now only view him through a glass security window. Although numerous, the stress of these encounters has been suppressed and rarely dwell within my thoughts. Law enforcement has its' down side, for which I credit the development of the infamous police sick sense of humor. In order to tolerate some aspects of life, combat culture shock and overcome occupational depression, members of the fraternity perfect a method of making light of the bizarre. At an early age, my dad unwittingly prepared me for such times. Toiling on a small Montana farm, regardless how difficult or unpleasant the task was, he found a way to insert humor and make the job fun. As the job wore on, he continued to modify our attitude with his wit and gritty perseverance. I give him credit for guiding me in absentia through many hours of grim duty, which for the most part will be forever suppressed. I am able to clean up a small number to make them suitable for publication. Sharing them requires a difficult balance. Vulgarity in a story is easily transferred to or associated with the story teller, yet a lemon pie is not complete without the meringue. Many names, limited to only the first, are real. Others for obvious reasons are completely made up. In all other aspects, the "Downside" chapter is presented as truth, without theatrical embellishment.

Fort Huachuca was an important U.S. Army Post located approximately 90 miles from Tucson. It was headquarters for communications for the Northern Hemisphere, and also Headquarters for the Army Intelligence School. It had a large population and was larger than any city in Cochise County or southern Arizona. The entire military reservation was the property of the U.S. Government, and therefore all civilian criminal activity, and selected military criminal activity was under the jurisdiction of the FBI. Fort Huachuca and Cochise County in its entirety were my working responsibility.

The Post Commander of Fort Huachuca called me one afternoon. He was an admirable leader whom I had come to know both personally and professionally. Out of respect, I always referred to him as Colonel. He attempted to respond accordingly by referring to me as "Agent Schreuder." However it became so clumsy in short order that I admonished him to call me "Dorwin." Since he was approximately equal in rank, but several years my superior, he willingly obliged. He appreciated that I spent many hours working indirectly for him, in the effort to discretely investigate criminal acts and eliminate undesirable personnel on his post. The amenable relationship was not without benefits. I was at times a guest of honor at Post "Dining Inns", was a welcome guest at the Executive Temporary Quarters, (a ritzy on Post guest quarters), the Officer's Club as well as the Post golf course. (A privilege I rarely had time to enjoy.) It was not uncommon for him to ask me to stop by his office to discuss a problem. After a few such visits I was able to determine from his tone whether it was going to be serious or an off the record inquiry. This call had the serious tone.

In his office, Colonel explained that the Hospital Commander reported an incident of "possible child abuse" to the Post law enforcement. The Hospital Doctors believed that the mother was mostly responsible for the abuse, and she was the civilian dependent of a U.S. Army enlisted man, residing on the Post.

Child abuse reports were not unusual at Fort Huachuca, and I sensed more of a problem was yet to be unveiled. The Colonel, seeing the questions in my gaze explained. Because of the extensive abuse, it was reasonable to believe that the father had to be knowledgeable and perhaps a participant in the neglect. I continued my quiet gaze, because this was still a matter handled at lower levels and not something that the Post Commander usually concerns himself with. Speaking through a tight jaw, he said his concern was that in spite of regulations to the contrary the hospital had failed to promptly report the abuse, and preliminary investigation by base authorities disclosed similar unreported incidents. The Colonel wanted me to in conjunction with the individual case, determine if there was a pattern of activity on behalf of the hospital staff wherein they were covering up such cases in order to improve their social statistical achievements. If that were the case, both civilian and military personnel would be involved. It would be a jurisdictional matter that I would have to work out with the Post Criminal Investigation Division, (CID), and the office of The United States Attorney.

I started my investigation by calling the United States Attorney in Tucson. His reaction to the details presented was that he was quite willing to prosecute in Federal Court, anyone abusing children, and that any associated document falsification was a problem of the U.S. Army. I anticipated this would be his response, and had already made appropriate arrangements with CID.

This left me with medical records to review, a few Military Doctors to interview, and the parents to interrogate. It was a slam dunk case. The hospital records were appalling. There were numerous cases where young abuse victims were being returned to their parents because inexperienced doctors were unsure of their requirements under new privacy laws, and were unsure of the military response and other regulations. Civilian medical school had not prepared them for this responsibility, so the common response was to do nothing other than treat the child and return it to the parents. It was an administrative matter that CID handled, but I had the pleasure of scaring the hell out of several staff members for failure to report a felony. It angered me that hospital personnel were more concerned with the welfare of their own careers than the welfare of children. The Colonel was satisfied, but there still was much more to do.

After conducting the background work, I proceeded to dealing with the victim child and the parents. I'll call the parents "Dick" and "Jane." The kid, a five year old, had multiple cuts and bruises on his head and face. Many were "older wounds" that were inflicted possibly weeks before his admittance into the hospital. Most disturbing, he had two broken arms that hung from his shoulders like limp leather belts. He walked with an irregular gate indicating other damage to his legs. He was not taken to the hospital until neighborhood mothers reported his condition to the Military Police, who then took the child to the hospital. I went to the hospital to personally verify the child's condition. It was one of those times that I would just as soon forget. Now I would deal with the parents.

Dick and Jane were disgusting specimens. Dick was a motor pool soldier. His job was mounting tires in the tire shop. Jane was a "mousy" late 20's low life socialite, with a reputation of sharing her body in the neighborhood. Neither was bright enough to contrive a reasonable denial, and both gave statements of admission to assault and child abuse. They said they had disciplined the child because he "wouldn't behave." I left Fort Huachuca the afternoon I interviewed them with one task in mind. Tomorrow I would arrest them, and put them both into Federal Custody in Tucson.

By mid-morning the next day, I had presented the case to the U.S. Attorney, obtained arrest warrants, and recruited Hank, another FBI Agent whom I have described in "Riding Shotgun" to help me transport Dick and Jane from Fort Huachuca back to Tucson. We had them both in handcuffs by noon.

My vehicle was a very civilian looking thing. It had four doors, a big engine, hidden lights and siren, and very good seat belts. I used the seatbelts to my advantage many times while transporting prisoners to Tucson. On this trip, I secured Jane handcuffed in the front seat. Because of the long distance and time involved, I was mildly compassionate, (largely to minimize the constant whining) and cuffed her with her hands in front of her torso, so that she could sit normally on the front seat. The seat belt was then fastened through the cuffed hands so that the hands were immobilized on the lap. Hank put his prisoner, Dick into the back seat in a similar fashion. There were no leg irons or other restraints. These weren't what one would call dangerous criminals, just disgusting ones. I drove, Jane beside me and Hank rode in the back with Dick.

The ride was without conversation, mostly due to the revulsion we held for our prisoners. Nearly half way back to Tucson, we passed by Benson Arizona. When Hank had agreed to help me with the transportation, he had asked if he could stop briefly to conduct business at the Benson Police Department. It was hot that afternoon, as I pulled into the Benson Police Department parking lot. "Roll down the windows Hank, and don't forget we're out here!" "OK, this shouldn't take more than 15 minutes," he said.

As soon as Hank left the car, Dick began to complain that he wanted to smoke.

"This is a no smoking car," I said. "How the hell're you gonna smoke tied up like that anyway?"

"I can lean down and get'um out'ah my pocket like this." As he spoke he demonstrated his snake like ability to bring his chest down to his hands and slipped out the cigarettes that we knowingly let him keep during our arrest search.

I was mildly amused and said "OK, let's see you light it."

It became obvious that Hank hadn't pulled Dick's belt as tight as I usually did, and that the lighter was also in the shirt pocket. After a couple minutes of contortions with me watching from the front seat, he got out the lighter, lit a cigarette which he had mouthed from the pack.

"Well I'll be damned" I thought. It is for a good reason that we travel with one Agent next to each prisoner, just to keep things under control.

The windows were open, and I didn't really care if he had a couple of puffs from his stupid cigarette before I got out and took it from him. But as soon as he got it lit, Jane started whining from the front seat that she wanted a "Drag" off the smoking cigarette. I'll have to admit that I took a little pleasure in refusing.

Dick with his lips closed around the smoking stick mumbled, "Turn around and I'll get it to ya."

With her hands still bound in her lap, she rotated her head around until she could mouth the middle of the cigarette while he leaned forward toward the front seat. Bemused by their contorted efforts I watched while unassisted they transferred the lit cigarette from mouth to mouth.

Then it happened. Attempting to rotate the cigarette from mid stem to getting the filter end into her mouth, she turned forward, leaned toward her lap bound hands and dropped it....into her lap.

I don't know why Jane wore a dress that day. Perhaps it was so she could look like a good mama in court. I don't know, but it was no ordinary dress. When the glowing embers dropped, the synthetic fiber (polyester?) immediately burst into flames, and spread, like fire in cellophane. She screamed, and I jerked into action. The damned fire was quickly engulfing her crotch. I began slapping her crotch with my bare hands. The fire was spreading quicker than I could swat. I switched to rapidly rubbing her crotch and thighs with both hands with her screeching in fright and pain. Flames were starting to spread up her belly when my last frantic rubbing snuffed the spreading fire. When the fire was out, I could to my embarrassment, see all she had to offer. Her scant underwear provided no protection and must have been made of similar material. Scorched pubic hair lay on the seat between her legs, like sesame seeds off a bagel. Luckily the material burned with amazingly little heat. Whatever heat there was appeared to rise away from her thighs. She complained of being burned only on her arms above the cuffs. I identified with her pain, because I had no hair left on my mildly throbbing hands. But neither I nor she had any blisters from the burns. I reached down between her legs for the still smoking cigarette, and snuffed it out. I remember thinking "This is a new experience." She was now a ghastly sight, but definitely out of the mood for smoking.

I just got the two prisoners settled back into their seats, when Hank came out of the Police Station.

Entering the car he exclaimed "Damn, Schreuder! What you burning in here?"

"Dick decided to try one of those cigarettes", I said.

Hank frowned and said, "What the hell's it made of, horse hair?"

I wasn't yet in the mood for humor, and carefully explained the accident, because I knew that the prisoners would probably use any misstatement to their advantage.

Hank caught the jist of my caution and added, "Well, it's their fault, they should have done like you told them."

"Yup," and I started the car.

When we got to Tucson, Hank took Dick into the jail. I waited in the entry lock up for a jail matron to arrive. I was quite uncomfortable with the appearance of my prisoner. She stood beside me with the entire crotch of her garment burned away looking like a naked cowgirl in chaps. The matron arrived, gave us both a glance and did a double take on the exposed privates of the prisoner.

"That's different," she said.

"Yeh," I said. "I don't think that dress was made for clumsy smokers".

The matron replied, "Well, no matter, she ain't gonna be wearing it in here anyway." The matron disappeared with the prisoner.

I walked out into the fresh air, relieved to have eased out of a potential problem. Hank came out of the holding area rolling with laughter. He had already shared my experience with the admitting jailer.

"Hank", I said, "You sucker, unless you promise to not tell this to anyone else, I'm gonna make you walk home, right after I take your shoes."

"It's OK Dutchman," he said. "Just so you're out of matches."

The "Boys" at the office had a good laugh at coffee the next morning. And another day began.

RANCH RIDERS

An old Montana farmers' saying is "Whether it's cold or whether it's hot, we'll always have weather, whether or not." Similar philosophy applies to many situations, whether it relates to weather, or not. My own related philosophy is that "Life is a collection of experiences", whether they are good, or bad, they are to be remembered for what they are worth. There always seems to be an element of luck in the creation of those experiences, again whether they are bad, or whether they are good.

I have always had more than my share of luck in collecting experiences. Many have been without the joy of luck, as we feel it in the usual sense. However, when the experience encountered is interpreted as a matter of luck... that one was in a particular place at a particular time, then luck performs the introduction. Thereafter the management of the experience has little to do with luck. The outcome is the result of the input. It is to that notion that I credit my great treasure of experiences. I hold no belief that my competence or incompetence has allowed me to collect so many, but it is the outcome of several that allows me to proudly speak of them.

Perry called me on a Thursday. It was August 2010 and he was concerned that he did not have enough personnel to adequately provide security for an important executive meeting that was to begin in just four days on Monday. Perry had been a co-worker during several years of occasional employment where I worked as a private contractor providing security consulting for a large private guest ranch in the Bozeman Montana area. The ranch, located northeast of Bozeman, is owned by a major eastern corporation, and is used as a retreat for executives and for customer relations promotions. The ranch has over one hundred guest rooms, is decorated in vintage western themes, with entertainment centers, outdoor recreation, and spares no cost to provide a memorable experience to all guests. The security staff assures that guests receive safety supervision in risky activities (rafting, climbing, riding, skiing, etc.) and that all executives and celebrities are shielded from public recognition or harassment.

Perry had been promoted to full time security supervisor at the ranch. He was younger than most of the other persons working security. The preferred security agent was retired law enforcement, usually FBI or management level police officers. The product they were buying was the talent and experience for calming terror, anger and hysteria with polished B.S. and a large spatula. Perry asked that I be at the ranch Monday morning for the 6:00 am briefing. It was short notice, but he was an old friend, the pay was good, and as for work, there was no "heavy lifting."

I left my house in Bozeman at 4:30 am. It was a little over an hour's drive to the ranch if I took the short cut through the Bridger Mountains via Brackett Creek. I drove my old Chevy Pickup because no one in his right mind would take a decent car 40 miles over rough gravel Montana roads, infested with deer at that time of the morning. When I got to Brackett Creek, the sun was up, it was cool, with just a few light clouds. I began thinking that this was going to be a great day for outdoors, no matter what the assignment. I got through Brackett Creek with only a near miss of a "White Tail" with a fawn, and slipped through the still sleeping Clyde Park.

The road to the ranch from Clyde Park looks like it was made by a drunken cowboy dragging a hay rake. There is an old joke still surviving among the local bar stools about the "pot holed" route. Legend says that one evening an old cowpoke, Lem, was relaxing in the Clyde Park tavern, and pretty well soaked his mustache in whisky. His multidirectional departure was in the wee hours of morning, and at sunrise his hat was discovered at the edge of town in a large pot hole. The well-meaning residents picked up the hat, only to find old Lem under it. Expletives were exchanged after which Lem exclaimed, " A'l fergit what ye said if yu'll jist shut yer face, and hep me git ma hoss outa this damn hole."

As I dodged pot holes, the road curled past ranch land, beside fences both straight and dilapidated, grinding through more gravel, over "Chicken Crick" (sic) and past a trout filled lake. Finally I passed under the arched ranch gate grandly planted at the edge of the Crazy Mountains. It was 5:42 AM. ; time for bacon and eggs before the briefing.

Perry said there were 80 guests at the conference. All were executives and spouses from large corporations. My assignment was to escort 16 of them on a motorcycle tour to Yellowstone Park and return. The bikes were being provided (all Harley's) by a rental/touring company out of Los Angeles. The tour company was providing four professional bike riders as guides. All I had to do was drive a new Chevy Suburban at the rear of the motorcade and see that the ranch safety policies were followed as well as provide the usual company courtesies. Because of the inherent dangers involved in motorcycle touring, I was to take with me, an emergency medical technician. (EMT) OK, thought I, Yellowstone Park for the 5th time this year, but it's a nice day. I wonder who the med tech is. I had been with several on other outings, and a good partner could make a long day more enjoyable.

I met my EMT partner at breakfast. Cindy, as she was known, was loading up on coffee to jump start her day. She was a middle aged female from New Jersey. I had worked with her about a year ago on a kayaking trip down the Yellowstone. She was OK....not my definition of excitement, but a good person. I could see that her co-workers liked her because two of the strongest loaded all 200 pounds of her EMT equipment into my suburban. Like I thought....no heavy lifting.

We escorted a ranch bus into Clyde Park. Waiting there was a 40 foot long semi-truck loaded with 25 gorgeous Harley Davidson Motorcycles, and three dudes that looked like they just crawled out of a cadaver. They were the bike riding guides, but their supervisor, a fourth escort was all Los Angeles businessmen. In addition he also had a black suburban with another driver to provide service if any of the bikes broke down. I found myself again feeling quite unnecessary, but as usual cost is never considered in these operations, and silent obedience is a profitable tactic.

The contracted tour leaders presented their briefing, explained the tour procedures and rules, and described the intended route. At the appropriate time, I inserted myself into the discussion with the "unfun" stuff. All riders had to be motorcycle certified, licensed, in good health, and assure they would abide by the prohibition rules. There would be no alcohol consumed during the ride. I checked my watch. "Great",

I thought, "For no more than an hour of this I have already earned $40."

We were about to depart, but I had to wait for Cindy to make a quick bathroom stop in the store across the street. She returned with another cup of coffee. I remember thinking that she obviously was a "sipper". In my experience, all "sippers" were also "wetters." Our route into Yellowstone wasn't designed by the plumbers union. Rest stops are rare. I wondered how she would handle it.

We roared out of town in a cloud of Harley smoke, disturbing even the earth worms. Our first stop was in Livingston to allow the riders to adjust their leathers to the Montana freshness. My partner made another rest stop and returned with two bottles of water. Yup, a "sipper."

Yellowstone was on that day unremarkable. Surprise! That isn't where this story is going. I was disgusted with the tour leaders for not showing their clients more, but realized they knew nothing of the Park and were just looking at a road map. Again, quiet observation was my perfected contribution. We left by the same route we came. We were expected at Chico Hot Springs for a catered lunch, and arrived exactly on time. At least these tour guys were aware of something.

During lunch, I again puffed out my chest, sucked in several years of inactivity, and reminded all riders that the beverages of choice were lemonade and ice tea. Again an unnecessary act because these people weren't a bunch of bundled testosterone on crotch rockets. They were sophisticated rich business persons out for a leisure ride. Half a day had passed and this day was looking easier with every hour.

After lunch the tour leaders changed the plan. The riders were finally enjoying the weather and decided to detour through Bozeman, motor through Bridger Canyon past the ski hill, and return through what we refer to as the twin cities.... Wilsall and Clyde Park. A rest stop and possibly a refueling stop was planned at the exit of Bozeman.

As we passed the service station at the Bozeman exit, Cindy began screaming, "They didn't stop! They didn't stop! Dammit they said they were going to stop!"

"Well......Ya, I noticed that", as I kept on driving.

"But I have to pee!"

She began spouting curse words toward the tour leaders which by that time were ¼ mile ahead.

My only consolation was, "Well maybe you can make it."

With a red face she gritted her teeth and became belligerently silent.

After about 18 miles she broke her silence with "I can't make it. If you don't stop, I'm going to pee right here in the car."

I've had to explain a lot of things to the boys back in the office, but I realized that my situational repertoire did not cover this. I was getting paid to shadow and protect this group, but if I didn't respond to my assistant, she was going to become the incident of the day. Luck (again) provided me an out because I knew of a single little camp toilet next to the road at the crest of Battle Ridge just ahead of us.

Within less than a minute I screeched to a halt in front of the little building and told her, "Make this a record run, while I turn this beast around."

I must give her credit for her talent because she was in and out of there in less than 30 seconds. We were back onto the highway just as the black suburban trailing the group went over the hill about 1/8 of a mile in front of us.

We both saw it, as we crested that same hill. Off to the right of the road, down a steep bank was a shiny motorcycle. The black suburban had stopped above it, and the bewildered driver was staring down at two human forms lying in the weeds below. "Holy shit!" came out of Cindy as I slammed my door and headed down the bank. Somehow she kept up, and we both stopped beside the still and purple faced form. He was the last rider in the group. His wife had been riding with him on the same bike.

He was twisted and bent, however she was sitting upright, shouting at him. "I'm OK" she said. "Just take care of him."

Cindy murmured, "I'm not sure we can do much for him, but let's get started."

She started CPR and at the same time told me to get her medical equipment. I ran up the steep bank, (yes I did run up the bank) and grabbed the first AMT bag. This time the "Holy Shit" exclamation came from me. The damn thing weighed about 100 pounds and I had to carry it back down the bank. OK, I thought. I will do this. When I got to her with the bag, she took out some equipment and said get my oxygen bottle. OK, back up the steep bank to the truck. I grabbed the second bag, and noticed that the bottle was lying on the tail gate, separate. Knowing that the rest of that stuff must have some use, I brought all I could carry. Again it must have weighed another 100 pounds. I stumbled down the bank, bag and bottle in my hand thinking about.....it's easy. No heavy lifting.

Cindy gave me orders to get things out of the bag that I had no idea what form they took or what they were used for. I passed my first aid training with honors, but had no preparation for something like this. I had tried to call 911 but my phone seemed to be dead.

My mind finally began working. The first passing motorist stopped. Rehearsed responses came quickly. "Call 911. Stop any other cars. Come down here please, we need additional help."

Back came the response, "This is a dead area for cell phones, we can't contact anyone."

Marvelous! "Then jump into your car, and drive toward Bozeman. Call as often as you can until you reach someone."

"You sir in the red truck, do you have a phone?"

He shook his head indicating yes.

"Good, you go in the same direction and don't quit calling until you contact 911. Tell them we are at milepost 31."

I was wondering, "Damn, how far is it back to civilization."

I called to Jim beside the black suburban, "Take my ranch radio, and drive in the other direction. I know that on the hill toward Wilsall, you can contact the ranch. Have them call for help too."

To the lady beside us in the weeds, "Are you sure you are OK, what's wrong with your leg?"

"I'm sure it's broken", she said, "but save him, I'll be OK."

Cindy and I realized that regardless of spinal, nerve or any other injuries, unless we got this man started breathing, it was over. After 20 minutes of tireless effort, we both knew it was useless. But we kept trying.

"Where the hell is the ambulance?" I never felt so alone and so remote. I finally heard the sounds of sirens. What a wonderful sound.

The first arrival was a State Highway Trooper, and believe it or not, an old friend. She got out of the car and called my name from up on the road. I guess my very recognizable bald head was shining up out of the weeds. She assured me that help was on the way.

I don't find it necessary to provide all the gruesome details of the emergency scene. Our effort in lifting a 260 pound man, up a steep bank on an emergency back board was pushing the limits of even the most fit. The lady was carried in a similar fashion to a second ambulance. The gentleman rider was pronounced dead on arrival. His wife received surgery for fractures, and is doing well.

In the aftermath I began helping my friends in the State Police put things together. It appeared that the driver, the last bike in the caravan, experienced a medical problem. He remarked to his wife, "Oh shit", and drifted off to the right down the steep bank. He hit 5 rocks, the largest two being the size of a filing cabinet. His colleagues ahead of him never looked back, and rode off into the sunshine, not knowing that anything had happened.

I knew that the entire staff at the ranch would be in a complete frenzy, without information other than there was a bad accident. My watch indicated it was 6.00 pm, and I still had work to do at the scene, but not just then. I would have to return the next day to obtain photographs, measurements and further details. The State Officers said they would mark the pertinent spots with orange spray paint.

Cindy went to the Bozeman hospital with the victims. The driver of the black suburban was still in shock. He needed to return with me. I drove and it took another 40 minutes to get to the ranch. When I arrived, and attempted to get out of the truck, I realized that the ankle I thought was just sore was now *really* sore. In fact I couldn't walk on it without a great deal of painful effort. "Marvelous again, no heavy lifting." But an interesting challenge was yet to come.

While I was providing answers to the State Police, there came a question I stumbled over.

"Did you see the accident?"

"No", I answered.

"Did your passenger see the accident?"

Again the answer was, "No."

The Captain, another acquaintance of mine was less formal. "Well aren't you guys assigned to watch over these outings? What the hell were you doing?"

It was the same question that I was going to have to explain to the ranch staff, to Perry, and to the "Big Bosses" in Texas and Virginia.

"I didn't see the accident because I wasn't quite there..... well not all there....well not there in time.....well, look my partner had to pee so bad, that if I hadn't stopped for 30 seconds, she would not have been able to function in an emergency anyway, and that 30 seconds was not only prudent, but was a safety precaution and the most reasonable thing to do at the time."

I paused to let it all sink in, "Watching the accident would not have prevented its occurrence. Being able to respond effectively was more important."

It's amazing how the truth bails you out of the damndest situations.

Desert Bombs

By the end of May, Tucson Arizona is hot. Spring seems to arrive sometime around mid-March and only lasts a couple of days before melting away into summer.

Thursday, May 24th 1973: I had just returned to my home in East Tucson after working a full day "on the road". It had been one of those seasonally hot spring days, and I was looking forward to retreating into my "swamp cooled" (evaporative cooling) house. But the phone rang about the time I got settled next to the kitchen counter.

All I had to do was say "Hello" and the flat business response dictated my activity for the next several days. "Schreuder, the office just got a call that a railroad train blew up outside of Benson. It was full of military bombs. I'm leaving my house now, and I'll pick you up as soon as I can get there. We should be able to meet the locals within less than an hour." – Click.

The caller had been FBI Agent Larry Bagley. Larry had been the agent assigned to the southeastern part of Arizona before I inherited the territory. He was a good friend then, and has remained one of my closest friends until the present. He later advanced to become the resident supervisor of a much larger populated Tucson FBI office. But in 1973 he was still establishing himself as a no nonsense hard worker with a practical mind and a good sense of humor. He had already learned some of the traits of our old mentor Kermit. Kermit was the long tenured senior agent at Tucson and was short on words and brief with explanations. Kermit was famous for initiating telephone calls wherein he would fire off instructions to subordinate agents without introducing himself, ask no questions, and hang up without waiting for a response. No one objected. We were an efficient paramilitary organization and we liked it that way. Larry would explain when he had the time. My immediate job was to figure out what I needed to check out a train explosion somewhere out in the desert, probably in the dark, and I had eight minutes to be ready when he arrived.

Larry lived a short distance to the west of me, and had to travel near my house on the way out of town toward Benson. He was there quickly as expected and barely rolled to a stop before I was in the car buckled up for the ride. Larry was assigned one of the better cars in the fleet. It was a new Chevrolet, nice looking for a Government car, flashing a white top over a blue body. Like all of our cars, it was a police pursuit model sporting a 140 mph speedometer, probably with the ability to peg the needle. However, just to make the job more interesting, the car rolled on cheap tires furnished by the lowest bidder.

The need to arrive at the scene post haste was multifaceted. As in any public disaster, gawkers and residents need to be evacuated to protect them and preserve the scene. Witnesses had to be identified before they departed as well as suspects, if they existed. Evidence needed to be secured. Additional hazards need to be detected and neutralized. In short, we needed to get there before everything got all screwed up.

We entered the I-10 freeway East about 12 miles from my house. The late day traffic was light. Larry quickly accelerated to 100 mph, the air outside was 100 degrees, and I was strapped in my seat with 100 different thoughts about how a second train in a month, loaded with US military bombs could explode. The first train had blown up in Roseville, CA on April 28, just a little less than a month before. That case was still being investigated as a possible sabotage. I knew there would soon be a lot of political and headquarters heat on this case. It happened in my assigned territory, so I would be living with it until completion. I had learned that all high profile cases offer the chance to be a hero, or a "dumb ass", often decided by the minutest circumstances.

Larry crested a desert ridge in the freeway and we saw ahead of us, three vehicles with flashing red lights on their roofs. We recognized them as belonging to a local "Do Gooders" group known as REACT. I don't remember what the letters stood for, but the acronym was partly self-explanatory. They were a group of curiosity driven, thrill seeking, busy bodies, sporting CB radios and coffee thermoses that reacted to every significant emergency and offered their assistance – perhaps in good faith, but usually became pain in the ass intruders. As they appeared in our view, Larry said, "Look up ahead! That REACT bunch must have picked up the information on their CB's and are already ahead of us."

I said, "Yup, that's them alright. I know the fat guy that drives that old Jeep."

Larry grinned and said through a gripped jaw, "Well, we'll blow their ass off the road."

They had to yield to our superior blue light, and we went by at over 100. They quickly disappeared in the rear view mirror and I thought confidently they would be one less problem we would have to immediately deal with.

Cactus, Mesquite and Palo Verde trees were flying by the window like a slurry of green pea soup, when I heard a loud rattle and slapping noise from the rear of the car. Larry gripped the steering wheel like the rope on a rodeo bull, and the car experimented with several fancy dance moves. The rear tire on my side had disintegrated at 100 mph. It was quite a ride for a few seconds, but Larry muscled the Chevy to a stop at the side of the road as if we had only pulled over for bathroom relief. We looked at the bare rear wheel....because there was no tire left to examine.

Larry grinned and in a tone mixed with adrenaline and relief from his spectacular bit of driving said, "I guess we better get the spare." He put the jack to the frame and I touched the wrench to the wheel.

The metal rim was so hot it burned my hand. "Holy crap! How are we going to get that loose?" I asked.

"Hold something against it and cool it off!"

"What the hell out here on the asphalt highway is cool?"

"Use your shirt!"

"Screw that, use yours!"

"Loosen the bolts, and we'll pull the wheel off with the straw seat cushion."

"How about the floor mats?"

"I don't have any? There's a bag that the tire tools were stored in."

"OK, I've got it."

As I looked up onto the road, all three of the REACT vehicles passed us with their red lights flashing. We were appropriately yielding at the side of the road, trunk open and jack still in place. They didn't stop to help. They obviously knew who we were, but had their own pride in once again being ahead of us. We removed the smoking wheel with a combination of shoe soles and tool bags and were back on our way soon enough to once again "blow the REACT team off the road." We went by without making eye contact as though we had never seen them before.

Including the traffic in Tucson, and a red hot tire change, we still traveled over 60 miles in less than an hour arriving in Benson shortly before dusk. Through radio contact we met the Sheriff of Cochise County, T. Jim (Jimmy) Willson. Together we then met with the area Superintendent of the Southern Pacific Railway. Sheriff Jimmy Willson was what I can only describe as "A good old Boy." Where I and most of law enforcement come from, that means a good down to earth person, grown up in the local area, hardworking, and trustworthy. The railroad Superintendent, Mr. Ralph Coltrin Sr. was a hardened businessman, and was everything one would expect from a person at the top step of the railroad boss ladder. Mr. Coltrin described the situation:

The US Navy was shipping bombs from a manufacturing location in the Midwest via rail to a port in California, where they would be transported by ship for use in Vietnam. Each rail car contained about 250 five hundred pound bombs. He wasn't sure how many exploded, but from a distance it appeared that several of about 15 loaded cars exploded. What remained of the center of the train was still on fire, and unexploded bombs were scattered over the surrounding area. He had no explanation for the bombs detonating. He had not been able to get close enough to assess further damage. The crew was not seriously injured and was being treated for minor injuries and shock. (There was something about a ringing in their ears.)

Larry said, "Well let's go have a look. We can go in my car." Sheriff Wilson got in the front with Larry driving while the Rail Boss and I jumped into the back. We didn't mention that we had no spare tire.

We rode the I-10 Freeway East 6 miles past Benson and turned south on Sibyl Road. Sibyl was a dirt road through a span of Arizona desert that supported few plants, and none taller than a couple feet. To the left, or east were the Dragoon mountains. The railroad wound around through this area, as a means of losing altitude after crossing through the Dragoons. It was dark when we came upon a crossing where Sibyl road met the Southern Pacific Railroad. From there I could see an orange glow on the tracks to the south. Larry drove off Sibyl into dirt tracks beside the railroad bed. One quarter mile further, the car lights illuminated three railroad engines still on the tracks. The windows in the engines were all cracked or shattered, and two were completely blown out. Larry slowed as we proceeded further, past several cars still hooked to the train, but in various stages of destruction. The orange glow grew into a roaring fire on the track. A railroad car loaded with lumber was still on the track, but was burning. Jimmy suddenly cursed, and Larry slammed on the brakes. A dust grey 500 pound bomb lay in the road in front of us. Larry eased the car around it, but in our headlights were several more. They looked like a group of sheep slumbering in our pathway. We all cautiously got out of the car to be greeted by the smells of burning lumber, scorched desert, and what I later learned was residue from exploded bombs. The burning rail car lit the area for several hundred yards. Ralph the rail boss walked over to the burning car. I noticed that the area beyond the fire appeared unusually dark. I walked only a short distance before I realized the dark area was a huge crater in the ground. The track was gone, as was any trace of the rest of the train. A black hole of unseen depth was still steaming with dust and burning debris. There were unexploded bombs lying in all directions. I looked in the direction of the burning lumber car to my left and saw part of the flaming car floor fall onto the tracks. When it fell, it didn't land flat onto the tracks. In the dim light I could see that under the burning mass were two more unexploded bombs. The collapsing floor falling onto the glowing bombs beneath it got the attention of the others, and prompted Larry to shout to Ralph, "Get back in the car! We need to get the hell out of here." Ralph may have even been on the car before the bottom fell out, but was inspired to join the rest of us in our retreat. All knew without saying, that in a few short minutes or less, the fire would ignite the bombs on the track, and may in turn set off some of the "sleeping sheep." Larry did not have room among the debris to turn the car around and began backing in the direction from where we had come. Sheriff Jimmy was shouting directions reminding Larry that we also had a bomb in our path of retreat. Larry found a clear spot to spin the car around and we dodged the roadway bomb again. We were not yet clear of the train engines when the first explosion occurred. I expected the worst, but was actually a little disappointed in the intensity of the concussion. A few seconds later, another much bigger blast lit the sky, and we saw a shower of sparks from the burning lumber car. It must have been the bombs under the car. By the time we paused at the Sibyl road crossing, we heard more explosions. Some of the "sheep" were awakening.

The rail boss was efficient. Before daylight, he had a repair train in place in front of the damaged engines. It was complete with repair materials, the beginning of a work crew, and a kitchen cook car. I mentioned that we would have a lot of work ahead to complete a crime scene search before the Southern Pacific began reconstruction.

He looked at me with all the confidence of a commanding General, and said "Starting tomorrow morning, I've got 48 hours to get our trains moving through here again. I'll give you 'till noon."

I looked at him with surprise thinking, "Crap! They've blown up half a mile of desert, and they want me to complete a crime scene in 5 or 6 hours."

I squeezed out, "Well, I'm sure we can work together."

He agreed, and invited the other three of us into his train kitchen car for coffee. It was well after midnight and we all needed to sit down and gather our thoughts.

The plan we developed was that the Army Explosive Ordinance Team at nearby Fort Huachuca could help gather up the bombs and make sure the area was safe from live explosives. As part of the crime scene, I would ask them to mark and catalogue the location of each unexploded bomb. The National Transportation Safety Board had already been contacted by the Railroad and a representative would arrive shortly after sunup. I would photograph the scene, coordinate the different teams, and conduct a trackside search toward the Dragoon Mountains. The sheriff would provide a security perimeter and road block the area. I asked him to also make a record of any vehicles appearing to scout the scene that were known to be from outside of the local area.

It was still a couple hours before sunup, when we were notified that the Commander of the Arizona Highway Patrol was waiting to meet us in Benson. Larry again drove us all back to

Benson, where we assembled at the Horse Shoe Café, an all-night "mom and pop" restaurant. Larry parked the car next to the railroad tracks across the highway from the restaurant. Trains were sorting cars in the rail yard next to the car, preparing to shuttle the work crew and more equipment out to the wreck site. We had a leisurely breakfast, settled on our strategy and waited for daylight. We needed one more quick look at the scene in the daylight before we finalized our plan. Larry and I planned to return to Tucson. There I would get my car and additional crime scene supplies and return to the scene on my own. He had a long planned vacation scheduled and figured he would get out of town while he still could. It was clear that I was going to have more help than I needed so he could escape with a clear conscience.

The sun was just coming up when we walked across the road from the restaurant to our vehicles. The noise of the trains was gone, so the first thing we heard approaching Larry's car was the engine running. He pulled on the door, but it was locked. We could see the keys in the ignition. The car was still running, and the doors were locked. I thought, "What a hell of a way to start the morning. At this rate it is going to be a very long day."

Five great minds went to work figuring out how to break into the car. The five minds consisted of two FBI agents, a County Sheriff, a Railroad Superintendent and the Trooper in charge of the Arizona Highway Patrol. A sixth, the Benson Chief of Police joined us so that there were at least two authorities in uniform. All were high profile, creating a grand spectacle at the edge of the highway, fishing wire through the window of a "plain clothes" FBI car. Several minutes of poor progress had passed when I walked around to the passenger side of the car. I tried the handle of the passenger door, and it opened immediately.

With the open door in my hand I said something like, "Well for @#$%&* sakes look at this."

Larry, without hesitating looked over and loudly chided, "Alright, which one of you dummies left the door unlocked?" It was an unforgettable classic Bagley comeback.

I got all the way back to Tucson, gathered my equipment, an overnight toothbrush and returned by the time other agencies were assembling. (My tires held together.) The scene was surreal. The crater was even bigger in the daylight than I had imagined. According to the railroad, twelve cars loaded with approximately 2,600 bombs had been hooked together in the center of the train. There was little remaining of any of the bomb cars. A trench 30 feet deep had been blown in the desert about the length of 10 railroad box cars. Four hundred sixty feet of track was blown up. Box car wheels stuck out from the dirt sides of the crater, and lay crooked in the surrounding desert. Spaghetti like strands of train rails wound their way through the rubble. All vegetation had been blown out of the ground five hundred yards around the track that apparently was ground zero. The desert was scorched for ¼ mile in all directions. Not even hardy desert clumps of grass remained. One hundred yards away, fence posts had been uprooted and flattened. And then there were the bombs.....scattered in all directions. Later measurements disclosed that several bombs were scattered in a 5000 ft. radius (yes that's five thousand feet) around ground zero.

The railroad crew appeared with two fork lifts, and operators began rounding up bombs from all directions in the desert. They recovered approximately 500 Bombs, meaning that about 2100 were exploded. I was not certain of the exact count because several were unearthed later when the railroad crew began grading dirt into the crater. I wouldn't be surprised if a bomb or two still lies today buried under the replaced railroad bed.

I spent the morning getting investigators to confine their activities to their own jurisdiction. I should explain that FBI jurisdiction centered on the Federal Train Wreck Statute, (which says it's against the law to intentionally wreck a train); the statute concerning destruction of Government Property (the bombs belonged to the US Navy); and the statute for prosecuting sabotage. (The US was at war in Vietnam and this explosion affected the war effort.) With all of those laws to guide me, I clearly had the primary jurisdiction, and needed to keep other groups focused on their particular expertise without damaging any evidence I needed to make a case.

I observed there were a lot of people wandering around getting in each other's way, with little direction. I stopped everything, and insisted we have an onsite meeting. It turned out to be a good idea that worked well. After a few minutes of very frank discussion, the Army went to work with the bombs. The National Transportation (NTSB) Agent's took over examining the remaining rail cars and the destroyed structures. We agreed that the Navy and NTSB investigators would work with the Army and transport all pieces of exploded box cars to a large hanger at Fort Huachuca where they would reassemble everything wherever possible. We agreed to meet daily to share information. The Sheriff and Arizona Highway Patrol would maintain security around the perimeter of the site. I interviewed the train crew, took photos and did a perimeter search.

By midafternoon, I had already formed my opinion of what happened. It didn't involve any type of crime....other than stupidity. The bombs were shipped in 12 vintage wooden boxcars. They were all coupled together near the center of the train. According to the crew riding in the caboose, they first noticed smoke coming from car number 38, numbering from the front of the train to the back. They radioed the engine crew, who attempted to slow the train. Before the train slowed a small explosion came from car 38, and they saw what appeared to be bombs drop out of the car. They jumped from the Caboose and ran toward a culvert for protection. They had just scrambled to safety when entire box cars started exploding. The concussions were so great that even though they were protected by the culvert, they could not look toward the train to see what was happening.

The train had come out of New Mexico into Arizona, rolling downhill for many miles. It crossed the Dragoon Mountains and coasted down into the lower desert toward Benson. The old boxcars had metal brake shoes and no spark guards. I believed the sparks from the wheels set the wooden floor of one of the cars on fire. From there some of the bombs heated up enough to set off the entire load. It was a simple solution, but I needed more evidence to prove it to East Coast authorities sitting in judgment.

I got into my "plain clothes" Ford, and headed up the rough dusty service road beside the railroad track. The road was two ruts cut into the rocky white desert clay. It was narrow, with the rail bed on one side and a rickety barbed wire fence on the

Pacific rails. What the heck, the rail line was closed, and I could drive all the way back to the scene. Alas there was no crossing that would allow me to get up onto the tracks. In a few moments reality set in and I decided it was no time for childish experiments. Today I wish I had done it.

When I returned to ground zero, heavy equipment was already pushing dirt into the crater. Fortunately I had taken all the photos I needed. I figured I could wrap this up in just a few more days.

I spent a couple more days visiting the scene, mostly to check on the progress of the other agencies. The crew at Fort Huachuca had assembled significant parts of a couple of box cars, including one that obviously had burned before exploding. It became clear that the fire started in the wooden car floor of car 38 just above the wheel and brake. Most of my work involved writing up the findings and submitting a few items of evidence to the FBI Laboratory. One of the items I submitted was the yellow/grey substance I gathered trackside east of the explosion. From what I had learned I believed it was Tritonal, a substance used inside the bombs. From my own chemistry education, I knew that the material was not explosive in the open air. However I wanted it positively identified because it would prove that the bombs were heated to the point of bursting open, at least a mile before they exploded. That type of detonation would definitely rule out a sabotage induced detonation. I sent the substance to the FBI Laboratory in Washington D.C.

Conclusion:

All agencies agreed on the results of the investigation. We shared our information, and the NTSB used several excerpts from my report. The conclusion was that car number 38 caught fire because the pin wheel effect of brake shoe sparks ignited the wooden floor of the box car. The fire heated the bombs until at least one "deflagrated" as a can of unopened beans would do on a camp fire. The inner material of the bomb burned intensely and eventually caused the entire car to explode. The resulting explosion caused a chain reaction, detonating all 12 box cars of bombs. Most interesting was that prior to the Benson explosion report, the Roseville California explosion was still being investigated as sabotage. That was because the fire in the floor of another wooden box car did not become intense until the train was parked in the Roseville train yard. The thoughts at Roseville were that someone had purposely started the fire with the intent of sabotaging the weapons. The Benson investigation caused the Roseville case to be solved, finding identical causes.

Shortly after I submitted the yellow/grey substance to the FBI Laboratory for analysis, I got a teletype identifying it as Tritonal, the material put into the military bombs. Along with the teletype, my supervisor got a similar one with an additional page recommending that I be given a letter of reprimand (censor) for shipping a flammable substance through the mail. I countered with the fact that the small amount submitted would not burn any better than the cardboard container in which it was sent. I also played dumb saying that I didn't know what the material was, and that's why I sent it in to be identified. The pinheads in headquarters didn't buy it and pushed for disciplinary action. However someone in our Arizona division strongly spoke up for me and the worst I got was a good ass chewing. I suspect my friend Larry was the strongest voice in my favor.

In perspective an overview after the fact is this: The government and S.P. Railroad sent a train load of bombs to California in April, palleted in old wooden boxcars. This type of car had a history of catching on fire; so many similar cars had been fitted with spark shields, but not the bomb cars. After braking the cars downhill into Roseville California one caught on fire. The resulting 16 car explosion caused an estimated $24 million dollars damage, injured 18 people and set off a massive investigation. No one figured out the real cause of the disaster and 28 days later another explosion occurred in the desert of Arizona, just minutes before the train arrived in Benson in time for the local high school graduation ceremonies. Again bombs were shipped in wooden cars, all coupled together in one group. All 12 cars exploded. However within three days, a small group of investigators in Arizona discovered the cause. The Roseville case was thereafter quickly solved on similar circumstances. However one of those Arizona investigators erred by sending a small amount of substance that was flammable through the mail. Because of that error, something harmful might have....could have happened. The discussion of how this person should be punished was extensive. It still gives me a warm fuzzy feeling to know that the government knows what to do about the important things. The FBI agents in "the field" strongly supported each other, because we knew that one "Oh shit" cancelled all of your "Atta-boys."

Desert Hideout

Summer 1972

Kermit Johnson was waiting for me when I arrived at the office. He flashed his most professional grin and said, "Check your mailbox. I think you're gonna need help on this one."

Within the first year of my assignment to the Tucson Arizona, FBI resident agency, I was designated as a "Road Trip" Agent. Headquarters for Arizona was in Phoenix. My work place office was located in downtown Tucson with nine other Agents. My specific geographic assignment consisted of all of Cochise County Arizona. The actual working area was at times expanded as far as Lordsburg New Mexico, and as far as sixty miles south of the Border into Mexico where the Phelps Dodge Company owned a large copper mining and smelting operation, employing many Americans. Administrative time or "time in the office" was kept to a minimum. Paperwork was a large part of production but was accomplished on my government car seat, linked to a thumb switch activated tape recorder with a microphone pinned to my shirt. I dictated my interview write-ups and reports while I drove to the next inquiry. Distances were great, and driving time was often used to catch up on dictation. I usually worked alone. When I needed help in a local situation I asked for assistance from a Cochise County Deputy Sheriff, or an Officer from one of the local towns. The task had to be either risky or of great importance to obtain help from other FBI co-workers. They all had an abundance of equally important assignments.

The local FBI boss, Kermit, bore the title of Senior Resident Agent. Kermit was a likeable, respected and experienced agent of almost twice my age. He was brief with explanations, impatient with incompetence and insensitive to what we now call "political correctness." New cases were assigned by supervisors in Phoenix, but Kermit reviewed all of the incoming mail. Most new work was assigned to Agents according to geographic area, or by specialty. (Some agents worked only certain types of cases, such as accounting matters, organized crime, or other specialized areas.)

Under any circumstances I always approached the mail box with anticipation, because many of the new challenges came in the form of requests (leads) from other FBI Offices throughout the nation. If Kermit said I was going to need help, it was probably an understatement, and held potential for some real adrenaline rushes. This had to be good!

My mail folder contained some of the usual leads; a couple of military deserters, a background investigation, a lead on an escaped prisoner, and a lengthy teletype from the Detroit FBI Office. The really "hot" stuff always came by teletype because, by organizational directive, teletypes were to receive immediate attention.

The Detroit teletype contained a detailed description of the membership and activities of a criminal gang believed to have successfully performed armored car robberies. The gang consisted of as many as 8 seasoned convicts with prior convictions for robbery and armed assault. The gang previously operated in the Detroit area and on the East Coast. They were the prime suspects in at least three armored car robberies where the losses totaled more than two million dollars. The Detroit FBI developed a confidential informant associated with the group. The informant advised that the gang was relocating to a remote area in southeastern Arizona with the intent of planning and conducting an armored car robbery in Phoenix Arizona. Possible towns near the location were provided as Sierra Vista, and St. David. The informant by necessity was going to remain in Detroit and would no longer be in frequent contact with the suspects. Detroit requested that the Phoenix office locate the suspects, monitor and analyze their activities with the goal of identifying the proposed robbery victim. The preferred end result would be to apprehend the suspects in the preliminary stages of the next robbery.

Kermit had penciled my name onto the teletype. In relation to this case, I was now the "Phoenix Office."

I read the teletype three times, making notes of the identities and descriptions of the gang. Statistically, bank robbers are plentiful. Armored car robbers are rare, simply because it takes organization, planning and hardened criminals to take on a vehicle built like a vault, and operated by two to three men armed with high powered weapons of their own. I needed to think this one through to assure that I developed a game plan that was better than the opposition. I ran some of the ideas by my co-workers and finished by using the telephone to cancel a couple of appointments I had made for that day.

Kermit had already retreated to his office. I stood in his doorway and said, "Well I'm on it."

He barely looked up and grunted, "OK". He said nothing else.

There were no questions about what I was going to do, or how I was going to do it. It meant that he trusted me and had confidence in how I would proceed.

As I turned to leave he said, "Call me when you're ready, and I'll send the boys down."

It was my turn to say, "OK", and I left.

It was sixty miles from Tucson to Benson, where I turned off of Interstate 10 and drove either south to Sierra Vista or passed through Benson onto state highway 80 to Saint David. I decided to begin in St. David. Usual procedure would be to begin inquiries with local officers like the Sheriff's Department; however I reasoned that notifying local officials at this point would be unwise. I needed to quietly gather intelligence on this gang without exposing our interest or creating alarm among the group. If I announced the situation too early and sought information through local sources, I risked having an officer accidently tip off the members with excessive or aggressive contact. No, I had to work this alone for a while.

The teletype mentioned that one of the ex-cons, identified as Harold Hummel, had "contacts" in Arizona. He was believed to be living somewhere near St. David or Sierra Vista. St. David was a very small community. I knew the Postmistress there. I could depend on her to confidentially fill me in on any new residents receiving mail in her area. As I approached the Post Office, I saw her pickup truck in the parking lot. Good, she was there.

The Postmistress was from the "Old School". If I asked for anything, she did her best to provide just a little more than expected and beamed with pride from being within my trusted circle. And she knew how to keep her mouth shut.

She saw me come through the Post Office door. As usual, she strode toward her private office, nodding that I should follow. If I encountered her in town, she enjoyed telling me about her grandchildren and her garden. But in the office we were both intent on business. With little small talk I explained that I was seeking information on an ex-con who may have moved into the area in the last month. I gave her his name and description.

She thought for a moment and said, "I have only a few new post office boxes this month, and even fewer new move ins on the rural routes." She checked her books, and went to a stack of box rental cards. She pulled out one and said, "Here he is; H. Hummel. He rented box 223, and gave an address of a little rental house that's just off of South Curtis Flats Road. To get to the place, you turn off the first dirt road to the west off Curtis Flats, and go all the way down to the wash. (Dry creek) It's a little house and the only one there at the end of the road."

I was just 30 years old, and she was an old lady. I didn't give her a hug, but I felt like I should have.

I drove down Highway 80 to the intersection of South Curtis Flats Rd. It was easy to find, and within less than a mile, I saw a dirt road to the west. The road went straight to the west for about ½ mile and disappeared in a field of weeds, and appeared to end near the dry wash. There, a few mesquite trees partially hid a low roofed small square cabin. I was unable to determine if any cars were parked near the building. Unfortunately there were no other houses in the vicinity, and the dirt road went to nothing other than the little house. There would be no reasonable excuse to drive the dirt road toward the house. I drove slowly past the dirt road thinking, "This is going to be real difficult to surveil."

From grade school forward, getting discouraged because of difficulties was never an option. I had to somehow identify everything and everyone associated with that cabin. I needed a place from which I could observe undetected. There was a farmhouse on Curtis Flats Road about 300 yards to the south from where the dirt road branched off to the west. Curtis Flats Road met Highway 80 a short distance to the north of the dirt road entrance. St. David was established by Pioneers as a Mormon settlement next to the San Pedro River. Several natural springs created an oasis in the settlement. It was the only place within miles that had large Cottonwood trees by the roadside. The farmhouse and the highway intersection were near a few big old trees. They would provide scant cover for a parked car, but would have to do. I would experiment with the location the next morning, at dawn. It was time to call Kermit.

The "boys" that arrived at dawn the next day consisted of three agents, each in their own discreet vehicle. One of them was my now longtime friend Larry Bagley. The other was Coy Copeland, who years later, with Bagley received notoriety from the Monica Lewinski/Presidential investigation. The third was Colin Dunnigan, now deceased. We were a total of four, which was two too many to locate at the surveillance site. The problematic location would only accommodate two with a view of the target. Both of those had more risk of exposure than desired. Two of us positioned ourselves in the little town of St. David, ready to follow anything that emerged from the dirt road.

We waited. Nothing happened. The occupant of the near-by farm house came out, looked around and re-entered his house. He re-emerged and got into his pickup truck. He drove past both surveillance positions, made a turn in the middle of Curtis Flats Road and stopped next to the Agent nearest his house. He walked over to Bagley and said, "You guys must be cops. What the hell are ya lookin for?"

Busted! There was no alternative other than to carefully explore the man's character, take him into confidence and explain as little as possible. He introduced himself as "Otto" and invited both Bagley and Copeland to his house for breakfast. In a short while, all four of us were eating a breakfast of bacon and eggs with Otto and his wife Jan. They were most congenial and willing to provide information concerning their new neighbor. Ah the joys of working with good country folks.

We learned that Hummel rented the cabin down by the wash from their neighbor. Jan and Otto described the landlords as a married couple and as "good people." The male was a traveling sales person of some type (Don) and the female was a school teacher (Harriet) and a close acquaintance of Jan. Harriet was acquainted with another school teacher who was the sister of Hummel. The sister had confided in Harriet that her brother had been into trouble with the law in the past. She assisted in his relocation to Arizona to give him a "new start on life." Otto and Jan said they had observed several different cars visiting the Hummel cabin. On occasion, some appeared to stay overnight. They estimated there may be as many as three men living in the cabin.

Both Jan and Otto seemed to be thrilled with the excitement of the FBI checking on one of their neighbors and did little to hide their enthusiasm. We admonished each to be cautious silent observers and to maintain strict confidentiality. I was relieved to learn that in addition to being a farmer,

Otto was a civilian employee at nearby U.S. Army Intelligence School at Fort Huachuca. He had a top secret clearance and understood what it meant to be told by the FBI to maintain a secret. He volunteered to loosely monitor the traffic associated with the nearby cabin and he was given our Tucson Office telephone number. (We did not have cell phones in 1972.)

Jan on the other hand seemed to be overly thrilled with the presence of four new men in her life and was bursting to tell all to her friend Harriet, Hummel's landlord. It made sense that my next stop should be ½ mile to the south to talk with Harriet. Together the two women could be a welcome asset if their excitement could be controlled.

Harriet and Don lived in a severely remodeled house. It was formerly a dairy barn, complete with cement floor and sewage gutter. After introductions, Harriet fluttered about the house providing a tour that I had little time for. However, my country upbringing taught me that one must always have time to be polite, and in the formalities I learned that Jan had already called Harriet, tipping her off that we were soon going to contact her. I made a mental note to remember that about Jan in future dealings needing confidentiality.

Before leaving, I learned that Hummel's sister Kris was a conscientious elementary teacher, living and working in Sierra Vista.

She was a struggling single mother. Her parents were no longer living and her only relative was her brother Harold. She had no money to spare, but had sacrificed to bring her brother to Arizona to get him away from his friends who were all past prison inmates. She confided in Harriet that Hummel had been incarcerated for theft, but did not mention anything more serious. He was allegedly looking for work locally but had not found any yet. I received a pledge from Harriet to not speak to Kris about our investigation and reiterated that she was not to mention anything about the FBI being interested in Hummel's activities. She agreed, but I wondered how long it would last. I remember thinking that I needed to keep on this one before it broke away from me.

I felt I was getting a good handle on Hummel. I knew where he lived, I knew enough about his sister, that I could get information from her directly if needed, or indirectly through Harriet. Jan and Otto would keep an eye on Hummel's Cadillac, a car about which he boasted to his sister saying he won it in a poker game. But I needed to learn who else was living with him. And I needed to learn who his visitors were at night. It was time to call Kermit again.

I devised a plan typical of a young agent with more guts than brains. We would walk down to the Cabin in darkness, get the license numbers from the cars, and if possible observe any people through the cabin windows. Kermit gave me three more agents. I only remember that the one who volunteered to walk down to the cabin with me was Scotty. Scotty was even younger than me. He had about two years' experience and wanted adventure.

We developed a plan that involved all four of us. Two agents would position themselves up at Otto's farm in their cars and communicate with us by radio. They were to be our backup if we came under attack. Scotty and I would arm ourselves with our handguns and carry shotguns as a primary weapon. We loaded with double 00 buckshot and solid slugs. We carried small flashlights, a paper pad and a pencil. It was a moonless summer night, but we wore all black clothing. My upper garment was a black windbreaker...in 100 degree heat. A black stocking cap topped off the costume. Scotty appeared the same, and even had smudges on his face. We wore shoes that had relatively flat soles to prevent leaving unusual foot prints in the desert dust around the house and on the road. We neglected to get the ear pieces for our radios, so we had to turn down the volume to prevent being heard by the gang in the cabin. There would be no radio chatter. Before leaving our cover at the farm, I reminded Scotty that all of our subjects were former convicts, had robbed armored cars while heavily armed, had assaulted and beaten their victims, and that Hummel had allegedly attempted to kill his former girlfriend by intentionally running over her. The message was clear. There was no room for error.

Scotty and I began walking. The two track dirt road to the cabin ran straight for about ¼ mile and then curved to the left for 100 yards to the house. The road was narrow, and closed in on us as we passed through an open field that grew chest high weeds. Huge "pig weeds" with large leaves bordered the road. They would conceal us if we had to make a quick dash for safety.

I whispered to Scotty, "If we have to make a run for it, head for these pig weeds. They will give us cover and we can crawl or lay in them until we radio the guys up at the farm to give us fire cover." I didn't tell him that I did not know if they had a dog at the cabin.

As we rounded the curve near the house, we realized just how dark it was. There were no adjacent houses. There were no yard lights. There weren't even stars due to a cloud cover. I saw nothing. I could not see Scotty, standing one foot away from me. We were guided only by the soft dirt under our feet, and the weeds at the edge of the two track road.

With audible concern Scotty commented that the dark could be rather dangerous. I could hear the tension in his voice. I related how even as a child, I was never afraid of the dark. I looked at it as a cover of safety. If we could not see, neither could anyone else. I opined that tonight the depth of the darkness was going to be our friend. He seemed to accept my confidence. I was also trying to convince myself.

Coyotes barked and rustled the creosote bushes down by the wash. We plodded silently toward the dim light of the cabin window. The window faintly illuminated three, possibly four cars. All were parked within twenty feet of the front door. A window beside the front door put out a faint light through a thin closed curtain. I realized we would not be able to use the flashlights on the license plates. Then the truth within one of those "Oh crap!" moments hit me in the nerve center. We would have to walk to the cars, and physically feel the license plates.

I thought, "We have to read them by braille. There are four plates to read and neither of us will remember the number without writing them onto the tablet. How do you feel a plate, hold a pencil, a tablet and keep a shotgun at the ready position? Damn."

I whispered to Scotty, "Tuck your gun under your arm and take the tablet. I'll whisper the numbers to you and you write them down. I'll keep my shotgun in my free hand. Don't shoot unless they come out firing. If we get separated, don't shoot me!"

It was good I couldn't see Scotty because reading his lips would have been less than flattering.

The cars were now directly in front of me. Thank God they parked them facing the front door. We duck walked to the back of the first car keeping the cars between us and the front door. The house was less than twenty feet from us. I could hear conversation inside, but my pulse was thumping loudly in my ears under the black stocking hat. I gripped the first plate. Crap… it wasn't an Arizona plate, and I couldn't tell color or shape of the small un-raised letters. I felt and whispered the large letters to Scotty, and then slid down the side of the car so that the faint light from the window obliquely glanced off the plate. There it was, Mich. It had to be Michigan. Great! One down and three to go! The next was easier. The dim light provided me with the Volunteer State and some numbers. OK, hurray for Tennessee! The next one was on an old Cadillac. Arizona was embossed on the plate thick enough to feel the letters. The numbers were also easy. Scotty kept transcribing my whispers. The fourth car was in the darkest shadows. I couldn't see it or feel the plate numbers. I thought, "I've got this far, I'm not quitting now." I paused in the dark and Scotty seemed to lose track of me. We heard louder voices and he looked in the direction of the window. I tried to whisper not to look at the window because the light would surely completely blind him. He realized his mistake, and hunched down holding his hand out to the side, shotgun still under the arm. I reached out and touched him, signaling where I was. We squatted motionless for what seemed like 30 seconds before I again reached for the mystery plate. As I felt the frame I found that it was loosely mounted onto the car with two thin bolts. Could I get them lose? I twisted and the first came free. The second stuck until I spit on my hands and wet the bolt. Both nuts dropped into my hand and the plate slid free.

Scotty had no idea what I was doing, and he whispered, "Come on. Let's get the hell out of here."

I stuck the mystery plate under my windbreaker and duck walked back into the darkness. Success!

I returned the whisper, "Now we have to get out of here."

During the planning stage I had fanaticized leaning against the outside wall of the cabin and hearing voices planning a big heist in Phoenix. What an insane idea! Reality now spoke loudly. This was not the place to play hero or Dick Tracy. We weren't equipped to outgun armed penitentiary parolees at a two to one ratio. I had to catch up with Scotty who was already several yards ahead of me.

I considered pulling a weed from the dirt and dragging it over the ground behind the cars to obliterate our tracks. As we were fading back to the edge of the weeds, there was movement inside the cabin and we froze at the base of the pig weeds. The door didn't open. There was cursing from within the cabin. It sounded like they were playing cards. There was no sound of TV so they could easily have heard any sound we made. It was time to go.

We retreated at least 20 yards before we stood up straight. I was sweating rivulets and Scotty was breathing like he just ran up a hill. I put my hand over my flashlight so that only a glimmer of light showed through my fingers. I read the plate I had removed from under my windbreaker. Damn, Michigan, I should have known. After writing down the numbers, I hurled the plate far into the weeds, well in the direction of the wash. I smugly thought, "Gone but not forgotten."

We still couldn't risk using the flashlights. Darkness still blinded us to where we were guiding ourselves by brushing against the roadside weeds. We rounded the curve a hundred yards from the cabin and then quickened our pace. Suddenly I felt a presence of something in front of me. I halted in on step and lifted the shotgun halfway to my chest. I heard a thump. Scotty screamed and fell to the ground cursing. Then I hear a thumpity-clop, plopity- clop running away from us. Scotty had walked smack into a horse that was resting in the middle of the road. The horse pushed back against him, knocking him to the ground, and then ran up the road into the weeds. Scotty was still on the ground loudly groaning.

"Scotty, for Christ sakes shut up! You're gonna live but not if you keep that up."

I stepped behind him because I wasn't sure if he might not still fire his shotgun. He wasn't sure either and was still in serious fright recovery.

Scotty gasped "I can't breathe!"

"Try shutting up. It will come easier."

"What the hell was that?"

"It was a horse, they run loose out here."

I was most grateful that he didn't discharge the shot gun. I would have doubled up laughing but right then we had the problem of being discovered from the sounds. Again we froze at the edge of the weeds and listened. No new sounds. Perhaps they thought we were just more barking coyotes. I was nearly hysterical in an effort to keep from laughing, but we would have time for that later. This night crawler act was still serious stuff.

When we returned to the farm house, two sleepy "back up" Agents had the audacity to inquire, "What took you so long?" I provided a brief explanation and peeled off my soaked shirt. I looked at Scotty in the dim light and saw that he too was wet with sweat, especially in the center of his blue jeans. I think he may have peed his pants. The matter was never discussed.

It was some time later, out of the presence of the others when Scotty asked with some indignation, "Why did you throw that plate away? You could have put it on the road and they would have thought it just fell off?"

I answered, "Scotty, that car was almost new, probably a rental. I need to know who is driving it. By this time tomorrow I will have every officer that patrols this area looking for a new Chevy missing a rear plate. When it is located the officer will have a legitimate reason to stop and identify the driver. The driver will then be released after receiving a warning concerning the lost license plate. We'll know who he is, and everything will still be cool. I'll just have to make sure that the officers know that the driver is potentially dangerous."

Scotty laughed, embarrassed that he had shown his inexperience. I said, "Remember, we are not in this race to take second. If these guys win, someone will likely die in the process." The thought made the evening's darkness even darker.

• • •

In spite of the exhausting night excursion, sleep was not easy when I finally returned home. There were high profile criminals in my territory, and I had not yet told the local authorities. Worse yet, I was responsible for removing the plate on the Chevy. Depending on who was driving the vehicle, he might not respond favorably to being stopped. There was a strong probability that there were warrants out for his arrest somewhere. I needed to get the Cochise County authorities briefed with no further delay.

The rising sun found me en route to the Cochise County Sheriff's substation at Sierra Vista. I had one of my co-workers call the area's State Police and the Chief of Police from Sierra Vista so we could have a multi- agency briefing shortly after I arrived. By 10:00 AM I had all possible participants, even the constable at Tombstone, briefed. They were advised to approach the suspect car without a license with caution, and only conduct a driver's license check, even if the driver had warrants in another state. The reasoning was that we going to prevent the commission of a very serious crime, and could relocate the subject later if our current mission failed.

It worked. The car was located at a motel in Benson Arizona. The Sheriff's boys kept the car under observation until they saw it moving. The driver was identified as Louie from Detroit. The car was a rental from the same area. Louie said he would be driving home on the weekend and would take care of the license. The officer told him to put the front plate onto the back and Louie responded immediately by using a screwdriver from a tool kit inside the car. The officer suspected the tool box was a burglary kit, because how many people carry a tool kit in a rented car? The officer thanked Louie for his co-operation and let him go without a citation. Great work!

Earlier that morning the Phoenix Office radioed me with the results of the other three vehicle license checks. The Cadillac was registered to Hummel. The Chevy was a rental out of Detroit. The FBI office there was working on determining who rented it. The second Detroit car was registered to a known member of the robbery gang, and the Tennessee plate was also owned by a car rental company. The Memphis FBI Office was identifying the lessee.

Within two days I had the identities of the three visitors with Hummel. They were all ex-cons but just having their names meant nothing. Then Detroit sent another teletype. They worked up a parole violation on Louie. He was not supposed to leave Michigan without his Parole Officer's permission, as well as not associate with known criminals. Detroit's plan was to arrest Louie and put the squeeze on him. Louie's choice was going to be to talk about his friends, or return to prison. I didn't want to nab him at Hummel's cabin because I thought it would reveal we had knowledge of their plans and meetings. We figured out a way to account for the arrest. We would in our post arrest conversation leak the information that we learned of his parole status as a result of the automobile license stop. If given the opportunity we would leak the same information to Hummel. I already had the opportunity. All I had to do was call Jan or Harriet.

Louie left Benson in the direction of Detroit shortly after his encounter with the Police, but no one observed him much past city limits. He could have been headed anywhere. Late in the day, a trip on Otto's tractor to the western field in back of his house disclosed that there was still one car, a light colored Chevy at Hummel's cabin. I wanted to be able to casually observe Hummel a few days more without being recognized, so I asked Bagley and two other agents to make the arrest of Louie at the cabin.

They wasted no time and within an hour, were ready to advance on the cabin. Otto reported a car was still by the Cabin door that morning. Bagley drove down to the cabin in broad daylight, prepared to do battle. One agent went to the back door, the other two to the front. They shook the house with their knock, and loudly announced their presence and purpose. No one responded. They repeatedly thumped the door but no answer. The front door was not locked, so a brief check inside revealed the house was unoccupied. Damn, they missed him. They left the cabin and searched through St. David, Benson and Sierra Vista. No Detroit Chevy was located. They returned to Tucson empty handed.

Did I mention that there was a small farm building, sort of like a woodshed, near the house? I guess not. Well there was this little building a few yards from the house - - - Otto sometimes had a Mexican farm hand working in his field during haying season. That evening when Otto came home, the farm hand told him a scary story. The Mexican said he saw a car drive toward the cabin that afternoon. Shortly before the car arrived at the cabin, he saw a man run out of the house carrying a shot gun. The man ran into the wood shed. The farm hand had heard from neighbors that the resident of the cabin was a former "Jail Bird" and he feared there was going to be a gun fight. If there was going to be a gun battle, he imagined that he too would be killed for being a witness. He hid in the ditch and watched. Three men with hand guns banged on the house door and eventually went inside. The guy in the wood shed stayed crouched down low with the shotgun pointed at the three outside the house. Eventually the three came out and left. The resident stayed in the woodshed for quite a while before returning back into the house with the shotgun. The resident left about ½ hour later. The farm hand crawled out of the ditch and snuck back to Otto's farm yard.

The next day, Otto told me the story. I always say I would rather be lucky than good, any day.

• • •

Several days passed with no significant activity. Louie, was gone. We didn't know who had been in the wood shed, but it was not Hummel, and probably not Louie. All of the players who had been in Arizona had been identified, but we didn't know where they were. The Detroit informant was not in close regular contact with the gang, but was still providing sketchy information confirming that the group was still planning on "A big hit." I spent several days watching Hummel, but had learned nothing other than his routine domestic movements. His favorite bars were in Tombstone, and at times he appeared to be driving just to be driving. I was sure he detected my surveillance a couple of times, even though I had changed cars.

I thought it was time to contact Hummel. It would be expected by him, and out of the ordinary for us not to appear. His residence had been visited by the FBI, obviously unsuccessfully looking for a fugitive. Why wouldn't we under normal circumstances return to interview the tenant? But before I met him face to face, I felt I should plant some, as we called it, "miss-information." My next interviews would be with Harriet, after which I would visit with Hummel's sister Kris.

Because I intended to interview three females, one possibly under adverse circumstances, I asked Scotty to work with me for a day.

Knowing their habits, it was safe to stop at Jan and Otto's early in the morning. We found that Otto had already departed. Our purpose was to determine if Harriet had mentioned anything about Hummel to indicate she had been in personal contact with him. In addition I wanted to know what Harriet's attitude was concerning the sister, Kris. I wanted to be sure that all players were still on our side, and were not detrimentally disclosing my own activities.

Jan was her usual hospitable self, offering coffee, food, and a soft chair to "rest your weary bones if you're tired." Jan still spoke well of Harriet and felt she was cautiously trying to help. After one cup we excused ourselves, because truthfully, we had much to accomplish.

We began the real work with Harriet. We found her in her St. David home. Her husband was gone as usual, and her extremely friendly attitude made me glad I had asked Scotty to share the experience. Scotty may have been a little naive, but he quickly read the situation. He flashed me a quick smile when yet another round of coffee was offered; this time along with toast. We accepted because I wanted to definitely create an ally to measure the after effect of our interview with Kris.

Harriet had spoken with Kris, but appeared to follow my admonitions to seek information without disclosing any. She reported that Kris was quite worried that her brother would soon get into more trouble. Her concerns resulted from his lack of desire to find a job, and the curious situation of his having money without working. Harriet disclosed that Hummel had on all occasions paid his rent with cash; two hundred dollars mostly in twenties and fifties. Harriet found it unusual that Hummel had on several occasions baby sat for Kris while she was occupied with her school work. Hummel apparently showed genuine affection for her young son. She felt that Kris would welcome a conversation with the FBI, to discuss her concerns about Hummel.

We left with invitations to return at any time, and a suggestion that if we visited during "happy hour" she would serve something better than toast.

As we departed, Scotty whispered, "What did that mean?"

I mumbled, "I haven't the slightest idea."

We drove from St. David to Sierra Vista, conversing about a strategy for interviewing Kris. We had to gain her trust. The consensus was that a straight forward approach would be best, if she was sincere about her respect for the law, and her concern for her brother's behavior. Her attitude would have to be determined within the first couple of minutes of the interview.

We called on the Chief of Police in Sierra Vista Arizona. Reed, "The Chief", was an experienced and dedicated Police Officer. He began his career in enforcement by taking a job with the US Government in the great depression. Cattle throughout southern Arizona and northern Mexico were dying from anthrax. The two Governments hired Reed and a couple others to ride into Mexico and kill all the living cattle, to eradicate the disease. Reed recalled that the Mexicans would often rather see *him* die that lose their cattle. Reed survived because of his tough character. He was now becoming a legend throughout southern Arizona and northern Mexico.

Reed was according to his assessment, "Part Mexican and part American Indian, with a pale face mixed into the wood pile." After killing cattle in Mexico, Reed came north to Sierra Vista, a very small town at the edge of US Army Fort Huachuca.

He got a job there as one of three police officers. He became the boss, soon after the city gave him a gun and a Ford Pickup truck for a patrol car. Reed spoke four languages – English, Spanish, sarcasm and profanity. In a couple of years, Reed had become one of my closest friends, remaining so until his death. But that's another story.

I used Reed's phone to make a noontime appointment with Kris. Afterwards I briefed Reed because I trusted his experience and judgment.

Reed's initial reaction was spoken with a frown. "Why don't you just arrest the Son of a Bitch? I'll let you throw him in my jail. You know he must have a gun, and ex-cons can't carry. My boys will do it here in town if you two candy asses are afraid to."

"We could do that Reed, if you want to entertain the other four or five of them while they look for a big money score. How long do think it would take for them to figure out how to bust Hummel out of this damn tin can of yours? Maybe you could make chili for him while he sleeps on your cot."

Reed's wife was Helen, also a very special person. She ran the political arm of the job, and was highly respected throughout the now progressive and growing town. She and Reed made chili that would eat through a paper plate on a cold day.

Reed smiled. He liked a good verbal confrontation. "Well if it satisfies your damn curiosity, my sources at the school say Hummel's sister is a good teacher. She's quiet, keeps to herself and works hard for the kids. She doesn't run around and doesn't seem to have a local boyfriend."

"Well it's nice to see you're good for something! How long has she been here?"

"How the hell should I know? I suppose now you want me to help you find the school house?"

"No. Remember I've been there to help your officers with a Color Crayon class. Besides we're using your tax money to take us all on a big lunch interview."

"You mean I'm invited?"

"Sorry Reed, we don't have that much money."

Much of the show from both Reed and from me was for Scotty's benefit. It was the way we did business openly. Behind the bluster, we knew each was covering the other's back, and no favor was too great.

As we were leaving his office Reed asked, "Are you gonna talk with Hummel after you wring out his sister?"

"I don't know yet. It depends what she says, and how it goes."

With a serious but friendly tone, Reed said, "Well, OK. Keep your legs crossed." Scotty looked at me like, "What the hell does that mean?"

In the car I explained. "Reed has a lot of original expressions. Coming from him, keep your legs crossed means be careful. Or it can mean protect yourself, but he delivers it with just the right amount of sexual connotation to make it humorous. It's his way of saying he cares and wants you to be careful. He even says that to his daughters when they leave the house."

Scotty mused, "What a guy!"

The moment Kris entered the restaurant; I recognized she must be the person we would be meeting. She was slight of build, with sandy hair that blended in with her tanned and unpainted complexion. She walked timidly, cautiously peering through narrow eyes, looking for her noon appointment. I rose and spoke to her. She looked startled seeing that there were two of us. She certainly did not look like the sister of a sociopathic killer.

The meeting went well. The plan was to apply no pressure. I played the role of just wanting to help her, which was not far from the truth. The problem was that we weren't going to be much help to her brother. I used all of my best manners and expressions with a soft low voice. We first learned about her, and then slowly guided the conversation toward Hummel.

Kris said she and Harold Hummel were raised around the Great Lakes. Hummel was her only sibling and he was eight years her senior. She had an abusive husband and was divorced shortly after her only son Charlie was born. Charlie just turned three. Hummel had been in trouble ever since she could remember. He didn't graduate from High School, and was imprisoned for theft by the time he was twenty one. Both of their parents died while Hummel was in prison. He had been released twice during ten years, only to be returned for committing more serious offenses each time. She had promised her mother that she would look after him, but doubted she could contribute anything to save him from himself. She doubted Harold's money was coming from gambling winnings. She doubted his visitors were just seasonal "Snow Birds." She now realized she had a greater responsibility to herself and her young son, where she at least could honor her parents by being a good citizen.

For me the story was all too familiar. For her, it was a difficult admission and a shameful tale. She humbly cried while telling about her parents. She shuddered when relating how Harold had intentionally run over his former girlfriend in a fit of rage. She wept when she admitted she didn't know anything further she could do.

I believed she was sincere. I had to begin the process of converting her to my side.

I explained that I had reason to believe Harold was still associating with criminal gangsters. I pictured situations where he may get himself killed if allowed to continue his pattern of behavior. I convinced her that if she helped me, together we might be able to prevent Harold or an innocent victim from dying. With tears on her cheeks, she said, "What do you want? I'll do anything."

She was either sincere, or real good. The first test was to have her determine how many people were staying at Hummel's cabin. If possible she should determine how long they planned to stay. I explained what was needed, without really saying why. I could have overloaded her with tasks, but she needed to pass the first test before we went any further. We ended the conversation by talking about her son Charlie. She remarked that the only thing Harold seemed to show any emotion about was Charlie. He liked to baby sit with Charlie and had on occasion taken Charlie with him on rides out in the desert. She still held a glimmer of hope that Harold would stay out of prison just for Charlie.

I gave Kris my Tucson office number as well as the Phoenix Office number. I wrote it backwards on the paper, with the explanation that if it was seen by the wrong person, it would not compromise her. I told her she could call the Phoenix number if necessary, and they would reach me any time, 24 hours a day, either by phone, radio or through the ever present pager tethered to my belt. She seemed relieved to finally have someone to confide in.

On the drive back to Tucson, Scotty and I decided it would be of no value to talk with Hummel. If Kris came through, we had him covered. We agreed. "Let him wonder how much we know, and worry about what we are doing."

Within a couple of weeks, Hummel and I became visual acquaintances, without ever speaking. Several times per week, when he looked around, I would be there. He knew he was being watched, but I doubt he knew for sure why. I visited regularly with Otto and Jan, who monitored traffic to his residence. His sister Kris was advising me concerning his friends. Harriet was retaining his cash payments until I could check serial numbers through the National Computer base for stolen currency, and local police officers were entering into their logs, the movement of his Cadillac.

I had him covered, but nothing significant was developing from it. He wasn't working, but he was spending plenty of cash dining in the best local restaurants, drinking expensive whisky in local bars, and burned dozens of tanks of premium gasoline. I had befriended the merchants, restaurants and bar owners he routinely patronized. They reported that Hummel never, ever, wrote or cashed a check. The local banks never heard of him, and could find no accounts under his name anywhere. So where was the money coming from? The Detroit informant kept reporting that the gang was living off of the bundles of cash they took from several armored car robberies. I had no trouble believing it but was unable to develop even a thread of proof. The only tangible evidence I had to confirm the informant's reports was our observations of gang members being present at Hummel's cabin. However none of his old associates had been seen in the area since the shotgun in the woodshed incident. Where did they all go?

One evening about mid-summer while I was at home, I received a phone call from our Phoenix night operator.

She said, "Mr. Schreuder, I have a female on the line named Kris. She says it is urgent that she speak with you. Do you want me to patch her through?"

I took the call.

Kris sounded upset. "Mr. Schreuder, Harold called me this afternoon and said he was going to be gone for a few days. He said he cleared it with his probation officer. He said he was going hunting."

"Hunting?" I thought, "Hell even if that were true, he would never report it to his probation officer, because ex-cons on probation were not allowed to have guns of any type."

"Did he say where he would be hunting?"

"He said he intended to hunt lions (mountain lions) in the Dragoon Mountains. He and a friend were planning on camping out there for about a week."

"Did you see him packing any gear?"

"No, he left before I got off work. I checked his cabin, and his car's gone."

I thanked her, telling her not to worry, and promised to call her if I learned anything to ease her concerns.

The next day, a quick check with the Detroit office disclosed that the probation officer knew nothing of the hunting trip, but as long as Hummel stayed in Arizona, he would not be in violation of his release terms. At least I confirmed that he was lying to his sister. Why would he have to lie about something that minor?

I thought about it only a few minutes before I decided to check the Tucson airport. The parking lot was large, but it would only take me about 45 minutes to check the entire lot for Hummel's car. It didn't take that long. Within ten minutes I saw it in long term parking; an old green Cadillac, with the now familiar Arizona plates. The lions in the Dragoons were going to be quite safe.

I called the Detroit FBI and spoke with the agent there working the case. We agreed to alert his informant and determine if any of the other gang members were traveling.

Three days later Detroit called me back. None of the "usual suspects" could be located, and the informant didn't know where they were. His only contribution was that they had been planning something, that didn't involve Arizona. We had little to do but wait.

Two days later, Kris called to say that Hummel had returned. He reported having a good time in the Dragoons, but that he and his partner had no luck hunting lions. That same afternoon, the Detroit agent called. The conversation was short and to the point. I don't remember it exactly, but it went something like this:

"Two days ago there was a well-planned Wells Fargo armored car robbery in Tennessee. They got off with about a million dollars in cash and close to three hundred grand in checks. One guard was shot but is in stable condition. The "MO" was the same as the Detroit gang. There appeared to be six members in the group."

Still... there was no positive connection to Hummel and his gang. Regardless, there was never a moment that the Detroit agent or I thought it could be anyone else.

Tennessee? Well imagine that! I felt like I had already touched the back of the car driven by one of the robbers. I called Memphis to make sure the agents there explored the possible connection between the rental Tennessee car that I had pawed in the dark, and their robbery. It wasn't long before Detroit, Memphis and FBI Headquarters were requesting that Phoenix (that meant me) increase our efforts to monitor

Hummel's activities. What the hell did they want me to do? Move in with him?

I thought Hummel would most likely have a fresh supply of cash, fresh green Tennessee money. Perhaps he would get careless....how, I didn't know, but I needed to watch him as close as possible the next few days. Kermit came through and assigned two agents to help me.

We set up a loose surveillance so that we could tail him whenever he left the cabin in his Cadillac. He usually didn't venture out early in the mornings, but always kept late hours. He frequently hung out in the Tombstone bars until closing time. It appeared he was winning the affection of one of the bar maids in a Tombstone tavern. That made for some long hours.

After a couple of days of seeing nothing significant, the other agents, (Bagley and Copeland) and I began to get impatient. We were justified. Here this SOB was sleeping late while we were up watching and waiting. He was living high drinking and dining until the wee hours of the morning while we did nothing but snack on Snickers bars and power devour coffee to stay awake.

On a Friday night, Hummel began his routine by having a few beers in Sierra Vista. He made the rounds there until almost midnight. When he drove toward the dirt road north of town we knew he was again going to take the country shortcut to Tombstone. The road was called the "Old Charleston Road." It was mostly gravel and rarely traveled at night. Hummel would soon learn we were following him. We really didn't care. We thought we might as well join him in Tombstone.

As soon as we got north of town, Hummel could see he had a tail. He began to speed up. This was going to be a fun challenge, because Bagley and I had often traveled this road as the quick route between Tombstone and Sierra Vista. I doubted Hummel knew the road as well as we did. Secondly he was driving an old Caddie. It had a heavy and mushy suspension. We had late model police pursuit cars with a real stiff suspension. The chase was on. In a short straight stretch a glance at the speed odometer increased my heart rate. Seventy Five was way too fast for this road. I reached down to the dash and shut off the air conditioner. My car had considerably more power with it off. What the hell, it was only about 80 degrees anyway. A short hill passed under us and I knew what was coming. The Caddie hit bottom in the next dip, and I could see sparks fly from the undercarriage. The tail lights were still visible through the dust, and to my surprise they were both upright. This guy was better than I thought. Two long curves had the Caddie fishtailing in the shoulder gravel only inches from sucking him down the bank into a roll over. I could see my friends riding comfortably behind me. I was hoping they were enjoying this as much as I was. One more dip spraying metal to rock sparks, and Hummel slowed down to a more reasonable breakneck speed. The Tombstone lights were soon in our view. Copeland radioed, "He must have to really take a whiz."

In Tombstone, Allen Street was the famous beat of Marshal Wyatt Earp and Doc Holliday. Some of the old buildings still remain in their original location, remodeled of course to modern standards.

Places frequented by Hummel were The Silver Nugget, the Bird Cage, the Longhorn, the Crystal Palace and the Blue Eyed Witch. In retrospect it's hard to believe I actually got paid a salary for visiting these places and befriending their proprietors.

That night, Hummel stopped at the Silver Nugget. He was known to fraternize with a dark haired bar tender/waitress there. We rarely followed subjects into establishments, but positioned ourselves so we could see any "out of place" associates. Tombstone was always full of out of state cars, so a survey of license plates would produce nothing.

The bar finally closed and we went for another wild ride. This time Hummel drove back to St. David via the paved highway 80. We could have summoned a local officer to issue a speeding ticket, maybe even a Driving Under the Influence (DUI) citation, but didn't want to disrupt someone else's sleep for nonproductive harassment. We concluded another week of work with scant results.

We again stayed in Sierra Vista overnight, planning to return to Tucson the following day. Reed knew we were working the area so I gave him a courtesy call by stopping by his office that next morning. I'll always remember his greeting.

"Jesus, you look like bleached dog crap! Why don't you get some rest before you head back? Go into that clean cell in the back of the jail and take a nap!"

The others had already departed. I was tempted to accept his offer but did not. But before I had completed this case, I napped in the jail more than once.

Several more weeks went by. The consensus was that indeed Hummel and his group robbed Wells Fargo in Tennessee, but again, there was not probable cause to make any arrests. Meanwhile the Detroit informant was telling FBI agents there was definitely a Phoenix robbery being planned. They were according to his reports, casing the Thomas Shopping Mall in central Phoenix. There was an armored car service attending to most of the businesses there, and it was a large complex.

Throughout the months I had been attending to the Hummel group, I had other work in the area as well. I was unable to observe his activities on a full time basis, and had to rely on my local helpers. Kris, was becoming more afraid of her brother, and frequently sought my guidance. She felt that if it wasn't for Charlie, she and Hummel would be totally estranged.

Harriet advised that Hummel was still paying his rent with cash. He usually paid in large bills. She invited me to come to her home to inspect the money and then said, "But don't bring the boy."

Oh, Oh, a red flag. I knew she was referring to Scotty, but was not in the mood to speculate what other message she meant to convey.

Jan and Otto reported they had on two occasions seen a strange car visiting the Hummel cabin, but were unable to observe a license plate. It was a dark sedan. The Tombstone girlfriend drove a little white Honda. The visitor was not her. So who was it? I didn't have a clue. Out of Otto's presence, Jan lamented that she hadn't seen Copeland since the first day she had given us breakfast and hoped he would be returning. I remembered wondering, "What's wrong with these women? It must be something lacking in the water!"

Within a day of Jan seeing the dark sedan, Kris called to say that Hummel was going to Phoenix for a couple of days. He said he just needed a change of scenery. I called the Phoenix Office and they set up a loose surveillance of the armored car operation at Thomas Mall.

The next day, Phoenix got a teletype followed by a telephone call from Detroit. According to the informant, five members of the gang had left for Phoenix with the intent of robbing the cash delivery/collection service at Phoenix Thomas Mall.

This story would be infinitely more exciting if I could report I was in Phoenix participating in the action at Thomas Mall. However practical operation dictated that I remain in Sierra Vista, to observe any associated activity to link our known suspects to the Phoenix activity. #$%&*

In Phoenix, I don't know who was "calling the shots" but I was skeptical from the beginning. They observed suspects appearing to be casing the Thomas Mall operations, but could not be sure enough to make an arrest. They decided they would have to let the robbery proceed as planned until they could observe an overt act. Communication from Detroit pinpointed the day the robbery was to take place. The armored car made its Thomas Mall rounds twice a day, at 10:00 AM and at 4:00 PM. The suspects were, on two separate days, observed collecting information at 10:00 AM. The group had a history of violence. Concern for the armored car workers made it necessary to brief them on the possible pending robbery. The security company was in the business of providing armed protection for commercial cash. It was not the FBI's job to protect them, but it was unthinkable that we would allow them to walk into harm's way without warning them of the impending danger. The security company was fully briefed on the operation.

The normal procedure for the armored car was to distribute and collect the shopping mall cash with one fortified truck, operated by one driver with two armed guards. On the morning of the planned robbery, as many as fifteen FBI agents and police officers were strategically positioned at the locations where the armored truck routinely stopped. Surveillance cameras were running. Radio communication was installed and operating between law enforcement at the scene and the cash transporting vehicle. Suspect vehicles were seen positioned near the loading zones.

And then.....when the guards got out of the armed truck, there were one, two, three, four of them wearing bullet proof vests, and carrying shot guns. A fifth exited with the money encased in metal boxes on a two wheeled dolly. The scene was such that even the dumbest con would turn tail and run. What happened?....Nothing!

Worse yet, no one was detained, no one was questioned and no one was specifically identified as a suspect.

When I heard the results I was furious. My initial impression was that I had spent three months without sleep chasing these SOB's only to result in fifteen cops and school boys letting them escape like birds in a bush. I was very disappointed and it must have shown.

Kermit and Bagley straightened me out. It only took a minute. Kermit suggested, "Before the take down, I guess we should have appointed you as the person to explain to any one of the guard's wife and kids how they were killed, and how sorry we were that we couldn't have prevented it."

I saw his point, but still felt they should have been able to collar at least one of them in the ready to rob position. Bagley suggested that no arrest was valid without probable cause, and there was no law against watching armored car employees working their route. Damn this job could be frustrating.

I played sports in High School. I ran track in College. I went through military boot camp. I served four years in the Air Force. I completed the FBI Academy near the top of my class. Whatever the stress, never during any of that time, did I ever embrace any thought of giving up. I began another week vowing that these bastards were returning to jail and my stamp of approval was going to be on the warrant.

It became obvious to me that Hummel didn't care if I was watching him. He didn't care if I was suspicious of his activities. His reward apparently was greater than his perceived risk, and he was going to continue his self-serving, indulgent, predatory life style; unless of course I could stop him.

I decided that if I was going to have a life of my own in the next few months, I had to win this game. It was time for open warfare.

• • •

The little white Honda was registered to Mimi. She worked at the Silver Nugget in Tombstone. The proprietor who hired her said she was a decent local girl, and came from a good family. He felt that Hummel played the part of a big spender, had a good line, and had taken advantage of her inexperience. He set me up with a surprise visit to interview her at work.

I took Mimi out to my car, parked on Allen Street, near the Bird Cage. She was young, barely old enough to work in a bar. She was not very attractive from the neck up, and was overly plump from the neck down. She was scared to the point of barely being able to speak. I too concluded she was not experienced. I wanted to immediately impress her with the seriousness of the situation, and scare any available information out of her before she descended into some type of romantic protective mode.

I dropped it onto her with terrifying emphasis. Hummel was a paroled convict. He was suspected of participating in gang activity. (I didn't say what.) He participated in armed assault. He argued with his previous girlfriend and drove his car over her while she lay in the icy gutter where he had knocked her semi-unconscious. Before I even began to question her, she opened the door, and threw up in the gutter. I thought, "OK, now I have her attention."

I convinced her that I had come to save her from some terrible fate, and that she should co-operate to help me determine Hummel's activities. I made it simple. I told her the most important thing that I wanted from her was to be alerted whenever he said he was going to be out of the area. If possible she was to find out where he was going.

I wondered if she would be able to pull it off. One thing I was sure of. None of their future conversations were going to take place in bed.

Fall was in the air when Kris called me to report Hummel was planning another trip. He said he was going to California to "take in the beach." It was a Friday and Hummel said he was going to leave after the weekend. My only hope was to set up at the Tucson airport parking lot, and determine what flight he took. Previous checks with the airlines failed to locate any tickets sold in his name, indicating he was using some type of false identification. I would have to observe him buying a ticket.

Jan was supposed to watch for his departure, so I could estimate his arrival time at the airport. There were thousands of tickets sold there every day and spotting one person was difficult. Jan called late in the morning, reporting that Hummel's car was gone. She hadn't seen Hummel. He had gotten by her.

Hummel never showed at the airport, and I didn't find his car in the parking lot. I eventually learned that he had driven to Phoenix and had flown out to New York.

About a week later I was sitting in Reed's office when my pager started chirping. It was a Phoenix call, and the dispatcher directed me to Roy, the reactive squad supervisor. That was not usually a good thing.

He started with a question, "You got any idea where that guy Hummel is?"

I knew better than to take that kind of bait. I answered, "No, I was hoping that you could tell me."

"Yup, I can. Detroit just sent a teletype - said that there was a big jewelry store robbery in Toronto Canada. The Mounties responded real quick and there was a hell of a gun fight. When the smoke cleared they had three of your Detroit boys and Hummel on the ground. Hummel didn't get shot, but they're gonna damn sure keep him in Canada for a while."

I was relieved and disappointed at the same time. I wanted his ass, but was getting real tired of following it.

"Do they want anything from us?" I asked.

"It appears they have a tight case and don't need anything from us right now. Why don't you get back to work and do something productive for a change?"

"Sure Roy, I'll be glad to."

"Reed, I think I am going to need a pillow for that cell this afternoon."

• • •

I met Kris that afternoon. I explained what had happened to her brother. She broke down and cried for at least ten minutes. She conveniently placed herself where she expected me to put my arm around her, but I didn't. I felt the same deficiency must be in the Sierra Vista water too. She said, "Charlie is really going to miss him, but I won't." I gave her a Detroit telephone number where she could contact other authorities to determine Hummel's fate. She was a nice person. I felt sorry for her. That much didn't break any rules.

Hummel had paid his rent several days in advance. As a result, Don and Harriet didn't rush Kris to dispose of the property her brother had left behind. However Don began to advertise the cabin for rent at the beginning of the next month, and was surprised when a couple from Texas wanted to rent it right away. Harriet worked it out with Kris to clean out the house on a Sunday. The new tenant moved in immediately, before she had the opportunity to remove a few more things from the wood shed.

The following Saturday, Kris with three year old Charlie in hand returned to the cabin to finally clear out the wood shed. The new tenant, Tom, found that Charlie was a curious little fellow. While his mother was cleaning out the shed, Charlie spent much of his time standing inside the living room pointing to the soffit between the wall and ceiling. As he pointed he kept mouthing the word "money, money."

Later that day Don returned to assure that Kris had satisfactorily removed all of Hummel's property. Tom mentioned the strange attraction Charlie had for the wall soffit and for repeating the word money. Don naively told Tom about Hummel and of his arrest, joking that maybe he kept money in the wall. Don returned home and thought about what had occurred. Even though it was late on a Sunday afternoon, he called me to explain what had occurred. I told him to meet me at the cabin early Monday morning and not to inform the tenant we were coming.

I met Don at the cabin at 7:00 AM the next morning. There was no sign of the tenant Tom. He had apparently moved his family and all his belongings out during the night. I was sure I knew the reason why. Don keyed me into the house. I inspected the area where the walls met the ceiling. The cabin roof was an open beamed ceiling. The rafters rested on top of the wall plate, and the space between the roof and wall was closed in with simple one piece soffit blocks. In anticipation of the task to be performed I brought a pry bar from my home shop. I went to work pulling out the soffit blocks. Each one was lightly nailed in. Once removed, they exposed a shoe box sized space filled with cobwebs dead flies and dirt. About six blocks from the room corner, the pry bar flipped a block onto the floor that contained no nail and was unattached. The space was empty. Really empty! It had no cobwebs, and no dirt. The space next to it was the same; easy access, cover not attached, and completely clean.

The explanation was clear. Tennant Tom had made a discovery. The discovery was worth packing all night and leaving in the early hours of dawn. Little Charlie had known where the cash was stored.

I put out an all-points bulletin (APB) on the name used by Tom, but could not find a Texas or Arizona vehicle registered to anyone with his name. So without a vehicle, an APB was not very effective. There were no responses.

Was Tom the Texan sent by Hummel or his gang to retrieve the money? I doubt it. Not with a wife and kids. The house had been empty. Any gang member could have broken in and taken the money with no trouble. Hummel probably was incarcerated, unable to make phones calls from Canada, other than to a lawyer. Gang members rarely trust their associates enough to have disclosed where he was keeping his money. Only Charlie knew. Hummel probably thought the money was secure and could wait for his return.

According to Jan, Harriet had lost her attraction toward Don, and after she learned how he had probably given away thousands they could have commandeered, she divorced him. In the years that followed I never returned to the old remodeled dairy barn. I thought it best not to revisit.

Otto, Jan and I remained friends throughout my service in Arizona. Ten years after I left and had been working in Oregon, I returned to attend Reed's retirement party. I stopped in to see Otto and Jan. Otto had retired and purchased a small farm in Texas. They were leaving the next week. I was fortunate to see them again.

They were an enjoyable part of a long story.

I will always wonder how much money tenant "Tom" found. It could have been as much as a quarter of a million dollars. I hope it was enough to make him and his family happy. Again, it's better to be lucky than good.....any day.

China Mary

Tombstone Arizona. Thousands of FBI agents across the nation envied me for being able to work there. Others interpreted the assignment as harsh deprivation and would have become psychotic attempting to adapt to the culture and customs of the land. I will always regard the good fortune of being the "FBI man" associated with Tombstone as one of my life's great experiences. I had no delusions of being the reincarnation of Wyatt Earp, or walking in the footsteps of Doc Holliday. But I shared and became a brief bit of history being a "lawman" within their realm of glory and infamy. I practiced my shooting on the same desert hillside where they honed their skills. I interviewed degenerates locked behind the original jail cells keyed by Earp. Indirectly, I even interacted with one of the famous residents interned in Boot Hill in 1906.

Knowledge and understanding of Tombstone history was essential for my success throughout the territory. Similarly, a short glimpse of Arizona history is necessary to fully grasp the impact of this story.

Tombstone is best known for having been a lawless town during the 19th century. It was a silver mining town, with multiple companies extracting the earthly riches. The miners worked 60-hour weeks and played hard on their days off.

In about 1870, hundreds of Chinese were employed in the construction of the Southern Pacific railroad through Arizona. When the railroad construction was completed, all the Chinese laborers were laid off. The Chinese managed to settle in near-by towns, finding work in the mines or being redeployed into the service industries. Several hundred Chinese settled in Tombstone during the Arizona silver boom of the 1880s.

Like most local settlements, Tombstone had its Chinatown. The whites called it "Hoptown." It hopped from Third Street to First Street and from Fremont Street to Toughnut Street. To avoid trouble with residents in other parts of the town, the Chinese hopped in and out of connecting private tunnels. In a town of more than 5000 at that time, perhaps 300 to 500 were Chinese who lived in their own quarters.

The "Tombstone Times" reported in a 2006 article:

Perhaps the most famous Chinese person in Tombstone was China Mary (nee Sing, aka Ah Chum), a plump woman from Zhongshan county. She usually wore brocaded silks and a large amount of Asian jade jewelry. She was influential among Whites and people of other nationalities, and in Hoptown her word was as good as that of a judge or banker. The Whites, who preferred Chinese domestic labor, soon learned that Mary was resourceful in finding workers. She guaranteed the workers' honesty and workmanship. Her warranty was "Them steal, me pay!" All work was done to the employer's satisfaction or it would be redone for free. Payments, however, were made to China Mary – not to the employee.

China Mary managed a well-stocked general store where she dealt in both American and Chinese goods. She was also remembered as a generous lady who helped those in need of money or medical care. No sick, injured, or hungry person was ever turned away from her door.

When Mary died of heart failure in 1906 (at the age of 65), *the town folks had a large turnout for her service.*

China Mary was buried in Boothill Cemetery beside her friend Quong Gu Kee, who died of "natural causes" on April 23, 1893.

Also buried nearby were Foo Kee, candy store owner, accidentally stabbed in a fight; Hup Lung, for whom no details are available, and two Chinese who died of leprosy.

Boothill Cemetery was so named because many unidentified, so called "nameless" people were buried quickly, with their boots still on.

I found that Tombstone was still a modern day hovel; a harbinger of roguery set upon the territory by a concentration of misfits seeking a place to seclude themselves from normalcy. Excluded from the troublesome social class were the working and responsible merchants, tourist guides and a few who were still searching for Jesus in faraway places.

My assessment of why Tombstone attracted an unusual number of eccentric personalities was because of the town's historical reputation. It was known as a place of visitation and hiding for outlaws, runaways, fugitives and ladies of the night. It's past riches fulfilled the dreams within get rich quick schemes and easy money. Tombstone also became the death place of many who were unable to rise to the level of fierce character needed to survive. And it seemed that many modern day bandits of assorted specialties fancied themselves as "Could have been winners" in that past society. These were the mysterious that came to visit. They came to identify with the characters prominent in the town's history. They came to feel the presence of Billy Clanton, and Tom McLuery who were both killed by Wyatt Earp. They came for George John (hanged by mistake), Dutch Annie, Indian Bill, 3 fingered Jack, Bronco Charley, Red River Tom, and Marshal White. Some passed through, others stayed until the historical shadow of romance faded, or until the law redrew their plans.

The town entertained thousands of tourists every year. Tourism was the main business and source of income. The mines flooded years ago, and were no longer productive. Some existing mines were converted to tourist museums and provided yet another historical attraction.

The 1970's population of modern Tombstone was about 1500. With the infusion of so many tourists, there was a need for a town Marshal. The Cochise County Sheriff's office provided enforcement for most offenses, yet during the tourist season, the Marshal was an officious keeper of the peace, and guardian of the stagecoach stops.

Tombstone's Town Marshal was Gordon. Standing at 5' 4", Gordon was not a fearsome figure to look up to, but he made up for it in girth. Gordon was almost as tall reclining as standing. His service belt featured a complete array of defensive utensils, a huge revolver, handcuffs, pepper spray, radio, sap, Billie club and still had room for any new enforcement toy that came along. His hat was large enough to shade most of his body while in the upright position. Gordon walked with a wheezing effort and spoke in elevated tones. But Gordon was a good soul. He was conscientious with an honest sense of fairness.

Gordon's office was in the old Tombstone Jail. The building had undergone some preservation remodeling and code upgrading, but still functioned with many of its original features. Two jail cells were from the original Wild West jail. The jail cells were mostly for show, because anyone taken into custody would soon be transported by the Sheriff to Bisbee. In spite of the jail being a historical building on the tour route, Gordon's office was usually in frantic disarray. But it looked like the home of a very busy working lawman.

Gordon's competition for attention in the local law enforcement business was the local Sheriff's Deputy, "Dusty".

Dusty was a younger man, athletic, very likeable, with obviously more professional training than Gordon. Dusty was ambitious and felt he could handle the area and the town on his own, without the assistance or advice of Gordon. Dusty also appeared to have ambitions of becoming the County Sheriff someday. Gordon and Dusty worked together for the good of the community, but only when they had to. They were not close friends. I worked well with them both, but guarded my comments by excluding any mention of either in the other's presence.

During the fall of 1974, the Tucson FBI received a telephone call from a man residing in Indiana, wanting to talk with "the guy working around Tombstone who may have the name of Shrader, or something like that." The call was eventually routed to me, and after some explanation of how he came upon my name from Tombstone merchants he launched into his own story.

About twelve years earlier, he was a lawless transient. He was an alcoholic, and traveled the nation writing bad checks. He was quite successful at his forgery and check scheme and had accumulated a significant amount of cash. He stayed in Tombstone for a couple of days in the company of one of the town's prostitutes. He remained drunk most of the time, but in lucid moments was concerned that the prostitute would steal his cash. He decided to keep the money safe by burying it, and planned to return for it at a later date. He bought a one pound can of coffee and dumped the contents. He placed the money, an estimated $15,000, into the can and sealed it with tape. He stole a shovel and in the dark of night walked into the boot hill cemetery. He needed a memorable location to return to, so he dug a hole beside the headstone of China Mary's grave. He buried the money there next to China Mary, and went back to his prostitute and deceitful profession. He said he went from one prostitute to another, from town to town, without ever returning to retrieve the money.

Continuing with his story, he confessed that, years later while in prison, he had become religious and after his release, he met "a good woman." He was no longer an alcoholic and had a responsible job. However the money buried next to China Mary was constantly haunting his conscious. He wanted to redeem himself by donating the money to charity. He explained that his wife, (the good woman) had a daughter born with a disability and was institutionalized. He asked that I recover the buried cash, and donate it to some local Arizona charity serving disabled children. The contribution was to be made in honor of his wife's daughter.

When questioned about the origin of the money, he said he already had served time for his violations and had no information concerning the identity of his past victims. He had also obviously been tutored concerning the statute of limitations and double jeopardy so that he was candid in his explanations.

I told him I would attempt to recover the money, but before I took any action, I would like him to repeat his story so that I could either record it, or have another agent listen as a witness to his testimony and to his desire concerning the disposition of the money.

He said, "Yup, that's why I called you. When I told those other guys I got worried that they would just dig up the money for themselves. So, I called a minister at the church in Tombstone, and he told me to call you."

That caught me by surprise and I said, "Wait a minute! What other guys? Who else have you been talking to?"

"Well, I called the town Marshal first. He said his name was Gordon. He didn't seem to know what to do about it, and didn't promise me he would try to find it. So then I called the Sheriff's office and talked with a guy named Dusty. He didn't seem to believe me, and then when I told him I had already talked with the Marshal, he got mad. When I was all done with them, I wasn't sure that they would give the money to the right place. So then I was asking about how to call the Highway Patrol, and the preacher said I should call you."

The only commitment I made to the caller was that if the money was still next to China Mary, I would return a call to him to discuss the disposition to his preferred charity.

I thought this was going to be interesting. I knew I could claim jurisdiction by opening an "Interstate Transportation of Stolen Property" case. But I had no idea how I would justify giving away the money. That would probably be up to the court. But I had to find the money first. I decided to begin by calling Dusty. Other calls followed.

It was as I expected. There was a figurative dust storm brewing in Tombstone. Dusty didn't trust Gordon. Gordon didn't trust Dusty. Gordon had gone to the city council. Dusty had gone to the county attorney. The county attorney was arguing with the Tombstone council on who owned the cemetery.

I offered the only immediate solution. "Why don't we all just get together and see if we locate anything first?"

I agreed to meet all interested parties at Boothill early the next morning.

When I got to Boothill, Gordon and Dusty were already there, sitting in separate cars. They both looked tired and bedraggled. I learned later that both had been up most of the night conducting surveillance on the grave site, and watching each other.

On the Northwest corner of town, highway 80 turns to the west toward St. David and Benson. Boothill Cemetery lies near the highway and at the end of Fitch Street. The cemetery is a frequently visited tourist stop, with the Boothill Cemetery Gift shop prominently at the edge of the cemetery entrance. The cemetery is and always was a dry un-vegetated parcel of desert landscape. It lies undisturbed in recent times.

I parked near the Gift Shop and walked toward the graves. Dusty and Gordon joined me, but kept me between them as we walked. Dusty immediately reported that there was a problem. "Look over there next to the cactus bunch. That's China Mary's grave."

I then saw the problem. Because certain graves in the cemetery were so frequently visited by the curious, the Tombstone Town Council had done some preservation work. China Mary's grave, along with several others had in the last five years been covered by a large concrete slab, slightly arched to shed the infrequent desert rains. The slab would have to be destroyed to explore the earth at the surface of the old headstone.

Gordon said he would contact the Town Council and get approval to remove the slab. Dusty replied, "Yah, like that's going to happen real quick."

Dusty was right. It took two days to assemble a back hoe and a town representative at the gravesite. I was there when the digging began. The hoe operator was an artist. He carefully removed more than enough dirt from all around the grave to expose anything that would have been buried there. Nothing! I telephoned the man who buried the money to confirm the location and depth. He insisted he barely put the can beneath the dusty surface.

Dusty asked, "Did the guy say exactly when he buried the money?"

"Twelve years ago in August", I said. "That would have been summer of 1962."

Dusty took a deep breath, turned toward the gift shop, and expelled all of the air in a string of curse words. The most I deciphered from it was, "I knew that S.O.B. never earned that money." And then there was more cursing while kicking his boots into the dirt.

Gordon was just looking at us both with a dumb expression.

I was the first to speak in real sentences. "OK Dusty, help me out, 'cause I guess I am missing quite a bit here."

"That lazy SOB that runs the gift shop never worked more than he had to, to buy booze. They were barely getting by and he struck a deal with the City Council to have his wife weed the cemetery. Not too long after that she quit and the council had to find someone else. Then all of a sudden, the SOB had all sorts of money and spent big to remodel the gift shop. I always wondered how he got the money to work over the building when he had to have his wife pulling weeds the year before."

Gordon now chimed in. "That SOB found the money!"

It was the first time in several weeks that Gordon and Dusty had agreed on anything.

I offered, "Well I guess there's no use in going over and asking him if he found the money."

Gordon was finally into it now. "You kiddin? That SOB would lie about a popsicle."

"Well I guess that answers my question." I thought, "A popsicle?" H-m-m.

I had to call the man and tell him what happened. I'm not sure he ever believed me. He wanted to confront the Gift Shop owner, but I explained that almost anyone could claim found property. And more important, no one could say with any assurance that the Gift shop owner was the finder. The opinions of the local officers did not matter. Under the circumstances, the temporary caretaker had not perpetrated a crime.

Once again, money had disappeared into the desert.

The town council recapped China Mary's grave and righted the headstone.

As for the gift shop operator, he ran a good business, and was by all observations working for his money. I saw that he was left alone to continue his work.

How Much Money?

I glanced down at my speedometer as a motorcycle overtook and passed me. I was traveling at 77 miles per hour. The man and machine appeared to be speeding close to 85 miles per hour. That was nothing unusual. But there was something different about this rider.

We were heading east on Interstate 10, nearing the little town of Benson, where State Highway 90 to the south intersects the freeway. The area was populated with large numbers of motorcycle groups. I say groups because not all of the motorcycle owners were organized into "gangs." There were ordinary riders, and there were "Bikers". Biker gangs known as outlaw gangs operating in Arizona included *Gypsy Jokers, Hell's Angels, Banditos, Outlaws, Huns, Brother Speed, Devils Disciples, Mongols, Diablos* and a few others I have long forgotten. Many came in from California, New Mexico, and Colorado. Much of their "business" in Arizona involved drug trafficking. We were right then motoring in the direction of the Mexican Border, just 100 miles to the south. Also in that direction lie the cities of Bisbee and Sierra Vista. The latter was a growing business community bonded with Fort Huachuca, a large US Army Post. Bisbee was an ancient mining town, once rich and grand but now dilapidated, being re-born into a new identity supported by bikers and old hippies. Both towns had the ingredients for nurturing hooligans.

This biker's "ride" was normal, but classy. It was a large "Harley", loaded with chrome accessories. A California license plate hung from the rear fender, but I couldn't read the numbers. The big two cylinder engine roared loudly under the "high rider" chrome handlebars. The rider sat back, over the large rear tire, with his scuffed black boots resting high out front near the smaller chrome front wheel. His long straight black hair flapped free in the wind, restricted only by a multi colored bandana. Large sunglasses gave him the space alien bug eyes featured in science fiction drawings.

What made him different? He was riding alone, wearing his "colors". His jacket bore his club logo and patches. As he eased past me, I saw clearly the club identification of the *Mongols*. I was aware of the presence of all of the Motorcycle Gangs in residence in Southern Arizona. *Mongols* were not known to be among them. They were thought to be mostly in California and Texas. Their membership consisted of mostly persons of Mexican descent, who were not allowed to join the Hell's Angels because of their race. In the early organizing, Mexicans attempted to join Hell's Angels chapters, but were rejected. Hell's Angels were "whites only." As a result, the two gangs were fierce enemies. That's what struck me as unusual. Arizona was also Hell's Angels country. A lone rider of any gang seldom displayed his colors, and especially not in enemy territory. The predominant gangs in this territory were Gypsy Jokers and Outlaws. They seemed to have a "business pact" with the Angels and were no friends of the Mongols either. No wonder he was running over 80 miles per hour.

I kept him in sight until I saw him turn south onto highway 90. That road led to Sierra Vista and Fort Huachuca. I just happened to be going that way myself.

I lagged behind, far enough to be inconspicuous but just close enough to keep him in sight. Just before we reached the outer edge of Fort Huachuca, the rider turned east onto a dirt road, toward a group of low class, ratty, trailer houses about a mile away. I made a mental note to later check out that area, and to discuss my observations with my friends, the Sierra Vista Chief of Police, and the Cochise County Sheriff's deputies. They would want to know if there were any new players in the burgeoning drug trafficking.

My interaction with Biker Gangs had been increasing. Most of it involved thefts of government property, or interstate transportation of stolen property. The drug violations were investigated by the Drug Enforcement Agency, and the local departments. This day, I had other important things on my schedule. I had to check out a proposed cover identity and job for a person being placed under the (WP) Witness Protection Program.

• • •

In the early days of the WP the FBI monitored and arranged for protection of their sensitive witnesses. Years later the responsibility was reassigned to the United States Marshals. On this day, I was notified that a certain female was going to be a major witness against upper level organized crime figures on the West Coast and Hawaii. It was going to be my job to keep track of her, and make sure she remained safe until she was called to testify in Federal Court. After that, she would again change her name and be relocated to begin a new life.

FBI headquarters and our Phoenix Headquarters offices made most of the administrative arrangements. Through various sources, she (we'll call her Velma) obtained a job in Sierra Vista. However Velma was no ordinary person, nor would she be employed at an ordinary job. She was an "exotic dancer", specializing in belly dancing. She was going to be employed at the Saber Lounge in Sierra Vista. The Saber Lounge was well known to be a hangout for soldiers, bikers, hookers, and other nefarious characters. The owner regularly employed a string of "dancers" to keep his lounge full, and the patrons happy. My instructions were to assure that "the placement was secure" and to guard against the "compromise of the witness's safety" by "maintaining complete secrecy from all citizens and authorities." OK, I got it. It meant that I was to tell no one, but I was supposed to check on this woman and keep her safe, all by myself. I wondered if the genius behind this placement realized that I lived 90 miles away.

My thoughts were, "This is really going to be great! In addition to my regular over assigned duties, I am going to have to baby sit a Belly Dancer, working in a hooker joint, while performing my regular duties wearing a suit, recognized by many in town, sneaking around meeting a big boobed blond in secret for her own good." Really!

Several telephone calls during the following week put together a plan. My supervisor worked in the Phoenix office which was staffed and operational around the clock. Theirs was to be the first telephone number on the witness's emergency list, and mine was the second. However I was "Knighted" to respond to any problems, and was responsible to assure her safe appearance in court several months in the future. It was in the mandate that I check on her welfare periodically.

When Velma arrived in Sierra Vista, I had my first meeting with her at the most benign place I could think of. I frequently stayed overnight in Sierra Vista. After work I routinely jogged around the High School Track. Other Citizens walked in the area of the track and football field. Velma was told to go for a walk, alone.

People in her predicament often did not understand how much they were vulnerable to discovery. They often compromised themselves by carelessly misplacing personal letters, or other documents relating to their old identity. Even a forgetful misspoken word could arouse suspicion in an associate.

Strolling around the High School track, I laid out the rules in a very businesslike tone. She was going to be responsible for her own safety, and was only to call me if she needed help with her secret existence. She was to obey all laws, keep a low profile, and above all tell no one her true identity or speak about her prior associates. She was not to leave the area without first telling me, and was to stay in contact with me before, during, and after any travel outside of the immediate area. I gave her the key to a Post Office Box I had rented in her new name. I explained that she was to use the P.O. Box for her regular mail, and was to check it daily for messages. I too had a key to the box and messages from me would be placed in the mail box with a certain water mark stamp on the envelope. Any message within the envelope would be cryptic, but would identify where we were to meet, or the time place and telephone on which she would be called. She spoke little and I only asked her enough questions to be able to recognize her breathy smoker's voice in a telephone conversation.

I could tell at that time, she was thinking much more positively about this new arrangement than I was. As she walked away toward the school, she appeared anything but discreet. What I observed was a five foot six inch stalky but sleek twenty something blond, built for attention, walking with a mid-section swing, clad in white shorts and a pendulous bare midriff top. She turned to look back as she crossed the school yard. I was the only person she knew and trusted in Arizona. I hoped that she made friends quickly.

I had previously surveyed the apartment where she would be living. She did not have a car, but could easily walk to work at the Saber Lounge. Groceries and other business stores were also close by. Communications with her needed to be secret. It is important to remember that during the 1970's we did not have cell phones. The pay phone was our mobile link to the telephone world. I noted that Velma's apartment did not have a telephone, but had a pay phone just outside the entry. That was important. If she responded to a phone in her room, probabilities of another person being there at the time were great. But if she frequently used the pay phone to make routine calls, it would not seem unusual for her to occasionally receive one from me. The pay phone provided much more security. I placed the number behind my credential identification and wondered how soon the first crisis would arrive when I would need it.

• • •

The image of the Mongol bike rider still rode in the back of my mind. I walked into "The Chief's" office where he was meeting with Cochise County Chief Deputy, Frank. After the usual verbal barbs and attempts at embarrassment were exchanged, we got down to business. I spoke of my observations concerning the out of place biker, and they responded with questions.

Frank asked, "Where did you say he turned off?"

"He turned on that dirt road to the east just as you get into Huachuca City. He went on down toward that group of trailers about a mile to the east."

"Did he stop there?"

Hell, I don't know. I can't see more than a half mile through your county road dust."

The Chief, Reed, responded, "Well it was early in the morning. You should have still been sober."

Frank inquired, "Did you go down there later?" (He suspected I had, and was saving something for the end of the story.)

"Yup I did, but it was about three hours later. There are five trailers down there; all of them trash heaps. The road ends at the wash behind the back of the east trailer. There were three bikes parked around a couple of the trailers, but none of them were the one that passed me. I couldn't get close enough to see the license plates. I didn't see any people. A couple of barking mutts caused me to turn around and leave."

Reed grinned, "Well why didn't you knock on the door, tell them you were from the church, and go on in?"

Frank was more serious. "I know a couple of guys that use to live out there. They were involved in that bar fight and shooting over in Tombstone about a year ago. They sometimes hang out with the bunch that runs that bike shop in the tin warehouse north of Fry Boulevard."

I asked, "Yes, I've been wondering what goes on in that old building. Is that a legitimate operation? Who runs that place?"

What followed was a long description of alleged gang activity by several outlaw biker groups in the area. It became clear that neither the Police Department, nor the Sheriff's Office had any trust or rapport with anyone in the motorcycle culture. They were unaware of the activities occurring in the old warehouse other than there was not a licensed business activity or person associated with the location. The tax records indicated the building was leased for storage.

At the conclusion of the meeting, I announced that I was going to spend some time, getting to know about the biker culture in Cochise County. Both Frank and Reed laughed and wished me luck.

• • •

During the next couple weeks, I did my work, examining each incident for some reason, some excuse, anything that I could use to visit the old tin warehouse, and talk to the people within. Finally an event occurred that gave me a natural opening.

A refrigerated rail car parked on a siding at Benson Arizona was broken into. Forty cases of beer were taken. Both pickup tracks and what appeared to be motorcycle tracks, were present next to the broken rail car door. A day later, a rancher along the San Pedro River between Sierra Vista and Tombstone called in to complain that there was a group of Bikers partying on his property, and they appeared to have a "whole pickup load of beer."

It was not an important case, but it was Federal – Theft from interstate shipment. No United States Attorney would consider prosecuting the theft of forty cases of beer in federal court. But it was a reason for me to talk to some of the local bikers.

In the meantime, Velma reported that she was doing fine. She liked her new job. She liked Sierra Vista. She was making new friends, most of them bikers who frequented the Saber Lounge. In fact she said she attended a great party near the river "over toward Tombstone." The guys showed up with a whole pickup load of beer.

Marvelous!

I micro planned my approach to the group at the tin warehouse for several hours. My foremost goal was not to solve the beer theft, but to establish some sort of relationship with the bikers. This had to be done in stages. I learned as a child that marching down to the river and throwing in the line would only scare away the fish. Sneaking up, slipping in the bait, and waiting with patience was a wiser approach.

My first appearance at the old tin warehouse was little more than an introduction. I used the official approach, badge and all, and explained I was looking for a certain pickup truck and the owner. I described the beer hauling pickup. Of course no one there even co-operated to the extent that they admitted knowing what a pickup truck was. I didn't push for answers. Instead, I took verbal notice of a nice looking custom motorcycle that was being assembled in the center of the cement floor. A couple of the men who appeared to be mechanics showed me their work with pride. They cautiously discussed their creation until the pickup truck seemed to be completely forgotten. Throughout the conversation, I was able to get a good look at the building and contents.

The warehouse was indeed old. It was wood framed with corrugated tin forming the outer structure. The roof was insulated, as was part of the sides. However shards of sunlight darted through the walls, and the large rolling metal doors thumped in the wind. Everything inside was dirty, except where the tools were kept, and where various bikes were stored. There were additional bike works in progress, from engines to frames. Benches were randomly placed around the perimeter and several stools stood near the assembly areas. The benches gave an impression that the large area could also serve as a meeting place for a couple dozen people. There was no cash register or indication of retail sales, or retail stock. The side walls and dark corners contained stacks of what appeared to be used motorcycle parts, and an occasional crushed beer can.

I concluded my visit with small talk about motorcycles, my own interest in car body work, and with a lie that I use to ride motorcycles in my college days. I left with a friendly word, and I am sure that after my departure they were all laughing about how dumb I must be. If so, that is just what I wanted.

I waited two weeks before returning. After all, I had other matters that needed investigating, and this biker thing was going to be just an interesting experiment.

• • •

One of the things troubling me was that a local soldier, Kyler, was missing from Fort Huachuca. He had been missing for 30 days and was classified as a deserter. That resulted in me being issued a warrant for his arrest. Deserters from a large military installation were common place, and I processed ten or more a month. They were usually located near their hometown USA or found loafing at some old girlfriend's house. However Kyler was different. He was married. He and his wife lived in Sierra Vista. She worked at the Saber Lounge as a dancer. According to Police reports Kyler and his wife were known to have domestic disturbances in the past. The wife did not report him missing until military authorities inquired concerning his absence. County authorities at the request of the military were looking into the possibility of foul play and were in the process of investigating his wife. As a result, I was sitting on the case, monitoring the county's progress. I only had a deserter warrant, and had no other jurisdiction or authority to conduct a homicide investigation. Aggressive questioning by me risked stepping on the county's case. Still, there seemed to be no trace of Kyler, and I too began to doubt that he was still alive.

When I returned to the biker warehouse, it was a hot spring afternoon. I had cruised by several times to make sure the timing was right to find as many people as possible in the building. I removed my tie, and was wearing only a short sleeved white shirt, brown polyester slacks, and brown Cow Town cowboy boots. My revolver was locked in my car, and the small pistol in my boot was not visible. Under my arm I carried a case of cold Hamm's beer.

When I walked into the work area, in the presence of eight bikers, you could have heard a wrench drop. No one said anything.

I looked toward the middle of the group gathered around the sparkling custom bike and said, "I figured that if you bastards liked beer well enough to pry open box cars to get it, I would bring some over and we could all share in the spoils." As

I spoke I threw the beer case on a low table at the rear of the bike.

The silence was broken with a few chuckles and then outright he-haw laughter. A couple of rough looking characters whom I had never met before didn't get it, though I was sure they knew about the beer party and theft.

When the laughter subsided, a huge ugly dude walked toward me and said, "You think you can just walk in here and start drinking beer?"

"Well...Ain't that what you usually do with it?"

He frowned and growled, "Who the #&$% are you?"

It dawned on me at that moment where I had met the guy before? This was big Bubba from our first meeting at the Horney Javelina in Tucson. Yes, the extortion case involving the tavern. Although it was a couple years back, I recognized all 6 feet 4 of him. Now he looked even bigger. I took a step in his direction, and said "You should remember me. We're old friends. We met in Tucson a few months ago. Remember? My name is Schreuder with the FBI."

I saw the realization come across his face. "Old friends my ass!" "I'm not drinking with a #&$% cop." He turned and stomped out.

The room of faces looked at me in silence. I reached for a beer and said, "Well.... does anyone else have any severe allergies?"

One face stepped forward, reached toward the table and said, "Ah, not to beer anyway."

It was the beginning of an interesting afternoon. All seven of the remaining bikers stayed. They were as curious as I was, but certainly with different questions. My goal was to appear as an OK normal guy, even if I was a "Cop." Through my subtle actions, I let them know that perhaps I wasn't as stupid as they originally thought. They realized I knew most of them were in on the beer theft, but yet for some reason I chose not to hassle them about it. That really puzzled them, but left them cautiously relieved. I never mentioned the box car incident again, not even during follow up visits. It was an unspoken truce and the start of an unusual relationship.

I tested the relationship regularly on Friday afternoons. I changed nothing, not even the brand of beer. Week by week I worked on being excepted and trusted, but progress was very slow. We were different from each other and knew it, but barriers were being removed. I learned their affiliation with other biker gangs was mostly mixed. They were a conglomerate of scattered groups brought together by their existence in Cochise County. Some were Gipsy Jokers, Huns, and a couple of Banditos. They were discussing forming their own Sierra Vista Club, but some of their previous clubs required that they vowed to never join any others. I suggested they form a more social domestic group, but the suggestion was not "macho" enough to satisfy many.

I finally made real progress when the custom, chrome low rider was completed. It was displayed proudly in the center of the warehouse floor. They asked if I wanted to sit on it. Of course I responded with enthusiasm. They cheered when I rocked back in the seat with my arms up on the controls. Then I had an idea.

"Hey guys this is really great! My mother would never believe that down here in Arizona I made friends with a bunch of guys in a bike shop. I'm going to go out to my car and get my camera, and want someone to take a picture of me with this bike and all you guys."

The FBI provided me with a camera that was always in my portable crime kit. I retrieved it, and on that day, nine of the moteliest dudes ever assembled were photographed with me sitting astride a custom Harley low rider.

I wanted to be sure I could keep the photograph, so in case someone was going to realize what had just happened and change their mind; I closed up the camera and jogged out to store it in my car. I was just in time to catch a potential intruder next to my car. He was a biker who had been in and out of the warehouse. He didn't appear to have harmed the car...yet... but was hands on examining it very closely.

I pretended not to be disturbed by his stealthy presence, and asked, "Oh, do you want to check out my car?"

"Ah, yah, sure."

I stifled my anger and in a friendly accommodating manner I opened the door, showed him the radios, the high speed 140 mph speedometer, the emergency light, and even popped the trunk so he could get a glimpse of my very ugly military type shotgun. Lastly I opened the hood so he could size up the engine. When I thought he had seen enough, I suddenly slammed down the hood and moved close enough to breathe on him when I spoke.

I looked straight into his eyes. "Now you've seen it. And if I ever catch you about to mess with it again I'll tear off your balls and feed them to you."

He blinked with a startled look, and said, "I'll bet you would. OK, you're cool. You're cool. OK, OK."

I interpreted that as granting me freedom from further "anti-Cop" harassment. I knew that word of my verbal assault would get around, and I wanted it to.

"Good!" I said, and I slapped him on the back with a firm friendly hand, threw the camera into the car, and we both returned to the warehouse. He grabbed a beer, and I thought I saw his hand shaking as he opened it.

Prior to the photograph I knew them only as "Grease Monkey, Ears, Tobi, Gear Box, Fussy, Boss, Bubba, Mudman, and one weird dude named Gary. There were others, too many to remember, with strange names and a small minority that actually went by domestic real names. Triumphantly I had a photo of them all, and could begin research to identify as many as possible.

My friends Reed and Frank were astonished when I showed them the photo. I kept them informed of my activities for several reasons. I knew they had their own informants and were probably aware that I had been frequenting the old warehouse. I wanted to be sure they understood I was working with a law enforcement purpose in mind, and not joining in some sort of racketeering scheme. I also wanted them aware because if things took a turn to the worse, and I disappeared, there would be a starting place for my recovery. The photo gained county wide notoriety among law enforcement, and was used extensively until most of the attendees of the tin warehouse were correctly identified.

Through all of this, the County's investigation into the disappearance of Kyler was going nowhere. His wife was openly cavorting with a biker. Guess who…..Bubba. They suspected that she had Bubba or his associates kill Kyler and dispose of him. But the greatest flaw in their case was that they did not have a body. They had nothing to prove Kyler had been harmed, and therefore did not have a regular homicide case.

• • •

The months drug on, and Velma was becoming a problem. She would disappear with her biker boyfriends, and not return for several days at a time. I learned her favorite male friend seemed to be Grease Monkey, or Monk as he was sometimes called. He was the chief and best mechanic hanging around the tin warehouse. He was one of the more normal ones, so I didn't worry about the relationship. She was becoming more complacent with her secret identity and took chances with the company she was keeping. Her style of living was anything but low key.

I was well established with the Fort Huachuca leadership and was an honorary member of the Officer's Club. One evening I was invited to attend Stag Night at the Club as a guest of the Post Commander. My military service acquainted me with the tradition and I willingly accepted the invitation. The grand finale of the evening, the featured entertainment, was an exotic belly dancer.

There for the first time, I saw that Velma was a true professional. She had muscle control and silky, sexy, moves that few in the Club had ever witnessed. Her musical movements were well timed and artistic. Even her costume was classy. She did not appear as a cheap body act. While she performed there were no "cat calls", no whistles, or off color remarks. She had everyone's attention and admiration. The audience realized they were seeing something special. Some senior attendees were heard to comment, "What's she doing in Sierra Vista?" I smiled at the thought that only I knew the answer.

Within the next couple of days I met with Velma. My intent was to admonish her to attract less attention, and have patience because she was soon to be subpoenaed to testify. It was then I first experienced her unbridled anger. Her vocabulary could have been a reference book for the ocean's warriors. In essence she said if I was so smart, why didn't I solve the Kyler murder case. According to Velma, "Everybody I work with and every p—k in town knows Bubba and Kyler's wife killed him."

I asked, "If you knew this why didn't you tell me?"

"Me tell you? Do you think I want to get #$&% killed?"

But further questioning resulted in nothing specific. I began to believe that in her own way she was actually trying to help. Most of her co-workers were reaching conclusions based on innuendos and insinuations that Kyler's wife engineered his disappearance after she began sleeping with big Bubba. An obvious conclusion was that Bubba had killed Kyler. The last anyone had seen him, the evening he disappeared, he was seen intoxicated at the Saber Lounge. His car was found abandoned in the Saber parking lot. Even when pressured, Velma failed to identify any specific person who seemed to be the most knowledgeable about the crime, or who might have been the source of the rumors. All I could do was explain that I did not have jurisdiction, and that she should stay alert for any clues as to who seemed truly knowledgeable.

Then again I cautioned, "Velma be careful! You have a much greater task to finish."

I felt inadequate so I decided to get more involved.

The one item that Cochise Sheriff's investigators lacked was Kyler. If they had him one way or another, they could proceed differently. I had a warrant for his arrest. I decided I would find him.

I met with my friends Reed and Frank, as well as Sheriff Jim Wilson and the Undersheriff, Jim Judd. We all agreed that it would do no harm for me to enter the investigation, even with limited jurisdiction. Realistically it was impossible to separate the homicide implications from a search to locate the missing soldier. But they acknowledged that an expanded search could not inhibit their case.

I had already worked through the usual leads. A search of his property on Fort Huachuca, interview of his military associates, a review of his Army records, and contact with his parents through one of the FBI offices in his home state, all turned up nothing. All information pointed toward a stormy relationship with his wife, a jealous outlaw boyfriend, and his disappearance after becoming intoxicated at the Saber Lounge. He was last known to be passed out in his own vehicle which was parked in the Saber lot at about midnight on a Friday night. The predominant theory was that he was taken from the car, and in some way disposed of.

I was out of leads, but not out of ideas. The main suspect was Bubba. Bubba was a biker. The Sheriff's detectives did not have any means of getting inside information from the local biker gangs, but I had been working my way in with them for just such reasons. I was not close enough yet to extract that kind of information, but there was one accelerant that hadn't been tried.

During my next Friday afternoon visit to the warehouse, I brought the usual case of beer. The end of week sessions had almost become a ritual. When I first began the routine, I worried that I would soon find the place empty on Fridays, but it was quite the opposite. Attendance now often rose to fifteen or more. Others sometimes brought extra beer, thus extending the sessions. They did not all appear as scoundrels, but were still from another world than what I was accustomed to. We often talked of local events, told a few jokes, and shared life experiences. They seemed profoundly surprised that I grew up a poor kid in the country, occasionally fighting with my class-mates in a rural school. I learned from all of them. I never took notes and slowly sipped my beer to remain unencumbered by the memory decay of alcohol. Sometimes on the ride back to Tucson, I would stop a few miles out of town to make notes on what I had learned.

But there was never any mention of Kyler. So this Friday, I broke the ice very abruptly.

I asked, "When are you guys going to tell me where to find Kyler?" I could hear a few suck in their breath, but I got noth-ing more than a couple of nervous laughs. I pushed it a little further.

"It seems to me that in a town this small, it would be hard for someone to do away with a guy, and hide him completely without some help, or without someone knowing about it."

There was still no response other than a couple of nodding heads. There was a nervous stir that went through the guys that belied their innocence. I knew then that the answer was here, but I had not found a way to get at it.

Conversation had been stifled and the atmosphere was abruptly uncomfortable, so I let it go; until the next week.

I was somewhat distracted by Velma during mid-week. She was being called to California to testify, but would return until she was called for the main Federal Trial. On her departure she informed me that "the girls" at the Sabre believed (for whatever reason I could not establish) that Kyler was removed from his car by Bubba and one of Bubba's friends. The source of the information was some unidentified person who had seen Bubba and Kyler talking, perhaps arguing earlier that night. Coming from Velma, everything was very unspecific. However, I had to remember that a few months earlier I had warned her to stay out of trouble and keep a low profile. It was good to have her leaving town. No one knew for sure when she would be returning.

My next visit with the boys at the warehouse began much the same. I entered with the intent of continuing the push for information about Kyler. I tried another tactic this time, and let other members select the conversation topics, and guide flow. The avoidance of talk about Kyler was obvious. It was clear that each member in the room was afraid to even mention the subject.

After a shorter time than usual, I faked a reason to leave early. I stood up on departure and again asked, "When are you guys going to tell me where to find Kyler?" Without waiting for an answer I said, "I can make it worth some money to anyone who wants to help me out."

With my departure, the session was breaking up. A few others were heading toward their machines. I slowly walked in the direction of my car parked away from the street behind the warehouse. I had the door open about to sit behind the wheel, when Tobi appeared shadowed by the building. He caught my attention and asked, "How much money?"

My heart leaped as I thought, "Fish on!"

I knew that however I handled myself during the next few seconds meant success or failure, hero or fool, shame or fame.

I paused and replied, "It depends on how much help I get". I let the statement hang there.

Tobi scratched his face and said, "I don't know for sure, but I know of a place out in the desert that might be it. If I'm right, how much money?"

Other bikers were disbursing around the parking lot, and we needed to have this conversation elsewhere. And I needed time. I had not discussed reward with my supervisor, or the Sheriff's department, and I didn't have a figure to offer.

I said, "I'll be at the Western Motel at exactly 7 tonight. Call and ask for Schreuder."

It was 5:15 on a Friday night, and I had work to do.

I started with a call to Phoenix. My immediate supervisor was Kermit in Tucson. But Kermit only kept operations in Tucson productive and real problems had to be referred to specific squad supervisors in Phoenix. I was lucky and caught the fugitive and violent crimes supervisor, Roy, before he went home. Roy was aware of the Kyler case, but to him the soldier was just another deserter. The idea of offering a reward for the location of a deserter was without president. This was also the 1970's and the FBI was quite stingy with reward money. They still labored under the concept that good citizens should volunteer their help, and the reward comes from just being civic minded. I had to explain that it didn't work that way in motorcycle gangs.

Roy was what we referred to as "A good old boy." He came up through the ranks of field agents, had spent years on the street as a working agent and had not been tainted with Washington careerism. Roy said he would have to consult the Special Agent in Charge (SAC) of the Phoenix Field Division. I told him I had to have an answer by 6:30 that night.

Roy was a good supervisor, and a friend, but the conversation became tense.

"For Christ sakes Schreuder, it's Friday night. What the hell you doin' down there now? Why don't you wait until Monday and I can discuss this with the SAC. We just don't hand out money to catch deserters. Hell we would be broke in a month if we did that."

I explained the urgency and told him that I believed I could get Cochise County to come up with half of the money. I picked a number out of my racing mind and said, "I think the source will go for about three grand, can we come up with fifteen hundred?"

Roy sighed and sarcastically said, "You want me to run down the boss tonight and ask him for fifteen hundred bucks just to find some deserter that you think is dead anyway! He'll think you've been smoking that stuff those wet backs are hauling around down there."

I steeled my voice to a monotone and said, "No Roy, I want you to verbally grant me the money right now because I am running out of time to pull off one of the best crime fighting breaks this community has experienced in a long time. Tell the boss it is urgent, and that the entire southern part of the state will recognize him and our involvement as an important participating force in law enforcement."

Roy paused and I could hear him cursing under his breath. Then he asked, "What if you don't find the body?"

"Roy, trust me! This is going to be a COD (cash on delivery) deal. When we get the body, he gets the cash. But I have to get him on the hook with a promise tonight before he gets cold feet. He's taking a hell of a chance, and could get himself killed if anything leaks out about his co-operation. I can't look weak with my commitment, and I can't put him off or I'll scare him back into silence. No one in Southern Arizona has a handle on this obvious murder, and if we don't act tonight, some killer is going to walk out of this."

Roy had by then calmed down and understood the political benefits of the deal. "Well, OK, I'll find the SAC and try and get you the money, but I'm not promising anything."

My calculated reply was, "OK Roy, I'll get the County's commitment for fifteen hundred, and tell them we'll put up the rest. You don't need to call me back unless you can't get the money down here by mid next week. Thanks Roy." Then I hung up.

• • •

I couldn't reach the Sheriff on the radio, but the regional Chief Deputy Frank picked up on my call. I arranged to meet him at his home south of Sierra Vista. He greeted me in the driveway, and I explained the situation. I was pleased with his prompt response.

"Fifteen hundred dollars; hell that's cheap. We already spent twice that much trying to figure out what happened to the guy. I'm hoping that the source comes through and we can pay him."

I chose the figure of three thousand even though I thought Tobi would co-operate for less. I wanted to impress him with a significant amount (remember this was about 1975) and also knew that he was in for trouble once I disclosed his identity to the County. There would be a lot of questions to follow.

The elderly proprietor of the Western Motel was an old friend of mine and other agents through the years. She had been housing me a couple nights a week for more than five years. She kept a special room for me, no smoking with a small refrigerator usually containing a couple pieces of in season fresh fruit. She knew most of my co-worker agents, and we affectionately referred to her as "Ma Frickett." Ma could be trusted.

This night, I burst into her office and announced that I needed a room for only about 15 minutes in which to receive a phone call. She beamed in anticipation because all calls had to go through her PBX switchboard, and she was the operator. We knew she listened to all of them, but usually didn't care. She knew how to keep her mouth shut, but loved to know what was happening.

As she ushered me to the room, I explained the call would come for me in about ten minutes, around 7:00 PM. Then I put my arm around her and said, "Mrs. Roberts, you don't want to listen to this one because knowing anything about this mess could get you killed."

She indignantly glanced up and said, "Mr. Schreuder, you know I never listen in to anyone's calls."

In reality she was one of my best sources around town. I knew she got most of her information from running her PBX board.

Tobi called at exactly seven. I thanked him for coming forward, and explained that the deal was going to be COD. If he directed me to Kyler, or to his body, he would get three thousand in cash. Then I was honest with him. I explained that if we found Kyler dead, the County would certainly have questions of him about what he knew and how he knew it. I admitted I would be unable to keep his co-operation secret if Kyler was found dead. Tobi weighed the idea for about a minute, but the lure of three thousand was too much for him to back out.

Tobi's information emerged haltingly. "There's a dirt road that goes from Sierra Vista to Tombstone called Charleston Road. Just before you get to the river there is a fence to the west side of the road. About fifty yards west of the fence there is an old dry well. I think there is a post next to the hole. We use to dump stolen bike parts and other hot stuff down that hole, 'cause it's real deep. A lot of guys know about the well 'cause it's a good place to get rid of stuff. If you look down there you might find him."

I took a chance and asked, "Do you know who put him there?"

"Hey man, I don't even know if he's there for sure. I just think that if someone wanted to get rid of somebody that would be a good place to put him."

I was clear this was not the time to get into an interrogation. Besides that, my job was only to find Kyler. I struggled to remember that.

I got Tobi's home phone, and told him I would call after I searched the location he suggested. He concluded by saying, "My wife doesn't know anything about this, so don't tell her who you are when you call."

I said, "OK", and he hung up. I didn't even know he had a wife.

• • •

I called Frank, told him the good news, and made arrangements to meet him Monday morning. I was 8:00 PM, Friday night, and almost two hours back to Tucson. Still, I was loving my job.

Monday morning, I was informed by the County Dispatch that it was Frank's day off. The dispatcher was reluctant to call him. "Too bad", I thought. "I know where he lives." Days off were constantly violated in our profession, and I knew Frank expected me to contact him as soon as I arrived in Sierra Vista.

Frank had several Mules in a desert pasture next to his home about 4 miles to the south of Sierra Vista. I found him out near the pasture fence, grooming an old Mule. Law enforcement officers often had unusual hobbies to serve as diversions from their intense occupation. The mule was probably a good listener.

I parked next to him and the fence and asked, "Would you rather spend the day with me, or that old mule?"

"My wife asked me the same thing just last week, and I didn't give her an honest answer, so you won't get one either."

Frank looked wistfully at the old mule, and I offered him an out.

"I'm going to drive out to where Tobi said the well was, and have a look at the scene. You want to go, or wait until I get back?"

"No, you're gonna need help. This old mule can get along by his-self." He paused and looked down at his worn boots. "It's my day off, so I ain't goin' in my uniform, but hold on 'til I get my gun."

We drove out Charleston road, and found Tobi's directions accurate. I parked on the road and we walked west past the fence toward a weathered old fence post. Appearing in plain view was a huge hole. The well was more than ten feet in diameter. It was on flat desert ground, and it would have been possible to drive a small car into the opening. It had no railing sides or protective berm. It was just a gaping hole that had no visible bottom.

We both stood back from the edge, afraid that if we got too close, the sides might cave in.

Frank squinted into the bottomless dark hole and said, "Holy crap, you could hide Custer's Army down there."

I picked up a fist sized rock and tossed it into the hole. It disappeared without making a sound. A second stone did the same, with no indication it ever landed on anything.

"My God Frank, how are we ever going to look down in there?"

We each experimented with a few suggestions, but Frank was familiar with the local resources and came up with the best ideas.

"We'll go in to town, to the Exxon station and get John and his wrecker out here. We'll attach some sort of seat to the cable, and lower someone down with a flashlight to have a look."

I realized what he just said and quickly interjected, "There's no way I am going down there!"

"Me either, but I have a new young deputy. We can send him down for the adventure."

I was still worried. "What kind of system can we use to hook him to the cable? Those sides are really dangerous. If he bumps the sides, there's a good chance they may cave in on him."

Frank, the hobby mule skinner had a plan. "I have a couple single trees. We can hook one onto the end of the wrecker hook, and the deputy can sit on it with the hook between his legs and hang on with the cable next to his chest."

I got it. "Just like riding a T Bar on a ski lift."

Frank stood on the desert hard pan and looked at me in a puzzled way. "I wouldn't know anything about that."

Back in town, Frank went for the new Deputy, Lee, and I went to the Exxon station. John the proprietor was another good citizen. I bought almost all of my gas at his station and had known him for several years. The thought of fishing for a body in a well was bizarre enough to capture his interest.

Within an hour we were back at the well. While John was rigging up his cable and positioning the wrecker boom to hang directly over the center of the hole, Frank gave me a lesson on desert pioneering.

"In the old days, before drilling rigs and back hoes, the settlers hand dug their wells. This one isn't very far from the river, so they probably figured they would hit water pretty close to the surface. The deeper they had to go, the wider the hole got. Judging from the size of the hole they went a long way down on this one. There is no indication of a stock tank ever being here during the last several years, so I wouldn't be surprised if it was a dry hole. The water table has receded several feet in the last fifty years, so many of these old wells have gone dry. If there's anything down there, that will work to our advantage."

The single tree was hooked to the cable, and a brave young deputy straddled the "T Bar" double tree. He carried a flash light and a radio. Frank told him that if he started getting short of breath, he should shout it out into the radio, and we would "wind him back up." (We didn't know what the air might be like at the bottom.) John had a length counter on the wrecker cable to allow us to know how deep the deputy was dropping into the earth.

The slow decent began, and Lee descended into the blackness. John had done a good job of centering the cable, so that Lee wasn't scraping the sides, or in danger of causing dirt to break loose and cover him. The first problem occurred when

Lee was at a depth of 40 feet. He radio began to fade out and quit. The radio became useless, but we could hear him from above if he shouted. We continued with him shouting up, and Frank shouting down.

The cable kept reeling out, deeper and deeper. Frank began to look very concerned, and asked John how much cable he had on the wrecker.

"About 100 feet, but I don't think we should let it all out. I haven't been to the end of it in over a year, and I'm not confident the end will still be safely fastened to the spool."

Frank turned pale. At 83 feet, we faintly heard Lee shout to stop because he had reached the bottom. The cable went slack. We listened intently, but there was nothing.

Frank couldn't stand the silence any longer and shouted, "Is it dry down there? What do you see?"

Lee could barely be heard. "There's a bunch of old boards on top of everything. OK, I see some old motorcycle frames. Frank! Fraaank! There's a body down here Frank."

We were speechless. For over a year, there had been no homicide case, because there had been no body. Kyler, presumably it was Kyler, had now been located, and my jurisdiction was abruptly ended. Any further effort by me would now be accounted for as "Police cooperation."

We were able to understand from Lee deep down in the earth, that the body appeared in tact, and was dry and mummified. He was unable however to move it due to other debris, and he did not have equipment or as yet a method to do so. He mounted the single tree, and was slowly winched to the surface.

A serious conference followed right there on the rear platform of the wrecker. The conclusions reach were several. The body had to be removed, but without bumping the sides of the well. It would have to be placed into a body bag to keep it in tact while winching it up. No less than two men working at the bottom would be required to get the body secured in a bag and attach it to the cable. It would not be safe to raise the bag, with the men still at the bottom of the well. Neither of the men could remain below while anything was winched up due to the extreme danger of causing a cave in from a slight tap on the well shaft sides. More help was going to be necessary.

Frank was a seasoned officer, with experience in search and rescue. Within minutes he radioed his headquarters in Bisbee. He briefed Sheriff Jim Wilson, and the Undersheriff Jim Judd. Other detectives with crime scene equipment and body bags were in route. For the safety of those returning to the bottom of the well, an ambulance with breathing devices was summoned. A generator with lights for below, and for above ground light after dark were brought out to the scene.

John and I conspired to fashion a suitable apparatus for lifting, all at the same time, two men and a large bag to the surface. Through a series of hooks and clamps secured to the cable, we built an apparatus that could lower and raise two men at the same time, one above the other. They would be able to hook the zipped container to the very end of the cable, leaving it to dangle beneath them as they were all three brought to the surface, suspended one above the other. The officer, second in line, riding in the middle, would be in the most danger. I guessed that would probably be Lee. The chief detective would be his partner.

As we prepared for the extraction, people began to arrive. Some of them I didn't even know. Dusk was creeping in, and a fire of mesquite and sage brush was started. Coffee was being brewed by the rescue and ambulance crew. Sandwiches were rumored to be arriving. Wheels spun in the desert weeds. Orders were given, rescinded, and re-given. In spite of all the bustle and preparation, we had no assurance of success. It was going to be a very dangerous operation. Eighty three feet was an incredible depth. One mishap and two more men could die.

The decent began at dusk. Two men, Lee, and the Chief Detective, I think his name was Douglas, were suspended one above the other on the single wrecker cable. Below them hung a hook and a small log chain. An electrical cord with a light was being fed over a pipe lying across the diameter of the well opening. The decent lasted several minutes until the cable reached the 90 foot mark, allowing for the upper man to set foot at the base of the well.

Radios would not work at the bottom of the hole. With the generator running, and a slight evening breeze rustling the desert brush, it was nearly impossible to hear the men below. Repeated attempts were necessary to make cable adjustments from above. After almost an hour, the signal was received to begin raising the two men and their cargo. Everyone breathed a thankful word and the slow upward winching began. The body bag apparently was not balanced properly to prevent excess swinging. If it touched or hooked onto the sides of the shaft, it risked causing the entire cable, officers and all to swing into the sides. The entire group had to be returned to the bottom and the cargo readjusted.

The second extraction attempt proceeded smoothly. Within five minutes, the entire pendulum was hanging above the desert floor, and soon lowered into a lighted clearing. All participants viewed the contents of the bag. What we saw was the remains of a man, baked and dried like the pieces of hide sold at pet stores for dogs to chew. He was well preserved by the arid desert air.

There apparently had been no invasive insects or parasites at the extreme depth of the well. The county medical examiner took possession of the unfortunate victim, and the entourage departed for Bisbee. I knew that the recovery crew would have no trouble identifying the body. A new phase of the investigation had now begun. I was jurisdictionally out of it, yet awkwardly in a position to learn more than most.

The very next morning after the gathering at the well, I was informed that Velma would be leaving Sierra Vista. She was scheduled to testify in Federal Court on the West Coast in three days, and the FBI wanted her moved as soon as possible. They were concerned about a security compromise, and wanted her to re-enter protective custody near the location of the trial. She would be relocated to a place of her choosing after the trial. I was directed to "escort her to public transportation" assuring she was "ticketed to her final destination."

I was indignant. Escort her to public transportation? I wondered aloud, "What the hell does that mean?" In Sierra Vista, that meant put her on a Grey Hound Bus. How secure was that going to be? Again somebody in a nice remote office made a decision without knowing what reality looked like.

She had been informed only the night before, and was told to pack her things for a permanent move. I also thought that was extreme, but considering the security aspect I accepted the conditions without objections. She was told that I or another FBI representative would meet with her by mid-day.

I was surprised to find her happily packing. It was only 10 AM and she was nearly ready to depart. She had given her good-byes to her friends the night before. She had worked most of the night preparing for her departure. I felt she deserved more than a bus ride, so I told her I would help her ship her largest luggage, and would drive her to the Tucson airport right after lunch. She had been provided finances to cover travel expenses. Some of the procedural details still remain confidential, so it is necessary to fast forward to the ride to Tucson.

Velma sat quietly in the passenger seat, as if afraid to speak. I still had the previous evening's events running through my mind, and was not very talkative either. We were more than half way to Tucson when I broke the silence by asking which airline she would be using. She replied that she would be spending the evening in a Tucson hotel, because it was past mid-day, she was tired and there were no "good flights" until early tomorrow morning.

I was turning that over in my mind when she warmly said, "You have really been good to me, and I will never forget it. I really appreciate all you have done, and would like to do something really nice for you before I leave." Then she hesitated, and said, "But I suppose the FBI won't allow you to accept anything from ordinary people."

Writing the statement on paper, doesn't begin to convey the real meaning and intent of the proposal. But I was alive and well and understood. There are times when inner voices speak to you. Just then, it was as if my old Dad was sitting on my shoulder talking to me. I could hear him repeat something I had heard him say many times over the years. "Every mouse trap is filled with free cheese."

I thanked her for her kind consideration and explained that she was correct. Accepting *anything* from the public we served was strictly forbidden.

She studied me with a questioned look until I said, "But there is one thing I would like to ask before we part."

She smiled and leaned slightly in my direction as if to accept the question on a plate. I spoke with no emotion. "What have you heard about who is responsible for killing Kyler and why and how did they do it?"

The look I received was interesting. In one eye she seemed about to cry, and in the other anger sparked like lightning.

She responded, rapidly spitting out words as if she had been slapped.

"Kyler was killed because he was a stupid asshole. He ignored his wife until she took up with something better. A couple of guys took him from the Saber one night and killed him. They did it while he was passed out drunk. They shoved long hat pins through his eyeballs up into his brain so that there would be nothing cops could find. Then they dumped him somewhere out in the desert."

She paused to breath and went on. "And yes I know what you are going to say next. How do I know it, and who told me, and how do they know it, and who are the guys that did it? Believe it or not, I heard it all through a motel wall. I was laying in the Ramada one night and heard a man and a woman talking in the room on the other side of the wall. I heard it all from them. They didn't do it, but were just talking about stuff they had heard. I don't know who they were, or where they came from. I don't remember the date, and nobody I was with used their real names, so you can't find it by looking at the records. No I don't remember the room number, because I didn't sign for the room. No I didn't go out and look for them in the morning because through all of this I have learned to keep my mouth shut and mind my own %&$#* business."

She leaned back in the seat and sighed. "So there Mr. FBI man, I have returned the favor. Now take me to the airport, I'm getting out of this #$%&* desert."

I walked her into the airport and assured she "was ticketed to her final destination."

Years later I am not ashamed to admit that I was sad to see her go. She was a strange mix of character. The visible part of her appeared lascivious; a personality laced with free thinking. Hiding under that cloak was a brave sole searching for honor and credibility. Did she not risk her life to speak for the truth and for what's right? I think of her at times, hoping she found the home she was searching for.

Even though I may have wanted to, I didn't wait for the plane to leave, I had work to do. I needed to get Velma's information to the Cochise County medical examiner, and to the SO detectives. I needed to get them all together to explain everything I knew before the pressure on them caused someone to "Cowboy up", and ride through the case alienating the few existing sources. I needed to get their money for the payoff. I had to get the other half of the reward from Phoenix. I had to hand up Tobi in a manner that would lessen the impact on him. I radioed ahead to Bisbee that I would arrive for an informational meeting at 5 PM. It was going to be a hard drive and another night away from home.

• • •

As I drove, I wondered about Tobi. Was he telling me the truth? Probably. Was he telling me everything he knew? Probably not. Would he tell me more? Maybe. No matter the response, the situation had now changed. The freewheeling beer induced discussions were over for a while. The gang would know that I had penetrated them. They would be suspicious of my actions. A few were secure and understanding enough to continue a sociable relationship, but their piers would shun them if they appeared too friendly. Would they suspect Tobi? I had been discrete and very careful with his identity, but now I had to identify him to the Cochise County hierarchy. I felt a responsibility to protect him from exposure that would put him in danger. Bikers were hard on "snitches." But the county thought differently. They hated bikers, and put them all in the same lawless class. I knew that the County would pounce on him for answers. I wondered how he would hold up.

Tobi was a frail small twenty something male. Matted long light brown hair drooped over his ears and forehead. His face was pale, and acne violated. Mottled teeth were separately spaced between swollen red gums. Horizontal eyelids hinted he could in some minor amount have Asian genes. He spoke in soft non-aggressive tones. If he had muscles, they were hidden beneath his loose fitting clothes. His only swagger came from being close to his supporting biker friends. Tobi was in trouble.

They were all waiting for me; Sheriff Wilson, the medical examiner, the Chief Detective, Frank, and the Count Attorney. The first news I poured into the circle was the possibility that Kyler was killed in an intoxicated state, via the use of long hat pin types of probes inserted into his brain through his eyeballs. That got their attention.

I had to attribute the information to an anonymous telephone call received on our telephone recorder in our office. I said the caller reported hearing the conversation through a motel wall somewhere in Serra Vista on an unknown date. That raised a few eyebrows, but there are hard and fast rules about protected witnesses. I knew there was absolutely no chance of developing Velma's information further or I would have covered it differently. They had enough information to explore the truth of the allegation with an autopsy.

Tobi's situation was more difficult. The Sheriff was paying him for information and wanted more of it. He and his deputies also had an unsolved murder in their county. Someone was going to take heat for the lack of answers, and if so, it was all going to be redirected toward Tobi. I cautioned them that a defector within a motorcycle gang was often disposed of. I suggested they first try to turn Tobi to their side. I opined if they could increase his cooperation and perhaps gain new information from heightened talk in biker land, they would be better off than having two unsolved cases after they found him dead.

The cooperation idea went well with Sheriff Wilson and the County Attorney, while the Chief Deputy looked at me as if to say, "How the hell am I going to do that?" Knowing how he operated, I wondered the same.

I accepted several rounds of accolades, congratulatory handshakes with expressions of sincere thanks, and headed my car toward Tucson. Unfortunately my family would again be asleep when I got there.

• • •

The next time I saw Police Chief Reed Vance, he stood in the open doorway to his office, giving me the "We need to talk" look. I went in, and he closed the door. I had worked with Reed for several years and I considered him to be the best friend I had in Sierra Vista. He was caustically blunt in mannerism, but honest, loyal, intuitive, and politically astute.

He looked into me with his dark eyes and said, "Your boy in the motorcycle gang is in for it. I hear he isn't putting out, and the county is going to eat him alive."

"I figured that would happen. But they've only given him a couple of days."

"Yea but finding a body in a well is big news around here, and the people expect Wilson and his boys to hang somebody's ass. They've been working on this for some time, and other than finding what amounts to dried leather in the well, they don't have a clue."

I had anticipated everything Reed was telling me, but I was sure he called me in for more than spreading bad news.

I gave him his chance to offer his thoughts.

"I appreciate your concern, but Reed, I can't find anything about this whole thing that is interstate. I have no jurisdiction what-so-ever. They are working on it with a five member brain trust and I can't even give them advice."

Reed stared at me and then said, "You could, but you just don't want to piss them off, do you."

"No I don't. I let them save face by keeping it quiet about who really was responsible for finding the guy, but they still seem embarrassed about it. Now my bosses in Phoenix are mad at me because I pushed them into spending $1500 to locate a rather unproductive deserter, for which they've received no credit. So now I don't dare go messing around with a county homicide case."

"But you are the only one in this whole ant hill that can get anywhere with those bikers."

"OK Reed, what do you think I should do?"

"Talk to the Son-of-a-bitch."

"Which Son-of-a-bitch?"

He smiled, "The biker, stupid!"

"Reed, it's a lose, lose situation. If I strike out and the county finds out that I even talked to him they will be mad. If I get him to roll over, they are still going to see red because I was in there trying to get a scoop and all the glory."

"Yea, I see what you mean. But what if I cover for you?"

"How the hell are you going to do that?"

"We'll get him in here for something petty, and cause him to ask for you. We can manipulate the little bastard around to wanting to talk to you, and then no one will have any choice about it. So get your ass out of here, and I'll explain it all to Sergeant Stanley and he will take care of it."

"OK Chief. You know, I'll have to admit. You aren't as dumb as you look."

The very next day, I received a call from the Sierra Vista Police Department, transmitted over the county radio network, that my presence was requested at the Police Station because a "Subject" was requesting to talk with me.

Crap, Reed was rolling big loud dice.

The situation was that Tobi was called in for questioning concerning some missing motorcycle parts. It somehow became apparent that I was the only person who could verify that he was working in the tin warehouse, or drinking beer there at the time the bike was stolen. Tobi needed me as a witness to get him off. I obliged and went to work.

I worked at gaining his confidence again after the trauma he had been through. He had been questioned extensively by the Sheriff's Department, but told them he had no specific information concerning the murder of Kyler. They in effect told him that he needed to come up with some specifics or he would become the focus of the investigation. He said he was scared, because all he was relying on at the time he contacted me, was rumor and hearsay from other bikers.

I pushed him to break one of their unspoken rules, and tell me who he thought killed Kyler. He reluctantly said, "Bubba".

"Why do you say it was him?"

"Because Bubba is one mean dude; everybody is afraid of him. Bubba was sleeping with Kyler's Old Lady. I even saw her riding on the 'Bitch bar' of his bike one day. If she wanted to get rid of Kyler, Bubba would be the only one she would turn to, to do it."

"Surely Bubba didn't do this all by himself. Who do you think helped him?"

"I don't know. He doesn't have any real good friends."

"Nobody?"

"Well, there's this guy that comes into town once in a while, maybe every two or three months." Bubba fixes up drug deals for him."

"So what's his name, or what does he go by?"

"I don't know, 'cept he's from California someplace. He's a Mexican guy; use to be a Mongol, and maybe still is."

"I thought this place was off limits to Mongols because you guys are supposed to have a pact with the Hell's Angles?"

"Yea, but this guy gets a pass because somehow he is a friend of Bubba's and he brings money into the area, and doesn't compete with the Angels. They probably get a cut."

"Have you ever seen Bubby with this guy?"

"No, we've, you know, been told to leave him alone because he just passes through with Bubba's OK."

"So do you believe the Mongol owes Bubba any favors?"

"Sure, he'd probably get killed without Bubba."

"Did you tell any of this to the County?"

"No!"

"Why not?"

"They didn't ask me."

I actually believed Tobi didn't know who performed the murder. In his culture, it was not acceptable to ask questions about other people's business. In addition, Tobi was not a leader or any important member in the local biker society. He was a little player on the fringe of the biker social circle. He apparently went home at night. He had a wife and two kids to feed.

I gave him some mild advice about always telling everything he knew to the Cochise County investigators, even if he was not getting along personally with them. I explained he should elaborate on what he had just told me, and said that if I learned he had not, I would be obligated to relay it to them, which would get him into even more trouble. He said he understood. I let him go. There was nothing more I could do.

The conversation had taken place in Sergeant Stanley's office. I made a few notes, and as I walked out, both Reed and Stanley were next to Reed's office grinning at me. Reed spoke first.

"Well Dutchman, did you crack the case?"

"Hell no!"

"What? We were counting on you. Don't tell me the FBI story is a myth!"

"I don't believe the little guy really knows much more than he has told us. He knows he is in trouble, and can't afford to protect anyone, because he has no one to protect himself."

Then with all the finality I could express I said, "He's pretty sure it would have to be Bubba that is responsible. Oh, and by the way, the Mongol guy I mentioned, the biker from

California, a little over a year ago – he's a friend of Bubba's and owes him lots of favors."

Without letting a second pass Reed said, "Glad to hear it. For a while there I thought you had wasted our time."

A few days later, the County Chief Detective told me what I already knew. Tobi had "given him a little bit of information." But it was still his opinion that the little guy was holding out."

I asked, "What are you going to do about the Mongol guy?"

"We'll identify him. We know the guys where you said he stopped that time you followed him. If he's the same guy, we'll get a rap sheet on him and see what we can develop."

I tried to give Tobi a little credit, and commented, "I'm willing to bet it's the same guy I saw, because not just any of them can cross all the way through Arizona alone without running into trouble. That's what caught my attention the very first time I saw him."

"Yea, you're probably right, but I don't know what that will prove?"

"Maybe not much, but it would be nice to learn if he was here the night Kyler disappeared."

• • •

Weeks went by, and it appeared that Cochise County investigators were dead in the water. All leads seemed to have dried up. They were still working on the Mongol biker, but nothing significant had been developed.

Then on a Friday afternoon as I was about to board the I-10 freeway ramp heading to Tucson, I got a radio call. It seemed that everything always happened on Friday afternoon. I was asked to "land line" the Sierra Vista Police Department. (That meant call by telephone to keep the conversation confidential.)

The results demonstrated that there are few secrets in a small town. The problem was that a woman, identified as Tobi's wife was frantically attempting to contact me. She had first called Ma Frickett at the Western Motel. Ma, respectfully Mrs. Roberts, had called the Police Department because she knew where I "hung out." The Police in turn radioed me. I told them I would return as soon as possible.

By the time I got back to the Police Department, Tobi's wife had gone home. She said she had left her children alone and had to return. I knew that Tobi lived in a little run down trailer on the North side of town, and reluctantly made my way there.

I expected the worst. My expectations no doubt contributed to my absolute shock from the encounter. The most beautiful woman I had seen in Sierra Vista answered the door. My first reaction was that I had arrived at the wrong address; but not so. I was ushered into a small but very clean single wide, old trailer. Two well-kept children were admonished to stay in the back of the trailer "while momma talks with the man." Except for her professor like grammar and diction, I could have thought I was talking with a former Miss Arizona. If you recall, my description of Tobi his appearance was less then complimentary. I won't be-labor the point, but I was in mind numbing wonderment how Tobi had met up with and married this remarkable person.

A summary of the situation was that Tobi was in jail. Cochise County authorities had picked him up on burglary charges. She was certain that Tobi had not done any burglaries, and that they had concocted the charges to make him talk.

She explained Tobi was picked up after he sold some mechanical parts to a used machinery/car/bike place in

Douglas. (At the time I thought, "Haven't I heard this before?") According to her it was a common business practice for Tobi to do so. He worked as a salvage mechanic in the tin warehouse. He made a living by buying wrecked or broken vehicles, disassembling them, and selling the usable parts. She said it was common practice and that he had been doing it for years. To his or her knowledge, none of the merchandise he handled was stolen.

Again I thought, "maybe, maybe not." But it didn't matter. This was not my toilet to clean.

She said, "I called you because Tobi told me to. He said you were the only police guy in town that would believe him."

"What does he expect me to do?" I asked.

With tears in her eyes she said, "I don't know, he just said to call you and you would know what to do."

"Well, I can't just go get him out. It's not that easy. Do you know if they have set bail?"

"I don't know, but we don't have money for that either."

"Mrs.; what's your first name?"

"Halley."

"Halley, you are going to have to get a lawyer. He's the only one that can give you legal advice now. I can't. Tell Tobi not to worry, because they won't convict him on something he didn't do. But even if he did break the law, the real thing they want from him is information about the Kyler case."

I explained that I would look into it, but that it would be unethical for me to do anything that was detrimental to an investigation currently being conducted. I asked her if she had a lawyer, and she said they couldn't afford one.

I gave her the number of the public defender's office, along with instructions on how to proceed to get help. She wanted my number. I gave her the number of the Sierra Vista Police, and the number of my Tucson Office.

She asked, "What if I need to call you after hours?"

"They can find me." I didn't need this woman calling me at home.

I went back to Reed's office. He was still there.

Once we were again in his office he said, "I thought I better stay and cover for you."

"Cover for me, why?"

"Well Jesus, did you look at her?"

"Did I look at her, man I've been talking to her for an hour and a half."

"I know, and you probably could have finished business in about fifteen minutes if you weren't tongue tied or hypnotized. She is one good looking, intelligent acting woman. How did that little weasel come up with her?"

"Nordstrom catalogue; they sell them under fashion accessories."

Reed laughed, "I think I'll buy one, I could use another secretary."

"Reed, I don't think she would fit in around this place. I'm going home"

Reed turned to leave, "Call Ma Frickett, she's worried about you."

• • •

I spoke with Halley two more times. The first time, I could tell she was prepared to ask me for another special favor.

She was dressed for more than housework, the kids were not present, and she appeared to be in a phony cheery mood. Immediately I thought, "Oh no, not again! What is it with women in this town? Maybe they all want out of it!" My old friend, the little on shoulder man with my Dad's voice jumped up to be heard. It was the same message, just a little different version, "The more cheese the bigger the trap."

Halley wanted me to vouch for Tobi, to lower the bail. He needed someone to testify that he was a family man with responsibilities and was not a flight risk. I told her that my agency would not allow me to do that, and suggested she contact friends or parents to assist with the money. That did not go over well, but she conceded that she would if she had to.

The last time I saw her, it was after Tobi had found a job in Benson. My reason for visiting with her was to tell her to express my congratulations to Tobi for somehow getting the charges dropped, and to wish them luck, because I was departing. I had just received orders to Portland Oregon.

Shortly after arriving in Portland, at my new duty station I received a call from the Cochise County Sheriff's Office in Bisbee Arizona. I was told Bubba, and another biker they identified as Lolo, a known member of the California Mongol gang were riding north on interstate 10 between Tucson and Phoenix when they were passing a truck and trailer. Somehow the trailer broke loose and struck the bike riders. Both were killed.

Approximately one month later, a Grand Jury Inquest was held in Bisbee concerning the Kyler homicide. Kyler's wife was absolved because she had a sound alibi the night Kyler disappeared. It was the conclusion of the Grand Jury that reasonable cause existed to believe Bubba was the person responsible for

Kyler's death, and Lolo was suspected of being an accomplice. However since both were deceased, the case was closed.

Epilogue

I cannot leave the stories of Sierra Vista without commenting adlib about some of the fine people mentioned in the previous writings. At the time of this writing, I am seventy one years old. Many of the FBI agents mentioned in other chapters still correspond with me and remain close friends. Otto and Jan mentioned in Desert Hideout remained in Saint David for several years before moving to Texas. Otto passed away, and Jan moved back to Benson. I am told, she still lives there. Mrs. Roberts' health deteriorated not long after I left. She was found one evening in her night gown, wandering in a field east of her Motel, unaware of her location. She died soon afterwards. Dusty, Frank, and Sheriff Jim Wilson all lived to retire from the Sheriff's department. Jimmy Judd became the Sheriff, and he too retired in position. Reed Vance became a lifelong friend whom I visited several times before his death. During my last visit with Reed, he was aware his long term battle with heart disease was nearing an end. The evening before I left Sierra Vista, towing my fifth wheel trailer, we had a barbeque at his house. We said our goodbyes that evening, with me planning an early morning departure. The next morning as I was hooking up the trailer, Reed appeared at my side with a 1/3 full jar of Miracle Whip. He said, "Here, you left this last night." The hardnosed old softie knew that this would be the last time we were together. He just wanted to say one last goodbye. It touched me deeply. He died within days. They named the new Police Station/public works building after him. His wisdom and advice followed me through many years of my career. Cochise County was a good growing place for me and left me imprinted with many fine memories. But I was willing to go. It was time to move on.

The River Rat Ice Company

J uly 12, 2014, the "Homesteaders Days" picnic was being celebrated at its usual venue, the Huntley Project Agriculture
Experiment Station, between Huntley and Worden, Montana.
I had just finished perusing the exhibits in the Agriculture
Museum, some of which contained artifacts from my father,
and a few from my childhood. I was thinking that a sure path to
feeling old is to observe your own childhood toys in a museum.
Unwilling to dwell with melancholy ghosts of the past; I got an
iced beverage and walked through the outdoor machinery exhibits. The little ice cubes were clicking on my teeth as I stood
next to a rusty relic of an ice cutting machine built by my dad,
Jake Schreuder, and his friends. I thought about how easily ice
was made now. It was in bits and pieces all over the park. In
contrast I thought, "If this old ice cutting machine could talk, it
could tell some great stories." Unfortunately the decaying iron
machine was well beyond the time when it vibrated with a voice
of its own. But standing next to the homemade relic, the voice
of my dad and his friends could still be heard in my memory.
I resolved that the machine's story had to be told. Dee, the
museum's curator agreed. It is with her encouragement that
I pass on the tales from my dad and his associates in the River
Rat Ice Company.

The Rural Electric Association (REA) was formed in 1937 and the Billings substation was the first electrical delivery point to the entire Yellowstone Valley beginning in the early 1940's. Prior to then, the little towns of the "Project" struggled with only the power of horses, humans, and a few gasoline engines. Homes were heated with wood, and coal if affordable. They were cooled only by a breeze through an open window. Food and liquids were cooled with ice, a substance which in rural America could only be made by the forces of nature, and preserved by pioneering ingenuity.

I was born about the time electricity was introduced to the Huntley Project. However, when I was beginning grade school, my parents were still referring to the refrigerator as the "ice box." The simple name was self-explanatory. Ice was put into a box with food that needed to be kept cool for preservation. The box was insulated and contained a water pan or drain to eliminate water from the melting ice. Ice boxes came in all sizes. Small ones in grandmothers' kitchens held only one block of ice with a little milk, butter and that special something served cold, while large ones like those in the Worden Creamery held all of dairy's treasures. Grocery stores and taverns had not only large ice boxes, but ice houses, where months' worth of the cold preservative was stored.

If there was no means to *make* such a large amount of ice, where did it come from? Ah, therein resides the story.

Dad and his friends were fairly self-sufficient. They gathered their own wood for heat and from the Yellowstone River cut their own ice for refrigeration. Both he and his close friends, the Dierenfields, lived only one half a mile from the river bank. Their close proximity made it a minor task to chop through the winter river ice with an axe and with a large hand held ice saw, cut blocks of crystal clear ice from the Yellowstone. Others, less fortunately located, often asked the favor of obtaining any extra ice they may have "blocked up." A few even paid for the favor.

Thus the idea was born. The 1930's were "hard times." Dad occasionally spoke of working at a job where he earned 10 cents an hour at night during the winter months, moving hay from fields to feed lots. He worked ten hours at night for $1.00 per night and tended to his own chores and cattle during the daytime. His friends struggled on the same economic level. Cutting and selling ice nearly in their back yards was going to be both easier and more profitable. Or was it?

Sawing blocks of ice with a hand saw was back breaking work. Lifting and hauling slippery ice blocks was no easier. They realized that mass production was going to be required to make any money. The river bank dwellers through teamwork and friendship created a mechanized efficient operation that eventually was named The River Rat Ice Company.

The first ice cutting machine was made by Dad, his brother Everett, and several of the Dierenfield brothers. A second was made and improved by Fred Rachele with the help of the original inventors. I believe the machine on display at the museum is the latter, and the first fell to the bottom of the river....another part of the story.

The frame of a Model A Ford was stripped of its outer body. With only the motor, transmission and axles still attached to the frame, it was mounted on timbers made into sled runners. The rear axles were positioned to protrude beyond the sled runners, and on the right rear axle they mounted a large "buzz saw blade." A buzz saw blade was a large steel cutting disc four to six feet in diameter containing large wood cutting teeth. It was normally used on a stationary hub to cut up large logs for firewood. The rear axle of the Ford frame was hinged so it could be lowered down onto the ice, causing the saw blade to slice as deep as one half of its diameter; a depth of one to two feet, depending on the size of the blade. The model A engine was coupled to the saw blade via the transmission and rear axle, which in turn powered the blade. The transmission gears provided speed control of the cutting blade which had to be adjusted depending on the thickness of the ice.

The entire apparatus was made without power tools or welders. Hand drills, hack saws hammers and fence wire were the norm.

It took at least two men to guide the dangerous uncovered blade along a straight line over the ice. The process also required guide lines on the surface of the ice so that the blocks were uniform in size. The guide lines were made by the "marker man."

Large commercial ice boxes required large ice blocks, while grandma's kitchen model accommodated something no bigger than we buy today for our plastic coolers. The ice blocks were cut to order to fit the needs of the customer; however production was slowed whenever small blocks were created. Storage and transportation was more convenient with larger blocks. Customers requiring smaller chunks of ice usually chipped the necessary size from a larger block stored somewhere in the home or at their local merchant. Some ice blocks weighed as little as 20 pounds, while the larger conformed to what a normal strong person could lift...from 50 to 100 pounds.

The marker man was responsible for engineering the size of the ice blocks. The measurements had to take into consideration the thickness of the ice, which often grew to a depth of 12 inches. (On several occasions after periods of -40 degrees Fahrenheit the ice became so thick the blade could not cut clear through it, and after cutting, the blocks had to be broken loose with a large 5 foot long crowbar.)

The marker man made the guidelines using a small circular saw blade mounted on a gasoline washing machine motor. The motor was in turn mounted on a sled-like apparatus guided by hand with oak garden cultivator handles. He would measure the required distance, scratch a few visible marks with an axe and saw straight lines between his marks forming a grid of rectangles. The buzz saw machine would then be guided along the smaller grooved lines.

Cutting apart the surface of the frozen river created a turbulent lake of floating ice blocks. It was far too dangerous to stand at the edge of the running water pond and grab the blocks with normal ice tongs. To retrieve the floating blocks, they created a large grapple hook similar to a giant "treble" fishing hook. However, the ice blocks were still too heavy to extract from the river pond by a single person.

Inventiveness was again employed to retrieve the floating ice blocks. They dynamited the river bank so that it sloped enough to get a truck near the water's edge, (an act which if performed now would have landed them all in jail). A wheel was removed from one of their sugar beet trucks, and a bare rim was put in its place. The remaining wheel on the other side was jacked off of the ground. A cable was attached to the bare wheel, and wound around the rim. The other end of the cable was fastened to the grapple hook. A wooden ramp was built and inserted, one end into the ice pool, the other end onto another sugar beet truck intended for the ice load.

"OK, you got it!" Throw the grapple hook into the back of the pond, put the cable truck into gear, let out the clutch, and pull the ice blocks up the ramp into the truck. The truck drivers stacked the blocks, filled the orders and delivered to the customer.

Here's the good part. They sold the ice for only pennies per ton. Unfortunately I cannot recall the varied selling prices of the ice, but I do remember it was significantly less than $1.00 per ton. A few cents were added for delivery. The average block probably weighed 30 pounds. Anyone who had the means to haul the ice was welcome to back up to the river bank for a load. The weight was usually determined by measuring the dimensions of the load. Large loads to commercial destinations were weighed at a truck scale at one of the local grain elevators.

Most of the ice harvest took place on the Yellowstone River at the end of roads North 11, 12, and 13. Occasionally the river would gorge, (form an ice dam and flood upstream.) Sometimes the backwater from the flood would freeze into large clear ponds on the side channel sloughs. If conveniently located, those ponds were also harvested.

Where was all this ice delivered? It went to individual ice houses scattered throughout the valley. Although all of this business occurred just a few years before I was born, I still remember our old "ice house". It was a large log building. Of course everything always looks larger when you are 4 or 5 years old, but this was a big cotton wood log structure. It had no windows and only one door. The floor was covered with sawdust from the wood cutting pile nearby. The ice was stacked on the floor, and individual layers were separated by "chinking" snow and sawdust in between the blocks. Snow kept the ice blocks from sticking together later in the warm season. The entire building was crammed with ice blocks, and the roof was covered with a thick layer of hay and straw. A heavy door insulated with feed sacks and sawdust kept the heat from destroying the merchandise. Throughout the summers, before the REA changed the landscape, my mother sold ice to Worden residents who did not have the luxury of an ice house. Mom said she often sold ice through the end of August. What kept things cool during September and the October beet harvest? I don't know, but they were usually back in business by the end of October.

Grocery stores and bars in town also sold Yellowstone River ice, from their similarly prepared ice houses.

A difficult environment created the ice, and made its harvest memorable. Sandwiches made for lunch were frozen solid by noon. They were thawed next to the engine of the ice cutter. A fire was usually built to warm the hands and toes of the workers. "Ice creepers" were made and strapped to their "overshoes" to keep them from falling, or slipping off the edge of the cut ice into the river. On one occasion a member of the cutting crew (I don't remember who), fell into the running water of the ice block pond. Luckily the pond was not then in the deeper part of the river, and the person was able to keep from being sucked under the ice by the water current. They pulled their friend from the pond, wrapped him in "coats from everybody" and put him into a truck while his clothing dried by the fire.

About the third year of operation, Dad was unloading blocks at home into our own ice house. The job was made easier by sliding the blocks down a ramp from the truck through the building's door. It was a two man operation with one pushing the ice from the bed of the truck while the one at the bottom slid the chunks away into the building. Dad, working at the bottom of the ramp, stumbled and placed a foot next to a large block, just as another slid rapidly down the chute. His ankle was crushed between the two blocks. Although it was later determined that a bone was broken, the remedy was tape and aspirin with no interruption of work.

The open pond, and moving current were always a danger. While operating the ice cutting machine, the large blade somehow jumped out of the cutting groove, and the rotating blade propelled the machine into the ice pond. Again, they were lucky. The gravel bottom stopped the machine from floating east. The contraption was resurrected, the oil drained, motor dried out with a "blow torch" and was cutting again within a couple hours. Somewhere near the end of their several years' operations, the original cutting machine again broke loose and dove into the river with the operators narrowly avoiding a cold death. Electricity was already outdating their business and the machine was never resurrected. The surviving one now sits alone at the museum.

Most of the participants were young daredevils. One form of entertainment was driving a truck out onto the thick ice. The challenge that followed was to see who could spin the most circles within a confined distance. Another contest was to see who could slide a truck the furthest after speeding off the river bank. They gave a whole new meaning to the term "going for a spin."

Dad and his friends reminisced about the long cold winters of the 1930's, and speculated about why the ice was so thick and plentiful then. Reasons offered were that Billings and

other towns upriver were smaller. Cities and industries were
not discharging warm water into the Yellowstone. And it was
colder. How cold was it? No one could drop in those one lin-
ers like Jake Schreuder. "It was so cold I chipped my tooth on
my soup." "You couldn't eat with a spoon because it stuck to
your tongue." "Our words froze in the air, so the only way we
could talk was to stand by the fire." "Our shadows froze to the
ground." "You didn't dare make an ugly face 'cause it would
stay that way." And truthfully, they had to start the motors of
their equipment on cold mornings by building a fire under
them.

The enterprise operated from approximately 1935 to 1941.
Although they called themselves "The River Rat Ice Company",
it was a "company" only in the sense that they were in the company of each other, surviving in difficult times. My father died
in December 2007, at age 94. He may have been the last surviving member of the group. Most of the names I remember, but
there were many, and to list them would only result in errors of
omission. Today you can find them generally still together on a
hillside near Ballantine.

"Learn How to Drive"

An ambition, the title for a lesson plan, or a derogative command, the statement "Learn How to Drive", excites activity no matter what its purpose. My first exposure to the statement came from my brother. But I am getting ahead of myself, and need to start at the beginning.

Farm kids learn to drive at a very early age. My brother, born almost five years before me, was driving farm equipment long before I began grade school. Naturally, I wanted to achieve more, and sooner than my brother in all things, and was persistent in my insistence that I be allowed to start driving. My father, in need of extra farm help was quite willing to accommodate my wishes, and began my training long before my legs were long enough to reach the control pedals on any kind of vehicle. "Driving" therefor began by gripping the steering wheel while sitting between my father's legs on a farm tractor. In those early days it was an intense struggle to keep the machine in its proper line, whether in a field or on the dirt roads connecting our farmland.

Dad's willingness to have me learn far exceeded his patience. That meant, he was pleased to have me available to operate a tractor, but expected me to learn all things in prompt order. As soon as I demonstrated that I could keep the tractor going straight, and in the preferred direction, he began channeling my enthusiasm into a useful activity. The same year that I began the first grade, at age six, he decided I was capable of operating the International Harvester tractor, hitched to a trailer, while he loaded the trailer with sugar beet tops.

"Beet top" collecting was a slow paced activity, well suited for learning. The dried foliage was all that remained after the sugar beets were harvested. The severed tops of the plants were first stacked in rows of small piles along the full length of the fields. Dad loaded the foliage onto the wagon by hand with a pitch fork. The beet tops were then transported to the feed lot where they were stored and eventually fed to our cows. My job was to drive the tractor, pulling the wagon along the row at a slow walking pace, while Dad pitched the beet tops onto the wagon.

This all seems simple enough, except if I sat in the seat, I couldn't reach either the clutch, or the brakes. However if I stood up, it was unsafe because I could quite easily fall off the tractor. The remedy was that Dad, with me in place on the seat, would start the tractor down the row at a very slow pace, and then hop off, leaving me to steer. When we arrived at the end of the row, I would kick the "off" switch with my toe and come to a dead stop just as I needed to turn around. Dad would then climb back onto the tractor, restart it, turn it around next to another row, and we would begin anew.

That procedure lasted for about one day. By then I was certain I could turn the tractor around by myself. Of course it involved considerable more risk, because Dad would not be able to mount the tractor quick enough to save me if I screwed up. However, I convinced him that because I was a big first grader, I was completely capable of, "turning around a stupid tractor" in a field of several acres. (No mention was ever made of the ditches at the end turn around points.) In transition, he accompanied me on the tractor for a few turns until I demonstrated I could crank the thing around without running into the ditch and "pay attention" to the rear tractor wheel so that I didn't turn too short and catch the trailer on the wheel.

Thus it began. I spent many hours riding on farm equipment with my Dad or occasionally with my brother, but was finally trusted driving in simple limited conditions. Of course my brother put me down at every opportunity, voicing that just because I could steer a tractor, didn't mean that I had "learned to drive." I took it, because I knew my time was coming. It wasn't long before I had mastered clutch, brakes, gas, and spinner on the steering wheel.

But I still couldn't really drive. The old 1936 International pickup truck my Dad drove was parked near the milk house every night. It seemed to mock me daily as I splashed by it carrying water to the chickens and did my farm chores. It needed conquering but it was going to be difficult. I practiced sitting in the driver's seat, but I could barely see out the windshield. To see ahead, I had to look through the spokes of the steering wheel. I could manage that with a little extra visual maneuvering, but getting my foot far enough onto the floor board to reach the old iron gas pedal required some real inventive acrobatics. To make matters worse, it was a "on the floor, stick shift." I realize that if my descendants read this, it won't progress through many generations until an encyclopedia will be needed to explain a "stick shift." Briefly, in that era it was necessary to step on a floor pedal, called the clutch, which disengaged the motor from the transmission. Removing the power to the transmission by depressing the clutch allowed the driver to change gears in the transmission by shoving around a long lever (stick) mounted on the floor. This all had to be done, while starting, or moving forward. Then the clutch, which was required to be held to the floor while moving the stick, had to be released while at the same time, with the other foot, applying just enough gas via a third floor pedal. Too much gas caused the vehicle to lurch into motion, while not enough gas would kill the engine.

OK, did you get all of that? With short legs, it was a daunting challenge. Well, we aren't done yet. Added to all of that was the problem of stopping. We now have electric power brakes on vehicles. Before then, hydraulic brakes used the advantage of hydraulic pressure to clamp the brakes onto the wheels. But none of that had been invented when the old '36 International was assembled. Its brakes were simply mechanical, meaning that only a system of levers and cables applied pressure to the wheels to stop. Stopping required that considerable pressure be exerted on the brake pedal to slow the pickup. I did not weigh enough to apply the needed pressure, and even if I had been the fattest kid in the valley, I still had a leg shortage problem. I overcame the limitations by standing on the brake and pulling up on the steering wheel. Using the wheel as a brace, I gained enough leverage to apply the stiff brake. I was sure I could triumph over my handicaps. It was time I really did "Learn to drive."

One day while returning from town with my Dad and brother, I exclaimed to my Dad that I could drive the old pickup just as well as my brother. The bold statement was audacious enough that my brother challenged me to prove it, because I had never driven it before. With both of us out of control about the idea, Dad gave in and stopped the old pickup right in the middle of the gravel road. Here I must say that it was a very stupid move on my part. Performing a difficult task for the first time, with my Dad as an instructor would have been more than difficult. But with my brother jeering and heckling it was a disaster. The venture of multi-tasking with both feet and hands, with limited vision in the face of merciless critics did not go well. I was removed from the driver's seat before we arrived home. "Learn how to drive", became a jeering insult. It was a memorable setback. For several days, I deliberated on a comeback.

A few days after the first pickup driving disaster, my mother was about to begin a task requested by my father. He asked that she drive to the far end of one of the pastures and retrieve some canvas irrigation dams so that he could use them at a different location later that evening. I went with her to help load up the dams and convinced her to let me drive the pickup through the pasture. She wasn't real adept at driving the old thing herself, so she agreed to let me try my hand. I did it. With her halting instruction, and few laughs in between, we navigated thistles, ditches, fence posts and cow pies. It was the beginning of hundreds of thousands of miles into the future.

I remember that the first journey motoring across the pasture in the old 36 International occurred when I was in about the 3rd grade. It was shortly after when I learned that all driving was not thrills and chills.

● ● ●

In the early days, Dad and his brother stacked hay with a three man crew. Dad brought in the hay with a buck rake.

The hay was pushed onto a stacking machine called an "overshot stacker." The stacker lifted the hay up onto an organized pile, or stack, shaped like a giant loaf of bread. My Uncle Everett worked on the stack with a pitch fork, placing the hay properly to form a bread-loaf shaped pile. However the overshot stacker did not operate on its own. The arms and rack that lifted the hay were raised by a cable on a system of pulleys. When the end of the cable was drawn out from the stacker, the mechanism rose upward and dumped the hay onto the stack. The apparatus was returned to the ground by moving the end of the cable back toward the stacker where it would retract and coil back into the pulley system. The backward and forward travel with the cable had to occur with each buck rake load of hay. My grandfather had pulled the cable back and forth on the stacker for years with a team of horses. However the horses were troublesome, in poor health, and my grandfather too was getting older. They changed procedure by adding an old International farm truck which they attached to the stacker cable in place of the horses. The truck was then driven backward and forward to pull out and to retract the stacker cable. However the truck operated with very different commands than did the horses. The stacker was raised by backing the truck at a regular speed until the stacker arms were vertical and the hay slid off onto the pile. The truck needed to be stopped at a precise moment, and was oblivious to my grandfather's frantic shouts of "whoa!" Whether in Dutch, German or English, the @#$%! thing just kept going.

I was soon recruited to "Drive the stacker." Boring does not begin to describe the misery of hay stacker driving. Vision backing up, stopping, and returning forward, in the same tracks, the same distance and speed several hundred times all day long. Imagine sitting in an old iron farm truck, in the hot sun all day long. Think about getting out of the truck frequently to pick up any hay that was spilled off of the stacker and getting back in for the next load. It was accomplished with no radio, no Ipad, no cell phone. My only snack was a drink from a canvas water bag. We put up hay for about 6 or 7 days, three times per summer. Graduating to driving the stacker truck was indeed an awakening. The romance of driving was fading. It was not always going to be fun.

I drove the stacker truck for about three seasons, until progress dictated another change. New more efficient machinery was purchased and a hydraulic loader now allowed my Dad to place the hay onto the stack without using the overshot stacker. My Uncle Everett still worked on the hay stack, but with much less effort than the old style stacker. To expedite transportation of the loose hay to the stacking area, I was now designated the buck rake operator. The hydraulic loader replaced the old stacker, and with me running the buck rake, Dad did not have to travel out into the fields as far to bring in the hay. Compared to the bi-directional tether of the old farm truck, the buck rake was exciting.

The buck rake was a wooden structure with long wooden "teeth" designed to scoop up the loose hay as it lay in rows in the field. The faster the buck rake was driven, the tighter the hay could be packed, and the more I could push up to the stack. The device was mounted on a small Case tractor that had a remarkably fast "road gear." It had a gas pedal similar to a car, and could be driven like a stock car at the races. The faster I drove, the more hay we could stack, and the quicker we were finished. For once, neither my Dad nor my Uncle complained about how fast I drove. I pushed that old Case to its limit. I had my foot flat down on the gas pedal all day. I speed shifted into high gear whenever I could, and turned corners with the front wheels throwing dirt. Dust would fly out of the hay, so thick it would plug the radiator on the tractor. The remedy was a piece of screen wired to the radiator front, and a temperature gauge that showed hot whenever I ran too fast with dust plugging the screen. There was no remedy to eliminate breathing in the hay dust. I wore large sun glasses to protect my eyes, but inhaled sickening clouds of dust. It was always too hot to wear a mask, and besides, only a sissy would cover his face. My "head" was usually plugged during the entire several days of hay harvest.

One trip across a hay field that I will always remember resulted from the assistance of my grandfather. As I mentioned, he did not operate machinery that could not be attached to his horses. However he still enjoyed working on the fringes using the old methods. One of his hay season activities was mowing and raking the ditch banks, and other hard to access areas. He did this with his team of horses, a horse drawn mower, and a "dump rake." Without describing a dump rake, its significant function was that it gathered the hay and "dumped" it into little piles that could be transported away with the buck rake.

A large drain ditch bordered one of the hay fields. The bank of the ditch was irregular but contained enough alfalfa to attract the attention of my granddad. He mowed it, and dumped the hay into little piles (called shocks) near the bank. One of the reasons it was not mowed with the regular tractor mower was that the irrigation district had recently cleaned the ditch, leaving large piles of gravel near the weedy edge of the bank. One of granddads hay shocks completely covered a large pile of gravel. I sped along the bank, swerving side to side, thumping into the little hay shocks, packing them in with my speed. I estimated that the last two would just fit, making a full load. I floored the gas pedal to avoid losing speed from the weight of the load. My rig hit the hay covered gravel pile max speed-full force, sinking the buck rake teeth deep into the dirt. The tractor stopped abruptly, catapulting me over the engine, across the wooden panel of the buck rake, and into the hay. During flight I apparently smashed my stomach on the steering wheel, and scraped my leg on part of the buck rake. But nothing was broken.....not on me anyway. One look at the wooden beams on the buck rake revealed a different situation. They needed some repair. The worst result for me was limping back to the hay stack and explaining what happened. Dad and Uncle Everett viewed the crime scene and I was forgiven. I believe they were actually relieved I had not been seriously injured.

• • •

As I grew accustomed to the machinery there were many days of driving tractors on the farm. It was there that I really came to know my Dad. I drove hundreds of miles towing him behind me on farm machinery. I was always the driver, and he was the machinery operator. There were summer days when I would become almost hypnotized by the routine of circling the field with the grain binder clinking behind me. When I would doze off and wander slightly out from the cutting edge, I would hear a whistle from Dad on the machine behind me. I always knew when I looked back, he would be pointing his finger inward toward the edge of the grain, indicating that I was wandering and should pay more attention. At other times, a whistle would mean that the grain was thinner in an area and that I should go faster or perhaps slower if it was a little green or immature. We spent many hours together, with me driving.

The local sheriff was also a part time farmer...or maybe it was the other way around; one of our neighboring farmers was also a part time sheriff. For practical reasons he never seemed to notice when an under-aged farm kid was seen driving on the side roads. It was not unusual to break a part on a farm implement. The machine usually had to be taken apart to be repaired. The broken piece was often taken to the local black-smith in Worden for "fixing." I was frequently tasked to take a broken part into town, to the blacksmith, for welding. At age 10 with no concern, I would drive the old 36 International pickup into town, park in front of the blacksmith, and watch while he welded and shaped the broken parts. We were allowed by community custom to drive into town during the day time for work purposes, but never at night for entertainment. After dark it was time for the parents to be present.

• • •

We were harvesting grain when I had my first (and only) mishap with the old 36 International pickup. We had filled one of the grain trucks at a field down near the river. Dad wanted to put the full load of wheat into a granary at my grandfather's farm yard a couple miles away. We had deposited the pickup at Grand Dad's so I was instructed to drive the load of wheat over to the granary, and return with the pickup. We were in full harvest mode, which meant I was to hurry. I was also responsible for hauling grain bundles from the field and pitching them into the thrashing machine. A "hired hand" would have to fill in for me while I transported the grain.

I was good at hurrying, but encountered a delay on my return. I met another farmer, who was moving his thrashing machine from one farm to another. Bill too was in a hurry, because everyone hurried during harvest. The machine was being drawn by him, operating a steel tracked caterpillar tractor. The road was narrow where we were forced to pass head on. I say forced to pass because either person waiting for the other at a wider place on the road would have involved wasting time, instead of hurrying. It was universal, everyone hurried during harvest. On one side of the road was a large irrigation ditch, and on my side was the roadside borrow pit, full of water draining from a nearby pasture. I slowed to almost a complete stop, yielding as much room as possible for the wide machine. I could see that if I didn't move more to my right, a long shaft protruding from the machine was going to hit the pickup right about in the center of the windshield. I moved over just a little more and then it happened. The passenger wheel sucked into the soft muddy shoulder and the pickup tipped into the gutter. I was only traveling about two miles per hour, so it was just a gentle tip, but the old pickup was almost on its side. Water was running into the cab through the bottom of the passenger door. I turned off the engine, and attempted to open the driver's door. But it was made with old fashioned steel and so heavy I couldn't get it open. I put all my strength to it, and felt it open, but realized that the other farmers were helping me get out of the truck.

I was too old to cry, but too scared to speak. Bill, the caterpillar driver immediately began giving me hell for running off the road. I was brought up not to talk back to older people but

I knew that this was not my fault.....well not much. I pointed out that he was going to hit me with the pulley shaft on the thresher. It didn't matter to Bill. He kept cursing about having to unhook the caterpillar to pull me out of the gutter. I thought "Well ain't that just too bad, it's my butt that ended up in the ditch, and now it's a big inconvenience to you." He hooked a log chain to the bumper of the pickup, wrapped it around the caterpillar hitch and yanked me upright and back onto the gravel road. There was nothing gentle about the extraction. I examined the pickup and found absolutely no damage other than a little water on the wooden floor boards and a clump of mud on the door. But now the chain was stuck in the bumper. Old Bill hammered and pulled on the chain but it would not unbind from the bumper. I wanted to say, "Well if you would have gently pulled the truck out instead of yanking it like a trout on a fishing pole, the chain would come loose." But I was still the kid and knew to keep my mouth shut. With a line of blue smoke cursing, he wound the chain around the bumper and said, "You can have your Dad get the damn chain lose, and I'll get it later." He hooked back up to his thrasher and was gone before I got the pickup started.

But now I was late in returning, and I had to explain why. I parked the pickup at the edge of the field, hoping everything would soon dry out, and returned to my tractor. To get to the field where my Dad was waiting to load my wagon I had to unfasten and open a barbed wire gate. I was still upset from the incident, and my state of mind contributed to another mishap. I let the wire gate slip from around my arm, and it sliced a long gash from my elbow to my wrist. I had nothing to wipe the arm up with, so I just let it bleed. It was a pretty flashy wound and looked good. I figured that if I appeared to be hurt, I couldn't get too much hell for crashing the pickup. When I drove my wagon out to my Dad to be loaded he greeted me with "Where you been so long?" Then he saw the blood on my arm.

I told him the story with as much drama as the truth would allow and to my surprise, he immediately sided with me, saying, "It's just like that damned old Dutchman to run a kid off the road." I told him that I still had Bill's chain stuck in the truck and his reply was something to the effect that Bill would get his damn chain when he got around to it

The arm soon quit bleeding, but I left the residue on my skin for most of the afternoon just for insurance. The old pickup fared much better. With the mud removed, it had not a scratch. It was cleaner than before.

• • •

By the time I began high school, the old 36 International had been retired, and I drove another pickup to school. It was a ¾ ton Blue Chevy. For the most part of the school year, it was my car, for driving to sports practice after school, entertainment, and even a rare date. Even with the heater on high, it was never warm in the winter, but was great fun on slick roads. On snow packed streets I could flip it end for end in front of the school, without ever sliding out of the proper lane. With tire chains and weight in the back, I churned through three foot snow drifts and plowed a track for neighbors to follow. It even performed well in a short drag race. But out of respect for Dad's truck, drag racing was never a frequent activity.

In 1959, Dad bought a new Oldsmobile. Wow, that thing really had an engine. However, it was his, and I rarely drove it.

I was given the older 1949 Oldsmobile. Now I had a car all of my own. I cleaned it up, and painted it a metallic light blue. With white wall tires, and "flipper" hub caps, it was a ride to be envied…..well I thought so. Every man has fond memories of his first car, especially if it coincides with his first dating experiences. I with my 49 Oldsmobile was no exception, but those are stories for another time. I always respected my car, and drove it carefully. OK, so I did drive it on the rail road tracks a few times, but that was because I needed to demonstrate that car wheels fit perfectly on the tracks. However even that has now changed, with wheel distances being widened.

It is true that I took care of my car. Our wild driving was done in another machine. Several of us in our high school class discovered that many old wrecked cars still contained good engines. We learned to remove the car body from the frame and replace just the seats and steering wheel. The cars were aptly named "frames." My friends Mike, Delvin, and cousin Bob all created frames. Because I was close friends with Delvin, and worked with him, I frequently was the driver of his frame. Frame maintenance and "testing" was usually a joint venture.

Frames became a local late teen's culture and shaper of behavior during the summers for the last two years of High School, and for a couple summers during college. My cousin Bob built a frame with a cutting torch. He cut everything off just above the windshield, retained the front seat and removed everything else from the front door hinge to the back bumper. The rough cut metal edges around the windshield were downright scary. We referred to it as the flying guillotine. My favorite, Delvin's frame, was a "flat head" V8 Mercury. It was completely stripped except for the steering wheel and the front seat. That seat was plush for its time. It was a one piece bench seat made of tough tan velvet type cloth and well padded. An improvised head light was wired to the battery, and held in the lap of the passenger after dark. The view from the seat was completely unobstructed. The only item forward of the seat was the engine and radiator. The bare wheels and tires would sling mud in all directions because there were no fenders. There was no dash board, no instruments, no seat belts, no windshield, and bugs in the teeth were the norm. It had no key, was always hotwired for starting, and had straight pipes out of the manifold without a muffler. Yes it was loud. The rear wheels had very little weight riding on them, making it difficult to keep the rear of the car from sliding in all directions. Spinning the tires was normal, and almost expected. The tires were always used, often discarded by someone requiring a safer amount of tread. The upper level expenditure for a used tire was often one dollar.

Three could ride in the seat, if both people on the outsides held on. Of course frames were not legal vehicles to drive anywhere. The illegality of it all made it a daring challenge, so with the exception of the state paved highways, we drove them everywhere. Well…almost everywhere. It was considered bad manners to drive them down Main Street in town, because the townspeople would complain and cause all frame drivers to "get a bad name." "Cruising" near town required restraint, otherwise we drove them up hillsides, into the outback, on the river's edge, up the sides of irrigation spillways, over and through ditches, into gravel pits, through fields, up shale hillsides, through a slalom course of cottonwoods, on railroad tracks, and even on regular gravel roads.

Forrest was our local Deputy Sheriff. He had a small farm, not big enough to support himself and a family, so he worked part time as the local Deputy. Ours was a tough community; his nearest backup was Billings, 30 miles away. Forrest was about the same age as my parents, and lived just two miles from us. While we lived on road 13, Forrest lived on road14. Forrest's most remarkable physical feature was he had a high pitched voice especially when he was excited. Because of the voice, he earned the nickname "Squeaky." In later life I realized what a great Sheriff, and exceptional person Forrest (Squeaky) was. To this day I have the upmost respect for his work with us when we were kids, but of course my view was a little different back then. That is not to say we didn't respect Forrest, because he went along with the county policy of letting kids drive when necessary. He was also very tolerant in dealing with us on other issues. However in the name of safety he objected to reckless-ness. Yes, Forrest had an attitude about frames, justifiably so because not only were they unlicensed, uninsured, and illegal, they were downright dangerous. Alas, the optimism of youth reigned triumphant and the latter point was totally lost on me and my friends.

Delvin and I had a friend who lived about 8 miles from us, near the Huntley Agricultural Experiment Farm. Her father had a reputation of being an adventuresome spirit, and was one of a shrinking minority who didn't sequester his daughter when we rode into view. On a warm summer evening near dusk, we decided to drive the frame over the back roads to visit her. We stayed only a short time, but it was dark when we began our return home. I was driving. Delvin held the headlight in his lap, illuminating the road in front of us. We approached an intersection not far from the paved highway near the Ag Station. I stopped before we got there, and we dis-cussed the presence of a car parked near the intersection. The car's engine was running, and its lights were on. We had been informed that State Patrolmen were aware of several "frames" operating in the valley, but there had never been a citation issued. I was apprehensive about driving past an unknown car at night, so close to the highway. Our confidence was shored up from the knowledge that State Patrolmen never ventured off the highways unless they were doing interviews concerning an accident. Then they never contacted witnesses in the evening after regular business hours. History and intelligence collection were in our favor. The unknown was probably not a State Patrolman. Delvin opined that it was more likely just one of the Ag station employees irrigating, and had the car lights on to help him change the water in the dark. We decided we should quietly drive to the intersection with our light off, and when we turned left at the intersection, we should speed away toward the river. We faultily reasoned that with a hasty departure we could remain anonymous within the roaring cloud of dust.

I cruised up to the intersection in complete darkness, with the engine turning at a hushed idle. I navigated to the left in the gravel intersection turning toward the river and home. The lights of the car were now at my back, about 10 yards behind me. I floored the old Merc V8 and it roared to life with that low level stimulating sound only straight pipes can create. The unweighted rear tires cut thin trenches in the dry summer gravel. Dust rose above the flying rocks behind us in a thick impenetrable cloud. The wind was soon rushing in my ears, but there was something unusual in the mix. I heard a different unfamiliar sound. I let up on the gas to be able to hear better and realized it sounded a lot like a siren. I glanced to the rear. Squinting through the dust cloud I could see lights were still there, following, but with an added red blinking one above the regular white ones. Oh hell!

We didn't know who it was, but it surely was the law. Delvin shouted, "Do you think you can outrun him?" It was not a good question. Not even the best driver could hold a frame onto a gravel road at anything more than sixty miles per hour. They were far too light. I was already probably doing sixty five with the rear end flipping like a spawning salmon. The frame would leave a dust trail that could be followed a half hour later. Everyone in the Valley knew who drove frames. Neither of us had a disposition for serious law breaking. We imagined a complete division of Calvary would greet us by the time we snuck home. I briefly wondered if I would be spending the night in jail. I was really afraid of State Patrolmen, but I knew it was time to stop and "face up."

I slid to a stop and hopped off the cloth seat. I stood to the side of the frame in plain view so the approaching officer could see me in his headlights. I froze there, hoping the lawman wouldn't shoot me out of anger.

The first words I heard coming out of the brightly lit dust cloud was, "What the God damned hell do you guys think you are doing?"

I couldn't believe it. What I was hearing was the familiar sound of an agitated high pitched voice. It was Squeaky. I was so relieved I could have hugged him. But I remained like a statue trying to put together some type of reasonable explanation.

Delvin came through first. "We were just trying to get out of your way."

It didn't go over well. But it was a possible opening. I added some truth. "We thought you were one of the Ag Station guys out irrigating, so we just wanted to get on down the road without bothering him."

Squeaky countered with, "Bother him? You don't think throwing a bucket of rocks over his or my car would bother him?"

I apologized saying that the gas pedal was hard to operate in low gear, and that sometimes I inadvertently spun the wheels.

Then came the final admonition, "You damn kids take this damn thing home and park it, and I don't ever want to see it on the road again. You're both gonna end up in the hoosegow driving this damned thing. Now I mean it! Get the hell home."

The only acceptable answer was "Yes Sir." We knew he had a ticket book. He also had handcuffs and a police radio. But he didn't use them. He was our neighbor Forrest.

Forrest farmed alone. He also had hay to stack, and both Delvin and I had stacked his entire crop in the past. Two days after the frame incident, Forrest called asking if I or Delvin would have time to help stack his hay for "a day or two." I got clearance from my Dad, and Delvin agreed we should work together. But Delvin did not have a car other than his Dad's fancy Chrysler. His personal transportation was either his horse or the frame. With confidence, Delvin drove the frame to my house, and together we proceed to Forrest's farm yard. Delvin parked the frame between Forrest's barn and his farm truck so that no passerby would notice its presence. Walking out toward the hay equipment, I saw Forrest glance at the still hot Merc engine, but it went without further notice or mention for the next two days. Now that I am older, I realize he probably secretly would have liked to take it for a spin.

One of the favorite activities with the frame was taking young ladies for "the ride of their life." Many of them were quite daring, and loved the open air cruise. It is important to know that we did not drive recklessly with friends aboard, and were considered by our peers to be responsible. But that didn't prevent us from staging pranks and scaring the wits out of the usually vulnerable girls.

A common trick was to pick up two cute victims, and drive toward the river, or some other remote area. With the two girls crowded in the middle between us we had to hang onto the seat to keep from falling off. Once we arrived at an acceptable remote destination, we faked being tired of gripping the seat and stopped the frame, suggesting a short stretch. Unknown to our passengers, the frame was stopped and started by simply connecting two wires together. It was therefore easy to shut the engine off, and with the wires disconnect, pretend that it would not start again. Once our victims were convinced that it would not restart, we would all head back toward town on foot. When we had walked a hundred yards or more, Delvin would ask me if I turned off the gas. I would reply that I forgot and we needed to do so, or gas would leak out possibly causing a fire. At the suggestion, we would both run back to the frame, quickly start it, and speed off in a direction opposite of our passengers.

They always realized they were the victim of a bad joke, and we never left them alone for more than a couple of minutes. Surprisingly no one ever became angry and we had many laughs over the prank. Fortunately no protective fathers ever caught up with us.

On one occasion, while cruising near Ballantine, we enticed a fun pair into a country ride. We chose to drive through a field of very tall weeds. Because of the weed's density and height, it was impossible to see much of the ground ahead. Delvin was driving, both passengers were in the middle and he and I were again hanging onto the cloth bench seat with one inside hand. At a quick pace, the weeds were snapping and flying over the fenderless wheels. Suddenly we hit a small irrigation ditch. The frame bounced up into the air, ejecting us in two directions. Delvin and I both fell off the ends of the seat. The frame continued airborne across the ditch, landed running soundly in second gear, and disappeared into the weeds, with both passengers still aboard, screaming in fright. We lay in the ditch looking at each other. Someone asked the other, "Are you hurt?"

The answer was a burst of laughter that re-occurs through the years at the mention of the two princesses riding our steel horse into the weeded wilderness.

There were times of simple misfortune coupled with the learning curve of inexperience. A Sunday afternoon found us bored and in town with a friend...Nancy. The three of us decided to return to Delvin's, home and take the frame for a ride. The challenge was usually to find something different to ride through, or a new area to explore. Our meandering brought us to the Ballantine gravel pit. The geology of the pit amounted to a massive hole in the side of a hill, with a road to the bottom. The road consisted of very coarse gravel, with large round rocks throughout. It was easy going down, and Delvin drove us to the very bottom of the pit. We checked the bottom area for arrow heads, and agate stones with no success. With our sights on the upper rim, we started back up the stony road. Oops! The rear tires began to spin on the rocks. There was not enough weight in the back of the old beast to give us enough traction to climb the hill. We tried several remedies, including pushing it by hand. It was pure suicide to stand anywhere near those rear spinning wheels throwing out rocks. The heat of the summer sun down in the bottom of the rock pit soon made it very uncomfortable both for us, and the frame radiator. Our only way out was to walk.

The walk out was easy for Delvin and me, but Nancy was wearing flimsy floppy sandals. She was not happy. It was nearly a mile into Ballantine, but we stayed together, arriving like beaten platoon soldiers. We caught a ride from another Sunday driver and convinced Nancy to stay with us, because we would eventually need three persons to extract the frame from the gravel pit. We were fortunate that the Sunday driver delivered us back to Delvin's farm yard where he fired up one of their John Deere tractors. Nancy and I returned to the gravel pit in my car while Delvin "putt putted" three miles down the road to the pit in the John Deere.

The scene at the gravel pit became a scary spectacle. We hooked the tractor to the frame with a long chain and attempted to pull it up the steep road. The road was so steep, the front wheels of the John Deere kept rising up off the ground to the extent that Delvin could not steer it. It was in danger of tipping over backward. I tried to assist by driving the frame while he pulled with the tractor. It still did not work well. For a while, it looked as if we may get the tractor stuck down in the pit too. Little by little, Delvin with great skill, steering mostly with the individual rear tractor brakes, jerked the frame forward while I drove it spinning the wheels. Nancy's assistance amounted to her covering her eyes and hyperventilating. Eventually we got where the road was not quite as steep. "Piece of cake", the two machines rumbled up out of the pit. We finally left Ballantine, tractor in the lead, frame following in the middle, and Nancy driving my car in the rear.

Thereafter Nancy never demonstrated much interest in cruising about on the frame. Her attitude was similar to several other girls in the community. Delvin and I could not understand their lack of interest. We surmised that frame touring was just not a girl thing.

• • •

D riving became more serious with each additional year of maturity. One summer job during my college days was delivering gasoline in an old Ford gas truck. The truck was owned by Andy, the proprietor of Watson Grocery and Motel. The business was also a service station and gasoline distributor. The gasoline was offloaded from railroad cars into large tanks at rail side in Ballantine. My job was pumping the gas into the truck at the rail tank yard and delivering the gas to farmers and ranchers in the valley.

One of the larger gas consumers was a rancher who resided across the Yellowstone River many miles to the north. The drive was grueling on the truck, and involved grinding my way over long hills and around sharp curves. The truck was old. A full load of 1,000 gallons of gas was near the limit of the truck's capability. And....the brakes did not work well. The main (master) cylinder on the brake system leaked fluid. Whenever the fluid leaked to a certain low level, the brake pedal depressed all the way to the floorboard and failed to slow the truck.

Of course I always checked the brakes before I left on a delivery, and added fluid when needed. Again inexperience kept me from realizing that with additional use of a faulty brake system, eventually it will fail sooner and under even less stressful conditions.

I was at the top of "Quigley Hill", (named after one of my relatives) in the rugged hills north of Pompey's Pillar with a full load of gasoline when I tested the brake at the beginning of the downhill roll. Hmmm! The pedal sunk all the way to the floor. I was without brakes!

"No problem", I thought, because I was in low gear. I would just stay in low and ride it all the way to the bottom. The weight of the load soon had the engine screaming from being pushed down the hill. Inexperience kicked my butt again, because the pressure on the transmission caused it to jump out of gear. "Crap! I should have held my hand on the floor stick shift and kept it in low gear. Now I found myself gathering speed in neutral with no hope of getting the stick back into a lower gear. I ground the gears into second, and realized I would be doing at least 40 mph when I got to the curve at the bottom of the hill. I was beginning to worry a little, because there was a lot of gasoline behind me. The truck was still controllable when the lower curve came into view – cows and all. It was open range, and a heard of Herefords was grazing on both sides of the curve with a couple lying in the two track road.

I began trying to slow down the rig by edging the wheels into the soft sand at the side of the road. I remember thinking, "This could develop into one hell of a barbeque." The horn still worked, and I used it to its full extent. The cows looked up, but few moved. They were too stupid to know that I was about to splash them, myself and the roadside with enough accelerant to outshine the moon for a week. The road appeared fairly flat around the corner, and I saw that the side was probably even softer near the moist gully bottom. With horn blaring, and sand flying, I scattered every one of those prospective hamburgers without spilling a drop of gas. The cattle responded by creating a lot of new cow pies. I contained my composure only slightly better.

I arrived at the ranch safely, unloaded and asked the rancher if he had any brake fluid. He granted my request, but was aghast that I had come so far without brakes. I made the return trip carefully, intent on insisting the truck be repaired before any further use. On my arrival, I was spared from using the speech I had rehearsed for Andy. The rancher had telephoned the store to tell them of my plight, "Just in case I never returned."

• • •

When I entered into the Air Force, and settled into my job as an investigator, I marveled at the fact I was getting paid, to drive around several states exploring and talking with people. Driving over the countryside to learn from local people was always interesting, but the driving was only challenging in its vast distances; except in the winter.

East of Chadron Nebraska is wide open prairie known as "the Sand Hills." The name explains everything. The terrain moves with the wind. In the winter, the snow only settles in one location for a short time.

I made arrangements to conduct an interview with a rancher at his home best described as somewhere near Cottonwood Lake, but east of Nebraska highway 61 and south of the start of the Snake River. There were no towns or land marks within several miles. It snowed a good eight inches the night before but roads in Chadron where I had spent the night were plowed. My car trunk was well supplied with winter survival gear and a good snow shovel. My attitude was typical of a Montana twenties something male, who wasn't about to be deterred by a little snow.

I got an early start, and was at the rancher's kitchen table by 9:00 AM. The conversation was short and when I left the rancher's house he cautioned, "You better git back to town before the wind comes up." I intended to.

As I drove through his pasture gate, I noticed the wind was already pushing wisps of snow, like ghost serpents, across my half hour old tracks. The sky was clear but a distant fog like whiteness was growing toward the west. Within ten minutes I was struggling to see more than ten feet in front of the car. The fast moving horizontal snow induced vertigo and a mild nausea. There were no visible references in the milk bottle world. I couldn't see the roadside fences, gutters or even an occasional clump of grass. But I knew that I had to keep moving north toward the main road, or I would be there until help came, or until spring arrived in a couple of months. I crested a hill, and could see that down the other side the road crossed a narrow gulley. Also crossing the gulley was a red picket snow fence partially buried near the left side of the road. I knew there would be a drift near the snow fence, but I hoped I could hit it hard and momentum would carry me across the depression. "Wahoo", I grabbed the wheel mounted stick shift and dropped the V8 Ford into second gear and sped up the engine. I hit the drift straight, but the snow was piled higher on the left and it pulled me in the direction of the fence. A strand of barbed wire crossed in front of the windshield and I fought the wandering hood ornament back into the road. The car ground to a stop in the road, but packed snow was now midway up the driver's door, and only slightly below the mirror on the passenger side. The wind was increasing and quickly filling the trenches I had sculpted. Great! I was stuck in the middle of Mother Goose's pillow with no one around but me.

I opened the car trunk and put on my winter gear; snow pants, hooded parka, boots and gloves. Of course the shovel was immediately employed, but I realized I might as well be sweeping water at the mouth of the Mississippi. Snow was flying everywhere. The wind was moving more snow than I was while swinging the shovel at maximum speed. I looked over to the snow fence, and wished it was nearer the car.

"Wait a minute!" I thought, "Maybe I could place it near the car." I got back into the trunk, and in the tool kit, found a pair of pliers, with edges sharp enough to cut wire. In ten minutes I had two long sections of the wooden snow fence removed from its posts and alongside the car. But the wind kept blowing the fence flat. Then I realized that if I could tramp the snow fence flat into the top of the drift, I may be able to drive the car up on top of the big mound of snow. If successful, I could then work forward alternating two pieces of fence underneath, and in front of the car.

I placed the first section of fence under the wheels in front of the car and shoveled until I could drive the wheels up onto the fence. It didn't work. The car was too heavy and broke the pickets in the fence. I had to make the support stronger. I went back to the remaining partially buried portion, and brought two more pieces up to the car. Then I tramped both pieces, thickness doubled, into the snow in front of the car. I tried driving onto it again. Great! The submerged fence held up the car. I slowly drove the entire car up onto the fence. I and the car were actually now on top of the snow drift. But it was still another twenty yards ahead before the snow drift subsided and exposed the road bed. I thought, "Great, now they will find me up on top of Mother Goose's pillow with a part of a picket snow fence, frozen stiff as a green cucumber and wonder what the hell I was doing."

With the car sitting on the top of the drift, I moved the other two pieces of picket fence to the front of the car, and again tramped it into the drift surface. Little by little, I kept driving the car forward, until the previous supporting section of fence was exposed behind the car. As soon as I could pull the sections free, I tugged them up to the front of the car, and began the process all over again.

The twenty yards seemed like twenty miles. The wind was brutal, and snow was swirling in every direction. It was hard work getting the fence packed into the snow surface solid enough so that it wouldn't break. I was sweating inside the winter gear, but didn't dare expose myself to the wind and flying crystals. I finally reached solid ground at the base of the next hill. The entire process took over two hours. The wind continued and with an exhausted body, I wondered how many more mountains I would have to climb before arriving at the highway. I attempted to roll up the fence in an effort to drag it along to the next drift, but it was broken in so many places, it was not going to be useful beyond the point where it now lay. I placed it near its original posts and got back into the car. It looked like it had been hit by a flying saucer.

Twelve more miles of road, threatened several times to keep me, and punish me for my winter arrogance. With the shovel, repeated attempts forward and backward, and finally a break in the wind, I returned to the highway about 3:00 PM. I saw not one car until I reached the highway, and thereafter they were few. I had found another place where driving was not always fun.

• • •

After the Air Force, I entered the FBI and enjoyed the four months at the FBI academy immensely. One of the courses briefly taught was pursuit driving. After I made just a couple of runs through the driving course, the instructor took me aside and told me he recognized that I had apparently driven a variety of cars under difficult conditions. His only admonition was that in the coming years, I should be careful and not "tear up the cars."

California and the city of San Diego was my first assignment. I had driven in heavy traffic before, but it took me a little time to become a California driver. I acquired most of the practical habits, but never gave in to the mantra of rudeness. The new job of cruising around the freeways was again fun.

Freeways in San Diego were wide. Eight lanes was a real big road for a Montana country boy. The bonus was that I was given as standard equipment, a police pursuit Plymouth, complete with big engine, rugged suspension, and a speedometer that went well beyond what I had ever seen before. It was good that I had reached a level of maturity where caution was a firm governor of so much horsepower.

I had been in San Diego less than a month. I was working inland near El Cajon, where the cool sea breeze gave way to the heat in the higher desert air. The office dispatcher nervously called for all agents in my area to immediately respond to an emergency at the airport. That was almost 20 miles away, down by the beach. The car had no air conditioning, and driving with the windows open was standard practice. I had grown fond of the drive back down into San Diego, because the rapid freeway descent into the valley cooled the interior of the car very quickly, as if walking into a plush hotel. The radio call I received made the temperature drop even faster. I still remember the emotional rush of speeding down the freeway with the emergency light and siren announcing my presence. Before me I watched eight lanes of traffic yielding as best they could, and the field before me clearing as if my chariot was bearing the king. It humbled me to know that I was expected to knife through all of those people, yet keep their safety as a priority, even before my own. It was a new excitement, which in 30 years never lost its effect.

As I drove, two incidents from my past briefly flashed through my thoughts. After I had become a Special Agent of the FBI, my mother put together a nostalgic little trophy in recognition of my achievement. She found in some of her old "keepsakes" a battered brown teddy bear that I had slept with as a child. Along with the bear, she discovered more of my childhood toys including a tin sheriff's badge, and a plastic "cowboy" gun with a holster. She pinned the star onto the teddy bear, and fastened the holstered six shooter to the bear's side. One evening I found the little guy on my pillow attached to a sign that read, "You've come a long way baby." At eighty miles an hour in California traffic her message flashed across my mind, and I thought, "Well mom, it's probably best that you can't see me now." The other piece of memory that emerged from my subconscious caused me to wonder. If my chiding brother were strapped in the seat next to me; would he say, "Learn how to drive?"

• • •

After San Diego, Phoenix was much different. It was hot most of the time. We had about sixty agents assigned to the city, and there weren't enough cars to allow each agent to have his own. I shared a car with Ralph. However sharing was not a problem because Ralph and I were one pair, of a two pair fugitive team. We worked together almost every day, and shared the driving of one of the best cars I have ever driven in the FBI. It was a 1969 Ford, and again a police special model. Ralph and I chased down a lot of "bad guys" in that car, and it was well known by the intake crew at the jail. Its best day of triumph came in February 1971.

We were staked out on the northeast side of Phoenix, in a rural/suburban area. A kidnap suspect was expected to return to the victim's home to obtain more ransom money. It was a high profile case, so we had several agents surrounding the residence. Due to the thinly populated area, we had to position ourselves at a reasonable distance so we would not be seen. Ralph and I were located so that we could see approaching vehicles, and direct others to close in on any escape routes. That location was at the end of a cotton field 100 yards from the house. The cotton had been harvested, so there were no plants to obstruct our view. Secluding ourselves in the field was my idea, because I was driving. It gave us a complete view.

The suspect was wary of being caught, so he approached the house, but did not stop. He continued past, and then took a short cut through a neighbor's lane toward another side road. He caught most agents by surprise, and Ralph and I were the only agents who could intercept him before he got to the main road. I should mention that we could only intercept him if we drove through the cotton field and emerged at the termination of the neighbor's lane.

The field was about 400 yards long. It had an irrigation ditch midway through, and entirely across the field. The ditch was about as wide as an office desk and three feet deep. I could see that the bank elevated on both sides. I floored the Ford and drove in the direction of the ditch.

Ralph yelled, "Hey, there's a ditch out there."

"I know, but it's got a good tapered bank."

"No shit! They all have banks."

"No, I mean if we hit it straight, we will fly right over it."

"What makes you so sure?"

"I've done it before."

There was no time for further discussion. The car had to absorb the initial front end shock precisely perpendicular to the ditch; otherwise we would roll like a car in a demolition derby demonstration. Reality struck; I was no longer driving a frame. This car had a bumper out in front of the wheels. We hit the bank doing about 40 mph. Dirt flew up onto the windshield as the bumper leveled off part of the bank. The old Ford became airborne, but the road grader effect of the front bumper forced the rear wheels to rise much higher than the front. We flew over the ditch just like a Merc frame in the weeds, but then returned to the cotton field front wheels first. The Ford seemed to hesitate there on its front wheels, like a cheer leader beginning a hand stand. Just as planned, our forward momentum carried us well beyond the ditch. The rear wheels finally came back to earth and joined us in the pursuit. We drove to the end of the field like a college half back scoring a touchdown. We behaved like two foolish kids in a hot rod Ford, but we beat the kidnapper to his escape road. We approached him head on, then ten yards before impact I broadsided our car in front of him. We had blocked his escape route. Ralph and I both clambered out of our Ford driver's door, not knowing if our exposed side was going to be rammed. The bad guy had a clear view of us with guns drawn, and looked to the rear only to see much more of the same closing in. He was smart enough to give up easily.

The next day Ralph asked, "Were you BS-ing me about driving across a ditch before?"

"Hell no, I did it all the time when I was a kid."

• • •

A year later, I was reassigned to Tucson. My first car was a turquoise Nash Rambler, with black plastic interior…..and no air conditioning. I sat out the miles on a straw covered wire cushion. I was routinely traveling more miles than any other of the eight agents assigned there. Eventually the supervisor mercifully assigned me a new white over yellow Ford. It had air conditioning. I wore it, and several other cars out during the seven years that I drove almost every road in southern Arizona. It was the yellow Ford that I became most attached to. Together, we had the best experiences.

I was responsible for attending to bad happenings at Fort Huachuca, 90 miles from Tucson. I received a call at 6:00 AM that a soldier had been fatally stabbed by his wife. The incident occurred in post housing, and the military police were securing the scene awaiting my arrival.

I drove the 90 miles to the fort frequently. I knew every turn, pothole and State Patrol Officer on the road. I knew they often set up a speed check point on the secondary road three miles after leaving the freeway. It was their job, and I respected it. They too respected that at certain times, my "undercover" car would be seen traveling a little faster than normal traffic, but I too was doing my job. It was a great mutual respect.

In route to the apparent homicide, I coached the speedometer up to 90 and was comfortably taking in the morning radio news. I turned off the freeway, cruising south along the edge of the Coronado Hills when I saw a State Patrol Car at their usual morning commuter monitoring place. The patrolman was parked at a wide turnout in a dip at the bottom of the hill. I glanced at my speedometer which was pointing just below ninety. I was the only person on the road. Long before I got to the waiting officer, he turned on his flashing lights. Obviously this was going to be a special greeting just for me. I was a little annoyed at having to stop, but he must not have recognized me and I needed to give him the courtesy of stopping. I jammed on the brakes and slid to a stop beside him in the gravel. I jumped out of my car and ran over to the officer before he could exit his car. His window was open, letting in big puffs of dust. It was then I noticed a younger man at the wheel. I had never met this guy. He was a "new kid" and he didn't know me from Bugsey Malone. I was wearing my weapon, with no coat covering it.

I quickly placed both of my hands on his window opening, and glanced at the screen on his radar. It was flashing 86. The speed limit was 65. Before he could speak, I said, "Wow, eighty six, that's not bad for a country boy in an old car." He was still speechless. I hurried through an explanation that I was with the FBI and had to get to a homicide on the Post at Fort Huachuca. The only thing the new trooper said was, "OK."

As I sped away, I smiled at the thought; the last time I pulled a trick like that the officer had a high "squeaky" voice. This guy seemed to have none at all.

I continued on to the fort, and attended to my duties. Later in the day, I went to my favorite lunch place in nearby Sierra Vista, and who should I see but the Captain in charge of the local State Police.

His first comment was not hello, but was, "Schreuder, you sure scared the hell out of one of my new troopers this morning." "What the hell were you up to?"

He was a good friend, so I took my usual liberties. "I was out on early patrol, and thought I would help out by contributing a little training."

The Captain commented, "You sure did. He told me a guy with a gun, driving like a mad man, stopped and ran up to his window, said he was a Fed, and sped away. I asked if he got the name, and he said no. Then he admitted that he never saw a badge or anything else other than the gun at his window and all he had a hold on was his pencil. Damn near crapped his pants. He said it was a yellow Ford, so I knew it was either you or you let some bastard steal your car. Either way, I figured it wasn't worth going after."

I apologized to my friend, and a few days later had the pleasure of buying lunch for the Captain and his new patrolman. He too became a friend for several years.

• • •

When I was assigned to the Portland Oregon division, I had enough seniority to be given the newest and latest of cars. In my thirty years of service I drove every make of American car, and enjoyed many exciting driving experiences. To review even a small percentage of them would soon become boring. I can summarize 30 years of driving at work by admitting I have exceeded all reasonable speed limits, driven over ice and snow where no dog sled should have ventured, crossed creeks and desert sand dunes, driven the wrong way on one way streets, made U turns in dense traffic, ran wheels up onto lawns, parked in the street to stop traffic, followed spies at night with my lights off, and blown out tires at high speed.

I estimate that during thirty years of service I drove almost one million miles in Government cars. Throughout that time I never caused an accident or dented a fender.

I always said when the time came that I was no longer having fun, I would retire. That day came late in November 1993. I decided to retire at the end of the month. On November 30, 1993, early in the morning of my last day at work with the FBI, I drove my assigned Blue Buick from the parking garage. I proceeded out highway 26, which was known as the Sunset Highway. It was a freeway that continued out of Portland to the Oregon Coast. When I got near the edge of town, I turned on the blue lights and the siren, and ran the car up past 100.

The telephone poles whipped by and the center line became a series of short white dots. The thrill was still there. I held the speed until the adrenalin subsided. I slowed and turned the car back toward town. I knew I would never be able to do it again. It was over....but for 30 years it was a great ride.

Diary II

Introduction to Part II

My role model high school music teacher had an impressive philosophical saying which was, "Always close the curtain with them wanting more." I have twice closed the curtain on this diary only to realize the performance remains unfinished.

I did not begin this journal just to tell stories. The intent was to connect my decedents with their past, and along the way chronicle my own character development, good or bad, and to document history in an entertaining manner.

I find it easy to write about youth and fun times, to tell humorous stories with rosy descriptions and finish with delightful endings; but to relive bad times...no I don't think so. It is no wonder I have avoided writing the last act.

OK, so the unpleasant is rarely fun. That's not a revelation, but if I am to tell my family the complete story, and tell it honestly I must expose at least a few dark events. Some memories have been buried; previously untold for the good of maintaining a positive attitude, and because one rarely improves his stature by tearing apart the character of another. It's my own admission that there are periods of despair in all journeys, from which healing was a slow triumph.

Adam J. Schreuder

I have decided to include in this diary several more work stories, only to demonstrate how my life grew and attitudes changed. I learned from my father's stories. Lessons I learned on my own too often came after the test. Looking back, unless I preserve them in writing I achieved virtually nothing. This diary is about the people. Real lives are not built from daily acts of excellence. Here are the lives and character of those I worked with, how they affected my life, how we survived, who we targeted, who we helped and who we destroyed. Details, specific times, evidence and descriptions have been minimized, even at times forgotten, to accentuate the human element. A few are portrayed with deservedly rude and brutal words, for in an adult world, most have known their ilk. This diary is about an ordinary farm boy on a sojourn through an unmapped maze, both following and leading, in a complicated society. In short I want the reader to know what it was like to be me.

When my name has long been carved upon my tombstone, I predict you my descendants, will find we were unusual people "back then", and I will make one self-serving statement. *We had good intentions.*

A Change of Venue

Relocation was not easy during my tenure with the FBI. There were no allowances for advanced payments, no house hunting trips, and no advances for travel expenses. We were expected to sell our house, pack up our belongings, and drive our family to the next location in a limited number of hours. After arriving at the new location, we were given only three days to get everyone settled, and begin work at the new duty station. When our household goods arrived at the new location, it was necessary to pay the moving company in cash upon delivery or pay additionally to have everything put into storage until a suitable house was located. When all expenses were tabulated, and not before then, we completed a travel voucher causing the government to reimburse us for all travel expenses. Real Estate fees were considered our own personal expense. Unless one had an outside source of money, moving was difficult for all personnel.

I used a commercial moving company to get to California and again from San Diego to Phoenix. But when I was reassigned from Phoenix to Tucson, I was a little short of money for the down payment on the Tucson house, an upgrade from my first purchase in Phoenix. After studying the moving regulations I learned that the Government would pay me for moving myself. To collect we had to pack everything ourselves, load the goods into a rented truck and weigh the contents. With a weight certificate, and an accurate distance measurement between residences, I could collect a fee in relation to the weight of my shipment multiplied by the miles shipped. I figured that we could make approximately three thousand dollars by moving ourselves. That would be enough to complete the down payment on the new house. The house had been selected from a group of "almost completed" new homes in a new subdivision in Tucson. Since I had been working in Tucson for two weeks before moving, I checked on the building progress regularly. The builder assured me the home would be completed by March 1st. (1971); which was on a Sunday, and allowed for packing and loading the truck on Saturday Feb 28th.

Everything went smoothly. Somewhere in this story, I must give credit to the boys' mother Judy, for her many efforts at moving. She packed our meager belongings so many times that she could accurately estimate how many minutes it would take to pack each room. She always did a good job and rarely complained – for the first ten moves.

With a U-Haul truck fully loaded, and the car pulling a mid-sized trailer, our entire worldly belongings were weighed at a roadside truck scales. With the all-important weigh bill, the truck rental documents, and a road atlas, I could collect 140 (distance in miles) x .28 (cents per 100 pounds) x 9,870/100 (total cargo in pounds divided by 100 = $3869.04. (These are approximate numbers). I figured it a dozen times and rejoiced in knowing that after paying for the tuck and gas, I would have just a little more than enough to make the house down payment, which was being delayed on my promise of payment immediately after I collected for the move. With a sigh and a feeling of great accomplishment we navigated Interstate 10 South toward Tucson.

We arrived at our new house, all together, after driving in a snowstorm....yes, snow in Tucson. A strong wind was blowing the snow nearly horizontal. It was refreshing in a strange way because none of us had seen snow since our last vacation in Montana, but I was hoping the storm would not last long. Unloading our belongings in a mini blizzard was going to be another problem.

I had obtained a key to the new house on Friday, but I didn't need it. The first thing I saw was the side window by the door was broken as well as a bathroom window. The doors were unlocked. The house was nearly as cold as the outdoors, and no wonder, there was no electricity. A look into the bathroom delivered another horror. There was no water either, and apparently the workmen had been using the toilets without being able to flush them. So welcome to the new house...no heat, no lights, no water, sewage in the house, and broken windows with no way to secure the doors. This move which started out so well was dissolving into something much less pleasant.

It was almost mid-day on a Sunday, with no chance of summoning anyone for repairs, so with a little thought we chose to unload everything into the house, mostly into the garage, and made arrangements for Judy and the boys to spend the night at another agent's home. Because we couldn't lock the house, I decided to sleep among the boxes to prevent another break in.

It finally quit snowing, but the wind was cold and unrelenting. The boys, Jack and Joel, (we didn't have Jason yet) were patient, but restless. We, as stressed parents, tried to keep them out of the way, but occupied at something to accommodate their own anxieties. It seemed that playing in the truck was the most popular activity, so I did nothing to discourage it.

Most of the truck had been unloaded, and it was about the time fatigue replaces good co-ordination. I was walking up the tailgate ramp, pulling the dolly cart when the cart tie down strap snagged on the ramp. I gave the cart a tug, but the strap remained snagged. In frustration I yanked on the cart hard enough to free the strap, but the cold steel cart handle lurched violently in my direction and smacked me in the mouth. Pain shot through my lip, but what bothered me most was the sudden discovery of a little hard rock in my mouth. It only took a second, with one quick breath of cold air to realize I had broken off my front tooth. Marvelous, it was still Sunday and I would be lucky if I could get into a dentist even the next day. In the meantime there was still a truck to empty and a family to care for; "One thing at a time."

I taped up the bleeding lip and on returning to the truck I noticed that the snow had turned to rain. The boys had left the truck window open, no, both windows were completely rolled down. I opened the driver's door, closed the window and glanced at the truck dashboard. "That's good; it didn't get wet, but wait a minute, where's the paper work?" Both windows had been open; the wind had blown through the truck for at least an hour. I looked for the weigh bill: it was GONE...blown away, out somewhere into the desert bordering the edge of our lot. Searching the desert for it in the waning light was useless.

With the arrival of darkness, the rest of the family departed for a real house with heat, water and light. I stayed in the vandalized house with a mattress and blankets on the floor, hugging my flashlight. The tape on my lip prevented me from breathing through my mouth and feeling the added pain of cold air across the broken tooth root.

It wasn't the coyotes howling outside in the yard, or the wind blowing into the cold house, or even the pain from the tooth that kept me awake. It was the thought of how I was going to certify and collect for the move without the proper documentation. That weigh bill was worth a month's wages, and I needed it to close the deal on the house. In the early hours of morning darkness I came up with a plan.

With the first arrival of construction workers in the neighborhood, I was bullying my way into the unfinished houses. I rounded up a plumber, and electrician and a heating specialist and brought them to our messed up house. Through them I placed a call to the general contractor's office and forcefully scheduled a glass repairman and a cleaning company to deal with the cluttered construction mess. Then I was connected to the General Contractor. The conversation was short because I was angry beyond my sensitivity training limitations.

"Mr. Lamb, I'm sure you remember our conversation of last week. On Wednesday you promised me that my house would be completed and ready for occupancy by Sunday March 1st. I am standing here in the kitchen, on March second, with broken windows, no heat, no electricity, no water, with construction dirt on the floor and poop in the toilets. I had to stack my household goods in the garage, and displace my family in another residence. What do you suppose that does for my appreciation and my confidence in your company?"

"Mr. Schreuder, I'm really sorry. I know I promised to have the house finished by March first, but I forgot that February only has 28 days."

He had the house finished and ready for occupancy by three that afternoon. A couple days later, he apologetically appeared with a gift certificate for two evenings dining at one of Tucson's finer restaurants.

After my calls concerning the house, I arranged for emergency medical leave from my own office, and found a dentist to do a root canal and temporary cap on my front tooth. Still thinking, "One thing at a time", but as quickly as possible, I called my former office in Phoenix and spoke with a couple of Agent friends. I explained the situation with the weigh bill, and asked them to locate the old weigh master at the highway truck station. They were directed to get a copy of the weigh bill, and if that wasn't available, they were to get a statement from him recalling that I came through the station on Sunday with a U-Haul truck, and a green Oldsmobile pulling a U-Haul trailer. I suggested they prompt his memory with the approximately 10,000 pounds total household weight, thus providing a stronger confirmation.

I didn't hear from them for two days, and was about to call Phoenix again when they called with their results. There were no records retained at the weigh station unless there was a weight or overload violation. It took a full day to locate the old gentleman who weighed us on Sunday. No matter how they tried, they could not get him to remember anything about us, the car, truck, or even a description of me and the family. It was as if he were asleep as I passed through. Had I not previously described him in detail they would have questioned whether they were at the correct weigh station.

Now what? After consulting with my co-workers, we thought I should call the transportation voucher section at FBI headquarters and determine if they would accept some sort of sworn affidavit outlining the circumstances, using as evidence the reality that my household goods did not just happen to appear in Tucson unassisted. It was worth a try, but due to the time differential, I would have to wait until the next morning to call the East Coast.

That afternoon, the weather had cleared, and the boys and their mother went for their first walk around the construction ravaged neighborhood. There were only a few finished homes; surrounded by unfinished framework and no finished yards or fences. Approximately two blocks from the house, they passed a large pile of construction trash. Judy happened to look down at the edge of the pile and saw a paper with the name Schreuder on it. She retrieved it from the pile and found she was holding the truck contract and lost weigh bill.

• • •

The reassignment to Portland was not something that occurred automatically. Although I enjoyed the work in Arizona, the allergenic climate was discomforting to me and most of my family. In addition to longing for the sight of a stream containing real water, and vegetation void of thousands of piercing appendages, I was anxious to work in a more challenging theater. The Bureau had jurisdiction over more than 120 Federal violations, and I wanted to experience more of them than only those occurring in an area predominantly comprised of Military and Indian reservations. Through some difficult negotiations and a little coercion, I was finally offered a transfer to one of three locations. I was allowed to choose between Portland Oregon, Milwaukee Wisconsin and Buffalo

New York. I chose Portland because it was closest to our home state of Montana.

A moving incident that tugs at my heart still, 37 years later, came from my son Joel. We had sold our Tucson home, watched as everything we owned was packed into an Allied Moving Van, and began our quest to learn new things in Oregon. We were on our second day of travel, motoring up Interstate 5 in my 1973 Chevy Suburban. My apprehension of the life to come probably permeated the thin veil of confidence I attempted to display. Silence had fallen upon us, leaving only the drone of the truck in place of the usually chattering boys. It was before the introduction of mandatory seat belts and car seats and Jack, Joel and Jason were stretched out in the back two seats, weary from the long ride.

Jason, the youngest, asked in an anxious, timid voice, "When are we going to be home?"

Before I could provide a meaningful answer, Joel replied in a tone of despair, "We don't have a home."

The comment struck me hard. Foreboding guilt and wonderment as to why I had submitted them all to this long termed and uncertain torture iced my spirit.

Thankfully Jason followed with youthful inquisitiveness and asked, "Why?"

It gave me a chance to gather my thoughts and provide a reassuring explanation about the prospect of a new nice home with green trees. In reality I was wishing that for starters I knew where to find a comfortable motel on arrival.

The house hunting was bleak, and we spent about five days in the Old Lantern Motel near Highway 217 between Beaverton and Portland. Because our household goods were scheduled to arrive within the week, we located a rental house near Tigard, on the outskirts of the conglomerate cities of Portland and Beaverton. We intended to live in the rental until we could build or find a suitable home. It seems unbelievable, but at that time, housing was scarce, expensive, and difficult to locate in a suitable location approved by the Bureau. (We were discouraged from living more than a few miles from the central office.)

The landlord of the Tigard house was a builder and I finagled a deal with him to rent one of his houses with a short term lease on the possibility I would buy it or one of the others he had for sale.

By then a week had passed, and I was already working, but management was quite understanding, and gave me the day off to meet the moving truck at our new temporary home. It was late fall, and raining. It was the first day of continuous rain, foreshadowing what would be hundreds of wet days to follow in the years ahead.

Moving was always hard work, because the movers only placed the boxes into the house, and the rest was left to us. Because the boys had already been enrolled in their new school as soon as we decided on the house, they were not immediately under foot. Their mother and I spent the day trying to make the strange new house into something that felt like home.

At midafternoon, a school bus dropped the boys at our doorstep, but there were four of them. I was certain that I had left Arizona with only three, so I looked to Jack for an explanation. He reported that Jim was his new friend who lived just a few houses down the road, and quite enthusiastically asked to be allowed to play there for an hour. It was a good neighborhood of relatively new houses and we visually checked out where Jim said he lived. We were reluctant to give our permission, however there was still more moving to do, and it was convenient to not have all four of them under foot. Jack left with Jim.

Just before the time Jack was to return back home, I departed to a nearby fast food store to obtain food for our evening meal. When I returned it was starting to get dark and still drizzling rain. His mother reported that Jack had not returned, and was long overdue. Quite concerned she he had gone to Jim's house where his mother reported that Jack had left at least 45 minutes earlier. The return home should have been less than a five minute walk. Fear gripped us both. It was almost dark, the kid was out there in a strange land, and not even he knew where.

The rest of the family stayed at home, hoping for Jack's return while I jumped into my car with an unfamiliar street map. I began a spiral search through the neighborhood, expanding out from the place where he was last seen. What did I expect to see? At best a soaked son, walking the street in search of what he thought would be his home. Feeling a prickly dread, I tried to deny my mind of any thoughts concerning other possible bad developments. I circled the area for a half hour seeing nothing that relieved my fears.

A few blocks away, Jack slogged along darkening sidewalks, drenched, cold, and upset, but was strong and admirably brave. On his return toward the new home in the dreary mist, he made a wrong turn. He continued forward until he realized that he must have passed the house. He backtracked, but was not aware of where he made the wrong turn, and each block traveled compounded his confusion. He was lost. He knew no one. He understood the reason behind the cautionary lectures and "Beware of strangers" lectures given by his father.

But brave as he was, he knew he was not going to find home before it was completely dark. Without help he would freeze in the cold night rain. But he didn't know his address, or even a local phone number. He was nine years old and alone on the twilight street.

From the street-side curbs he studied the houses. Most were new, but some had established yards. He concentrated on the "better looking" houses, because he remembered his dad saying he could tell something about peoples' character by the appearance and neatness of their house. Through an un-curtained window he saw movement, perhaps another child. He reasoned that in this situation, he was going to be the stranger, and he would have to find and rely on someone who lived in the neighborhood that could be trusted. He approached the house and rang the doorbell.

A man about his father's age came to the door. Seeing what resembled the last shipwrecked rat to swim ashore, he brought Jack inside and listened to his dilemma. Jack told him that he would probably recognize his family's new house, but was sure the all familiar Chevy Suburban and the "green bean" Oldsmobile would be parked in the driveway. The good Samaritan was aware of an unoccupied rental house a few blocks away. He put Jack into his car and drove directly to the house in question. There was the suburban.

The man thoughtfully escorted his wayward passenger to the front door, and was promptly greeted by a very worried mother. He also delivered a lecture to a mother whom he perceived was careless, mindless, and unthoughtful by abandoning her child in a strange neighborhood.

In 1976 there were no cell phones in ordinary households. I had no way of determining if Jack had returned, other than occasionally returning myself. On my second return, I saw a car pulling away from the new residence. With relief, and anticipation I entered the living room to find a cold and brave little kid hugging his mother.

No admonitions, lectures or additional warnings were given. It was a good lesson for all of us. In the following weeks, I noticed a new awareness in Jack, a mixture of caution and confidence. He showed more concern for his brothers in a new environment, giving them counsel, while devoting more attention to his new geography and well-being.

The day ended with cold pizza and for Jack a hot shower and his own bed in a new place. I was exhausted and sought relief for a sore back by stretching out on the carpet in front of the fireplace. No, there wasn't a fire, because a piece of dry wood was now a rare item. It was the relief provided by the flat floor that I sought for the next hour.

Before dawn the next day, I was dressing for work, and both noticed and felt, what appeared to be the beginning of a rash on several areas of my body. Pondering the cause, I thought back on past lessons about how extreme stress could cause body rashes. In spite of the annoying red spots, I argued inwardly that life had been a little tense, but I wasn't so tense it would result in a rash. I ignored the irritation throughout the day, and was relieved that evening to find most of the skin redness had diminished. To make matters better, I located a few sticks of wood; enough to make a fire in the fireplace. This time it was quite relaxing to again lie on the carpet before the fireplace. Nearly asleep, I begin experiencing a strange sensation, as though my skin was exposed to wind-blown sand. I abruptly sat straight up! "What the hell...that's it!" The carpet was full of fleas. They were dining on my tired carcass.

When we moved into our first rental house in San Diego, after we spent the first night unpacked, we discovered the place was full of cockroaches. The remedy was; relocate everything to the center of the rooms, and employ an exterminator. How could this happen again? Why does moving always have these ubiquitous problems?

My first visitation the next morning was with the new landlord. He was a good person, and understood my point immediately. Fortunately the exterminator treated the carpet and associated areas without having to empty shelves and drawers. I vowed to never be a renter again.

We lived in that house only one month. By constantly searching, we located a beautiful place in Cedar Mill, a subsection of Beaverton….but with a zip code and postal address of Portland. (That allowed compliance with the office rule requiring I live within a certain distance of the FBI office.) The house was located on almost 3 wooded acres bordering Cedar Mill Creek, with another small creek running under the edge of a second story roofed deck. It needed some work, but I intended to live there long enough to make it a show place.

This time, we had to do all the packing and moving, and bear the costs ourselves. I rented a U-Haul truck, brought out the packing boxes we had saved, and spent a full weekend packing and loading the truck. I took Monday off of work, determined to move the entire household by myself. My work associates were all busy, and I knew better than to ask anyone else to take a day's vacation to help me move. I wasn't concerned, I had done this before.

The new house was beautiful, but had a difficult entry. The garage and basement were on the lower level, with a full flight of cement steps to climb before entering the main living space.

That meant that almost everything had to be carried up the stairway. I had rented a good dolly cart, but couches, mattresses, tables and chairs were a serious struggle. My experience as a Montana farm boy kept me going, through hauling the washer, dryer and bedroom dressers up the stairs with the dolly. I finished well past evening meal time, so again we opted for a pizza supper, but dined out. I was too tired to eat, and almost too tired to drive, but found reserve energy from the brief rest.

Finally home again by 9:00 pm, we unpacked sheets, and got the boys ready for bed. I could barely keep from falling onto one of the mattresses myself. The first one to bed used the bathroom in the hall with no consequence. The next in turn was the second to flush, and began hollering. The toilet was running over the top of the bowl and spilling across the floor. Water ran out into the hallway soaking the carpet. I stopped the flood, but not before water had crossed the hallway. We entered panic mode, to find something that was not still packed, that would soak up the mess. Some of the water found its way through the floor and into the basement. A few packing blankets absorbed the rest.

In the meantime, there were still at least two family members that needed to use the bathroom before bedtime. There was a second bathroom in the master bedroom, several feet away from the defective one. The last boy to retire, went to the remaining bathroom, and flushed. Another flood crossed the floor in that part of the house. Obviously, the sewer line was plugged outside the house, or near the septic tank. There would be no more use of the facilities until we could get a sewer line company to clear the pipes.

I frankly explained the situation to the boys. "If you need to whizz tomorrow morning, you will have to go outside."

Somebody asked, "Can we whiz off the deck?"

I was too tired or argue or even care and answered, "OK, but do it off the back side over by the trees", and then thought about the impression the neighbors were going to get of us, the new people, when they look out in the morning, and see three kids peeing off the second floor deck of a high class home in a nice neighborhood. Welcome to the new home! My final thoughts that evening were, "At least there aren't any bugs."

EARNING A POSITION

At the time of my transfer, Portland was a much larger office than Tucson. Although I had worked in San Diego for a year, my reputation had been developed in Phoenix and Tucson. There were about 80 Agents in Portland, all curious about the new guy. Suspicion was aroused because of the transfer itself. It was clear that I had been moved under special circumstances, which were in reality family health (desert allergies) problems, but anyone with "special connections" was not welcomed into the established cliques until he had proven himself. My reputation was that of being an independent and successful "loner" because I had worked all of southern Arizona by myself. But Portland was a big city, in need of "team players", not loners. Within one full day at duty, I knew once again that I was at the bottom of the pecking order, and I must fight my way up. My new associates made it clear. I could have single handedly scalped Geronimo, found the Lost Dutchman gold mine, survived sand storms, eaten raw cactus, and I still wouldn't have been treated as an equal. No one cared what I had done yesterday; it was about what I could do today. Agents have little charity for other's defects or mistakes. I would have to reorder my universe into something new, something I and they found comfortable. I sort of liked that, and was only concerned about how long it would take.

In most FBI offices it was not uncommon for the new agents to get assigned the "crap" cases, sometimes referred to as "Dogs", or "Old Dogs" if they had been open for a long time. These were investigations that were unsolved or stagnant either because they had been mishandled, were not in favorable graces with the prosecuting U.S. Attorneys or for any other reason unpopular, not glamorous, and disliked. I was assigned the Granddaddy "Dog" case of the Portland Office on my first day. The case was one of the Bureau's first involvements with Drug cases, even before they were granted jurisdiction of some of the drug laws. LSD was being manufactured by a sophisticated group of college "intellectuals", in Oregon, and was being shipped worldwide. A young aspiring agent had begun the investigation, with ambitions of getting promoted to supervisor by managing a large high profile case. He stretched the investigation inserting as much sensationalism into the work as possible, involving numerous agents and "burning" hundreds of work hours. However through, in my opinion, poor surveillance techniques and other substandard practices the culprits learned of the investigation, ceased their operation and fled to, as best as I could determine, Nepal; a small country in the Himalayas between India and China, and a bit out of my reach at that time. Sensing the impending collapse of his glory balloon, he took the job of supervisor within another squad, and set the case aside to be assigned to the new guy, me.

At the time I inherited the mess, no one knew where the group had gone. They weren't even sure they had abandoned their manufacturing operation in the woods outside of Cottage Grove, Oregon.

So I became once again, the lone wolf, assigned only one large case, and was given an old gentleman agent about to retire as an assistant. He was a good old soul, but smoked, even in the car, and read aloud every billboard we drove past.

I worked the case for two months; getting nowhere other than learning it had become a worthless fiasco, largely unworthy of its initial attention. I, Lone Ranger or not, decided to quit figuratively sitting on the fence, and chose to make something happen. I told the aged gentleman Tonto, to pack his overnight bag because we were going on a trip. Striding into my supervisor's office, I announced that "Chuck" and I were going to Cottage Grove, to check on the LSD lab. He looked at me and gasped. Lee was an indoctrinated and experienced security (spy oriented) agent, who couldn't easily process in his individual consciousness the act of approaching the enemy head on, face to face. In his mind you continued to watch and report on the enemy in secret well after the war ended.

"You can't do that!" "Why not", I asked.

"Because we've worked on this an entire year, and no one has even taken the chance of going down there."

I mulled over that anticipated answer about two seconds and replied, "What you're saying is that I shouldn't do it, because we haven't done it yet. Well then, don't you think it's about time?"

"The place is an old barn out in the woods. We've only seen it from the air. If you drive in there you will spook the whole bunch and blow apart what's left of the case."

I had to appeal to his sneaky peaky mentality, so I suggested, "Look Lee, I've given this some thought. You guys are supposed to be hikers up here, and I've walked a few miles myself, and I'll guarantee you these woods will be a hell of a lot more cover than the desert mesquite trees where I've hidden the past few years. We don't even know that these people are still in Oregon. I'm not good at investigating ghosts, or shooting at something I can't see. I'm going to walk in there, and see if anyone is still living around this barn and old house. Chuck can drive in, drop me off a mile or so away. I'll take a radio so I can call him if I need help." I knew that last comment was the weakest part of my plan, but Lee wasn't thinking of my welfare, only of his own ass if I screwed up the case.

After some extended discussion I convinced the supervisor we needed some positive action to justify continuing to waste time gathering dated information on departed demons.

The drive down I-5 was interesting. I shamed Chuck in to not smoking, and he entertained us both and quieted his fidgeting hands by reading out loud every bill board advertisement between Portland and Cottage Grove.

At a rest stop near our forest road destination, we changed our clothes and prepared for a hike. Chuck insisted he go with me in case I got into trouble. The old partner could shoot straight so I agreed; although with him by my side we were going to wake numerous spotted owls, sounding like two crippled moose walking with crutches.

We stashed the car several miles west of I-5 at a fishing turnout. The hike to the residence and barn was uneventful. Only once did Chuck stumble over a downed windfall tree, careen into a small cedar, land flat on his belly and conclude with a loud expletive. Figuring the woods were full of athletic animals launching over logs, while singing out expletives, I had no worries and stealthily snuck onward.

Observation of the suspected drug lab from the woods disclosed there were no vehicles, no movement, and pathways were being grown over by weeds. We walked into the clearing like Daniel Boone looking for mushrooms, and saw that the barn door was open. A senior appearing citizen was operating a small tractor across the road from the residence, so I approached him, pretending to be interested in buying or renting the property.

I asked if he knew if the place was for rent. He gruffly stated, "It ain't fer rent yet, but if yer not a hell-of-a-lot better person than them that left, yee can fergit it."

With an opening like that I jumped into a productive conversation. I learned that the old gentleman was the owner and that our culprits had suddenly disappeared two months previous leaving the place in shambles.

He said, "I think they must have been doin' some kind of chemistry stuff in the barn 'cause they left a bunch of jugs and bottles, and there's broke up glass ever which way."

We got his permission to look in the barn. It was a "chemistry lab" to say the least. We were afraid to touch anything, fearing it was contaminated with LSD. I left with a camera full of photos showing an abandoned, once upon a time drug lab. We drove home the next day joking about soon having visions of colorful sugar plums dancing in our heads; a concern more realistic than the frivolity in which we addressed it.

A couple weeks later I had the case condensed into a simple open fugitive investigation, and learned that all of the suspects had fled the United States to exotic countries, using various passports and assumed names. To put the case on the shelf, all I had to complete was a few days of paper work. But I didn't rush into it because I wanted to have some influence on where, and what I would do next.

I was acquainted with, and had in other offices worked with, a couple guys on the reactive/bank robbery squad. They were good guys and a tight knit group. They were the "right hand" of the big boss, (the Special Agent in Charge) and were cautiously referred to as the "Palace Guard." A desk in that squad was my goal, but it would be the most difficult of any to attain. Somewhere I would have to slay my own dragon to be knighted.

Stepping off of the winning pedestal and beginning a new race at the back of the pack was not a new experience, nor should it have been. Anyone who aspires to progression and improvement must occasionally reinvent himself, invigorate his individual consciousness, learn anew and humbly demonstrate an honest "how can I help" attitude. The challenge was to accomplish the resurrection without cutting in front of, or offending another competing contemporary. One inconsiderate or uninformed gaff would indefinitely damn me to a fate equal to being sealed and hog tied in an air tight container fed only menial investigations sardonically appeasing social irritation. Portland was a large high production office, with something for everyone, and I didn't want to be among those picking up the crumbs at the bottom of the ladder.

My assessment of the situation was reinforced through an act as simple as my first visit to the Portland Police Station. I went there to speak with a vice squad detective; an inquiry about a drug dealer with whom he'd had past interaction.

Throughout Cochise County in Arizona, I was well known and reasonably respected. My arrival into a small town law enforcement agency usually generated a greeting of "Hello Mr. Schreuder", or in some "Hello Dory", or even "Be careful, here comes the Dutchman." Often I was greeted by the dispatcher or receptionist with the latest joke of the day. I was consulted concerning major decisions, invited to local ceremonies and a welcome guest at everything from military banquets to little Jimmy's birthday, and the pulling of Suzy's first tooth.

Portland was a cultural and professional contrast. The Police Station was an old drab grey, concrete building, not far from the river and close to a busy rattling draw bridge. The only parking spaces available were labeled "Police cars" or "Detectives only." At first sight of the no parking signs I smiled at the recollection of when I use to park near the Cochise County Jail, and the sheriff would have the trustee prisoners wash my car. In Portland, my vehicle was equipped with a card to place on the dashboard imprinted "U.S. Govt." It had to be used discreetly to prevent getting the windshield smashed.

Inside the Police Department, to reach the detective floor, I had to walk up a well-worn staircase, whose walls smelled of age and were stained from the diverse hands of the city; officers, victims, witnesses and miscreants. Attaining the working level, I gazed through a thin mist of smoke, wafting over a sea of desk bound bodies, mostly men, dressed for business with neckties and shirt pocketed writing pens, engaged in a buzz of activity, telephoning, scribbling on note pads, researching through reports and files, talking, gesturing, escaping only to the crusted coffee pot, and fossilized water cooler.

I was greeted by a sternly pleasant receptionist whose primary duty seemed to be acting as a protective barrier for twenty or more well-armed plainclothesmen, and secondly was occupied taking messages for the absent masters of several vacant desks.

She sighed when she finally became aware of my presence, saying, "And what can I do for you?"

I told her, "My name is Schreuder, with the FBI and I would like to see detective Derrick."

"Do you have an appointment?"

"Yes, I called earlier."

Without looking up she said, "He's in Vice."

"Yes, thank you. I know that, but I'm new here. I have never met detective Derrick, and don't know exactly where to find the Vice squad."

She looked up from her desk and with tired disgust in her tone she asked, "Where they gitten all you new guys?"

I wasn't sure who "they" referred to, but was slightly relieved to know I wasn't the only new person to intrude into her cosmos. I smiled, but ignored her question, and said, "If you'll just point me in the right direction I might spot his name plaque on a desk."

She didn't return the smile, but said, "Second desk beyond the partition with the wanted posters."

I found Derrick. Before I could say anything, he looked in my direction and inquired, "You Schreuder?

I extended my hand, "Detective Derrick I assume."

"Yah, they call me Chip. What do you want?"

I instinctively knew that this was not a time to try to endear myself to anyone, and was aware that the sooner he got rid of me, the happier he would be. I also sensed that I could have been Little Red Ridinghood and would not have been treated any differently. We had a professional conversation and I departed with a nostalgic longing for days past. As I retreated down the historic old steps my evaluation was, "Well, that didn't go to well." Refusing to be dejected I commented to myself, "Well, at least I didn't fall down the damn staircase! I'll be back."

• • •

As the office radio dispatcher worked with the agents throughout the city, I listened closely in my own car. Whenever there was immediate attention needed, usually at a bank robbery, I made sure I was conveniently nearby and could help with the routine procedures. At a fast developing extortion, I was "Johnny on the spot" knowing how to wire and hook up the telephone recording equipment, and had it operating before the traditional radio technician arrived. I discreetly stayed out of their way, but made myself available for any level of detail they felt like casting to an underling. I figured a useful tool often applied would finally fit their hand.

It was mid-afternoon. I had just finished checking a vacant residence for about the 20th time, when the radio dispatcher broadcast, "Ninety-one New, at Western Savings and Loan" and gave the address. A Ninety-one, meant bank robbery. I was less than three minutes away from the bank so I responded.

I wasn't the first law enforcement person to arrive, but was the first FBI agent on the scene. The local Police usually got there first, and after the FBI arrived, we assumed jurisdiction. The uniformed police helped wherever needed initially and the case was later resolved by FBI agents and city detectives. By established procedure, the first Agent to arrive is in charge until one of the regular bank robbery Agents arrives to assume command. I knew the drill, and had done it alone in Arizona on many occasions. I separated and isolated the witnesses, requested the camera film be processed, obtained the FDIC insurance certificate and requested an audit of teller cash. As other agents arrived, I made several assignments until one of the regular robbery squad members arrived. Things were totally under control, and the new in charge person had little to do. I assigned myself to interview one of the witnesses, and when I finished, obtained an additional assignment to complete a portion of the "neighborhood investigation", which consisted of canvassing residents or businesses in the area in search of other witnesses, determining escape route and searching for external evidence.

I never ever looked upon this activity as work. Remember, I grew up sloshing irrigation boots through fields of mosquitoes, and stacking hay bales in hot weather. This was pure fun, and I was getting paid a whole lot more.

After completing my grid, with no significant results, I walked back in the direction of my car. I noticed a Bus Depot sign a couple of blocks away, in a direction that would place it just outside of the grid drawn up and assigned by the supervising agent. In my previous world, many derelicts traveled by bus and since I had not yet seen the place, I decided to veer off course and look it over.

The building was typically old, and sparsely occupied. After my visual assessment added to the discomfort of a few waiting travelers, I proceeded to examine one more important location...the men's room.

I entered the all tile room with the echo of my footsteps following like a shadow. I saw only one person present, but he was in a stall with only his legs showing. I shuffled my feet as if I had a usual mission at the appliance hanging on the wall. As I stood there and watched the feet in question, it became plain that they were not pointing in the appropriate direction. Whoever was attached to the feet seemed to be standing at the side of the bowl. Something wasn't right.

I flushed the urinal and walked to the door, flung it open so that it returned closing with a bang. With the occupant thinking I had departed, I quietly walked back and stood near enough to the stall to watch the feet. I watched a single pair of adult hands remove the shoes. Then a shirt dropped to the floor, the same color shirt that I was told the bank robber had worn. The shirt was followed by the rustling of a paper sack and another pair of pants appeared at the base of the stool on which the occupant now appeared to be sitting. Then oddly, the feet rose up off the tile floor, and the second pair of pants was put on over the original ones, that I now realized were also the same type reportedly worn by the bank robber. "Well now" I thought, "I believe I have found my bank robber."

Although I couldn't yet see him, the robber had been described as about 5 foot 10 inches, and threatened to have a gun in a paper sack. I made sure my own weapon was ready to quick draw, and waited. It was apparent that my new friend was completely changing his clothing, was folding the garments and putting them into a paper sack. That meant he would emerge from the stall with his hands occupied by the baggage he was carrying. It also meant if he had a gun, it might still be in the sack. That was good! I waited, with my heart ticking away the seconds.

Finally he emerged, and I scanned him completely within no more than five heartbeats. Comically, next to his chest, he was holding a paper sack with clothing protruding out of the top, revealing a roll of money in his front pocket so large that it resembled a half roll of toilet paper.

I drew my .357 magnum and shouted, "FBI, drop the bag, turn around and put your hands on the door." He paled and complied.

"Now get down on you knees and cross your legs behind you, so that your legs are crossed at your ankles." Without looking back he did as he was told.

"Now put your hands behind your head and lock your fingers together." Again he complied, and I thought "This guy has been arrested before."

I placed a handcuff on one hand with it behind him then cuffed them both behind him to complete the arrest. His only words were, "Where the @#$% did you come from?" I left him still kneeling while I checked the paper sack. There was no gun. I stood him up and searched him, leaving the money in his pocket. Still no gun, phew!

Now I had a new problem. I was at the bus depot, with no radio, (It was before the days of cell phones) and I was three blocks from my car, and three blocks from the bank. Some of the other agents probably still be at the bank, so I grasped my double clothed "suspect" by the rear mounted handcuffs and guided him out of the bus depot as if I were pushing a wheelbarrow, with one hand on his cuffed wrists and my other carrying the bag of clothing evidence. It was a great, but cautious feeling. Walking on the sidewalk, I felt as though I was an ambulance driver working my way through traffic with red light and siren. All who observed moved over to grant me ample right of way. As we walked, the wad of paper money began to work its way out the top of the bandit's pocket The problem was becoming serious because I did not want to touch the money before other agents witnessed the spectacle, and also because I wanted a witness to its counting.

I could not have been more fortunate. Just as I navigated the last street corner, pushing my human wheelbarrow I was greeted by several Agents and two police squad cars having a conference in front of the Bank. Like a sportsman being deprived of a great fish, my catch was taken off my line and placed into a squad car.

All that followed was routine. The suspect was identified by the victim bank tellers, was interviewed by Agents, and was booked into the city jail. I lingered, acting as if I had only pulled a weed from a garden, but was thinking happy thoughts, hopeful that I had slain my dragon.

Three days later, I was reassigned. My new desk was located in the Reactive Squad.

LIFE IN THE FAST LANE

Working on the Reactive Squad was an introduction to a different pace. The word reactive was appropriate. A day planner was useless, and instead, I operated from a "To Do" list and an appointment calendar. The reactive agents were expected to "react" immediately in most instances, often as a group, to crimes demanding a quick response. Interruptions to our planned days were frequent. Sometimes one day stretched into two or three without a break, other than a bite of fast food gobbled from a sack thrown in your direction by a co-worker. Our most frequent responses were to bank robberies, interstate fugitives, extortions, and kidnappings, interspersed with an occasional barricaded felon holding a hostage. I was even lucky enough to negotiate three airline hijackings, a feat not equaled by any other agent prior to my retirement, and to my knowledge, perhaps because airline hijackings are now very infrequent, no one has as of this date negotiated as many.

Pursuing bank robbers was exciting and fun for several years. Eventually they became so frequent that I, along with several of my associates, migrated to other duties. But I am getting ahead of the topic. Our solution rate averaged in the 80% range because usually the 20% unsolved were recent robberies that had not yet been fully investigated. In addition perpetrators often robbed several banks before they were caught, causing the solution rate to fluctuate significantly.

I make no pretense that we solved so many cases because we were "smart", but realistically we were highly successful because the robbers were so "stupid." We developed a system that I eventually built into a profile lesson and taught at local Police Academies. I will explain robbery profiling right after I demonstrate what I mean by unintelligent bank robbers.

To begin with, bank robbing is a very poor profession. Prevention and detection has greatly improved since Bonnie and Clyde. The proceeds are usually quite small, elaborate high tech security measures are employed in most banks, and employees are trained to increase their safety and minimize losses. Typically when the robber announces his intent, or provides a robbery note, the teller immediately activates a silent alarm notifying law enforcement, which at the same time turns on multiple cameras. The serial numbers of certain bills in the teller drawer are previously recorded, and in most instances an exploding device filled with red dye is hidden in the money. When the stolen money is stuffed into the thief's belt or pants, it makes a wonderful mess out of his pants, and when in a paper sack, it sometimes blows out the bottom of the sack. The average take of a lone robber is about $600. Couple all of that with needing to plan a discrete escape, and being basically mentally challenged, while high on narcotics and you will understand why investigating agents had an advantage.

Keep in mind that during the several years I worked bank violations, we averaged approximately 250 per year. That large number provides a wide variety of experiences.

I'll share a few examples of criminals not on America's list of geniuses.

• • •

I t rarely snowed in Portland, but on one of those rare mornings when two inches of wet snow covered the sidewalks, we received an alarm. A savings and loan on the south side had been robbed by two men at opening time. The victim employees described the robbers a young men, wearing blue jeans, tennis shoes, hooded sweat shirts and ski masks. They departed through the side door of the building. A quick check outside disclosed tennis shoe tracks leaving the building and continuing down the middle of the sidewalk. We followed the tracks three blocks to a run-down duplex apartment. The tracks led directly to the apartment on the left. We forcefully banged on the door, and a young male answered clothed only in his underwear. We entered to find another male in the second of two twin beds. The first claimed they were both sleeping and that we woke him from a long late sleep. However hanging on two chairs near the beds were two hooded sweat shirts. Incredibly, both pairs of pants were hanging over the backs of the chairs, wet half way to the knees, with water dripping from the pant cuffs. We found the ski masks in a bedside drawer.

• • •

A lady, perhaps I should more accurately describe her just as a female, lived alone in a small cottage near the town of

Clackamas. She was unusual in form, being approximately 5 ft. 1 in. in height and approximately 250 pounds in weight. She would wear out a ten year mirror in just a month. She reasoned living would be better if she had more money and assembled a bank robbery kit. Her tools consisted of a brown grocery sack large enough to cover her head, in which she cut two eye holes. With a cloth glove containing a stick lamely appearing to be a small pistol, and one more paper sack for money she proceed to the nearest branch of the U.S. Bank *in which she had an account.* She parked her own green station wagon near the door, put on the head cover and entered the bank.

Employees, who immediately recognized her unmistakable barrel form, greeted her saying, "Hi Bertha. What are you doing with that thing over your head?"

Bertha, unfazed replied, "This is a robbery. Give me all your money!"

The employees were shocked, but were trained to offer no resistance, and complied putting several hundred dollars into the bag. Bertha jumped into her station wagon bearing her own license plates and sped directly back to her home less than two miles away.

Within a few minutes we paid Bertha a visit. I drew the short straw and began the interview with Bertha. She denied everything including even being near the bank that day. We obtained a search warrant under "exigent circumstances" via the telephone, and searched Bertha's cottage. In Bertha's refrigerator she had an ample amount of "lettuce", much of it bound in rubber bands. Bertha was eventually judged to be of "sound mind", and in fact put up a strenuous argument insisting her innocence. She claimed she had no idea how all that money got into her refrigerator.

There are always a few stories out about how robbers doom themselves by writing demand notes on telltale pieces of paper. There were many incidents where that truly did happen. I have witnessed notes unintentionally left behind, written on deposit slips from the robber's check book; notes on personal pads containing phone numbers, on the back of business cards, even on the back of personal checks. There have been cases where the thief has stuffed money into his pocket and dropped his wallet running from the bank. Others less fortunate have threatened bank employees with a gun, and accidently shot themselves. One shot himself in the foot while sticking the gun into his coat, and another shot himself in the groin while running from the bank. Another shot his getaway driver in the leg attempting a speedy departure.

Of course there were many others who had different approaches. One variance was to facilitate a better escape by not entering the bank; instead robbing the drive in teller. This was often performed by using a note, and by using their own car with the license plate covered. Well-equipped banks still had a camera system that provided images of the robber and his vehicle. Most banks were also equipped with bullet proof glass between the outside automobiles and the teller. Tellers were also trained to retain any demand notes that were passed through the drive in window. They were also trained to give the robber a small amount of money including the dye pack and recorded bills so they would leave without incident.

Incidents of amazing stupidity were frequent, and I must also include occasional lack of reasoning on the behalf of the victim teller. There were incidents when a robber drove up to the teller window and announced that he had a bomb, and threatened to explode it unless he was given money. The response varied from the employee cleaning out the teller drawer and passing the contents to the robber, without getting a description of the robber or the car; to the teller reading a note threatening a bomb and replying, "Well blow it out your ass", and stepping back from the window to call the police.

Many "would be" bombs amounted to 3 or 4 road flares taped together with black electric tape. One of the most famous notes ever written in Portland was given to a drive in teller. In the interest of decency I won't spell out the obscene words other than to say the robber couldn't even spell the four letter "F word". He made a three letter word by leaving out the letter C. The note which he passed through the drive up window read, "This is a *robry*. I have a *bom*. *Gimmy* all the *f—n* money. Don't call the *f–n* cops or the *bom* will self *detatinate* itself." (I italicized the misspelled words.) The note became a teaching tool that I used for several years during bank teller training to demonstrate the mentality of many robbers. One must wonder how this would be gangster was going to protect himself in the car with the self-detonating bomb.

The lone wolf bandits were what I profiled as the first category of robbers. The second was more sophisticated, employing a driver-lookout-partner. The driver could be female or male, and the car was either stolen, or often without license plates. Occasionally they were careless and used their own car, thinking that if they parked a block away no one would notice it. However it is hard not to notice someone running from a bank, carrying a bag, or a gun, and wearing a mask or some type of head gear. The same car was often used, and many cases were solved through the car. Being the getaway driver was not always a good occupation either. One pair of "buddies" robbed their third bank in Beaverton Oregon. The inside man got a little greedy and took time to demand money from two tellers. He departed out the front door and jumped into the waiting car driven by his partner. However a County Deputy Sheriff arrived just as the two were spinning away and nearly ran over the Deputy, who fired off a shot directly toward the driver through the windshield of the car. The car sped away, but we believed the driver was hit. We had a good description of the getaway car and it became the object of a city wide alert. Two days later we found the car on the 3rd floor parking garage of the St. Vincent Hospital. The driver was dead at the wheel, right where his buddy left him. It's true, there is little honor among thieves.

The third category was the gangs. Criminals who had been in prison came out schooled in the professional methods of bank robbery. They participated in bank "take overs" They operated with big fancy guns, sawed off shot guns, ski masks or Halloween masks and were a serious danger. They often went into a large bank, put customers on the floor, demanded money from all tellers, and verbally abused everyone. The worst situation was when they progressed with their "macho" confidence and began competing with each other to demonstrate who could be the most fearsome. Each robbery became more violent with shots fired through the ceiling and victims being pushed around or assaulted. Combined with many of them being drug addicts, category three robberies were a priority for the squad.

Fortunately, the gang robberies were often the easiest to solve. They spent more time in the banks. There were plenty of photos of them in action. The participants usually had a prison record. Most were on parole or at one time had a parole officer. Many were also known to local police officers, or prison guards. We quickly made the associations, identified their girlfriends and associates on the periphery who would rather co-operate with us than go to jail because of their temporary friends. It was always exciting "taking down" a gang of bank robbers. Whenever we could, we would try to locate them, and at a time when they were separated, make the arrests, all at about the same time. This prevented any of the group from getting the word of our raid, and escaping. It didn't always work, and that just made for more excitement through the thrill of the chase.

My working partners and I were written into the records of the U.S. Supreme Court, concerning one particular gang robbery. In the court record US v. Donald Gene Booth, United States Court of Appeals, Ninth Circuit, submitted April 15, 1981, a procedure used in the on scene identification of a robber was questioned and decided in our favor. Other legal procedures were at issue and the court argument comprises ten pages but since it was a personal victory for me, (and of course because I was specifically mentioned in the write up) I will enjoy summarizing it here.

The robbery was conducted by gang members, all friends released from prison. The bank they chose was a large one, in which I and the bank security officer had provided extensive training to the employees. During the robbery the gang forced all employees to lay face down on the floor, discouraging them from observing the action. Thereafter they vaulted the counters, looted the cash drawers and threatened employees and customers alike.

However the tellers were observant and provided good descriptions of three of the felons. One teller had a particular ability to notice and remember in minute detail. While lying with her face pressed against the marble floor she could only see the robbers from about the waist down. One of them walked within a few inches of her head. She later described him as wearing black penny loafers, worn grey at the toes, with dirty white socks, and checkered polyester pants. The checked material in the pants was small 1/8 inch checks, tan, grey and blue, and on his right thigh about midway between the knee and his pocket, he had a small three cornered tear. She went on to describe his voice and various features of the others, all wearing ski masks, brandishing guns, but her detail was impressive and specific. Other witnesses added a few more details such as height, weight and a Hawaiian shirt. A fourth man drove the getaway car. A description was broadcast to all uniformed patrols.

Less than an hour later a Portland Police Officer (Mitcham) observed a person later identified as Donald Gene Booth walking on the sidewalk, 3 ½ miles from the bank. Booth appeared to answer the description of the robber and after Mitcham requested a rebroadcast of the description he stopped to talk with him. Mitcham, a motorcycle officer immediately saw the details noted in the description, down to the small tear in the polyester pants. He told Booth to put his hands over his head, and patted down Booth looking for weapons. He questioned Booth, who said he was carrying no identification, and that he lived in Salem, Oregon, but was in Portland visiting friends. Booth admitted being on Parole from prison as a result of burglary convictions. Mitcham cuffed Booth, called for a patrol car, and had Booth transported back to the bank.

Prior to the return of Booth to the bank, as routine procedure we had witnesses fill out questionnaires which were description cards of the robbers.

From there I will quote from the court record. "FBI agent Schreuder told the witnesses that a 'suspect' who was not necessarily involved in the robbery would be brought in for identification. He also told the witnesses that the person would be handcuffed, but that they were not to infer that he had done anything wrong. Schreuder explained that the handcuffs were standard procedure for the protection of the officer, the suspect, and the witnesses. He instructed the witnesses to decide whether they had seen him on their own, without conferring with anyone else, and not to discuss anything among themselves until they had filled out their comments (in writing.)"

Further quoting the court record, "Booth, with his hands handcuffed behind his back, was then taken before the group of witnesses who viewed him for approximately one minute and then recorded their observations. The witnesses were subsequently interviewed regarding their recorded observations. After some of the witnesses identified Booth as one of the robbers, he was taken into a bank conference room where he was formally arrested and advised of his Miranda rights." The defense and a lower court argued that the identification by the witnesses should be suppressed because it was "so impermissibly suggestive as to give rise to very substantial likelihood of irreparable misidentification." However the US Supreme Court decided in favor of our action saying that the lower court applied the wrong standard in judging the activity. Referring to the identification by the three witnesses the high court wrote, "The district judge appears to have based his conclusion that the show-up procedure was inherently suggestive....(however)...we conclude that the district judge applied the wrong standard to assess the reliability of each witness's identification. The test is not whether there is a likelihood of

misidentification and whether the overall factors will result in an appropriate or fair identification. Rather, the district judge should determine whether in the totality of circumstance the 'procedure was so impermissibly suggestive as to give rise to a very substantial likelihood of irreparable misidentification'."
"Therefore, we remand to the district court for application of the appropriate standard."

I'm sorry to bother you with all that legal dialogue, but in short the US Supreme court said "Hey Schreuder, you got it right, even if you were figuring out the rules as you proceeded." It was a proud moment for all of us, because that method of on scene identification became the standard and guideline by which law enforcement now operates.

Now that we have seen the legal mumbo jumbo of the case, there remains a good side story. I recently spoke with Bob who gave his permission for me to tell it in detail.

The real workers on the bank robbery gang in question were Bob and Stan. They had put in many hours, identifying the suspects, surveilling them, and building a case sufficient to obtain a search warrant for a store (front) and associated residences. Prior to this robbery, Bob and Stan had carefully surveilled this gang of dangerous past jail birds for two days....a Monday and Tuesday. Their intent was to continue the surveillance until they observed them rob another bank. Knowing the gang was overdue for another robbery, both agents put in long hours gathering their facts, and the anticipation was growing intense.

There was one problem. On Wednesday (following the two days in a row of surveillance), Bob had a special court appearance. He was getting a divorce, and was required to report to court for the final decision. It was to be the end of a traumatic experience, and one which he wanted to put behind him. Bob told Stan that he had to take Wednesday off for court and Stan agreed, stating they would resume activities on Thursday.

However it was Wednesday, shortly after 10:00 AM that the gang robbed the above mentioned bank. Bob was in his Bureau car and heard the radio traffic. From the description and methods he knew it was "his gang of robbers" that made the hit. Bob and Stan both responded to the bank, but also intended to "Bust" them at the store front. At shortly after 11:00 AM Bob was in his protective vest, weapon strapped to his side, and prepared to assault the gang's headquarters. But events were delayed and the warrant wasn't issued by 12:00. Bob had to be in court by 1:00 PM, no excuses or his former spouse "would get the farm."

At the last moment Bob jumped in his car and sped to the Courthouse in Portland, blue emergency lights flashing. He couldn't find a parking spot near the entrance, and he didn't have time to drive around looking for one. He double parked the office car, with the blue light still flashing, and dashed into the building. Back then all of the problems in federal buildings had not yet occurred, and it was acceptable for law enforcement personnel to enter armed. Bob charged up the stairway and into the court room only slightly late, still wearing his bullet proof vest and wearing his .38 special.

The judge looked at him, reacted with a startled re-take look and said, "My understanding was that this was to be a friendly and civil proceeding."

Bob said, "Yeah it will be, but I gotta hurry."

The judge responded in words to the effect, "Well in your condition, we wouldn't want to keep your waiting. Let's get on with it."

According to Bob, it was one of the fastest court sessions he had attended.

• • •

On a bright sunny day in Gresham Oregon, on the outskirts of Portland, we assembled in a grocery store parking lot. We had located a pair of men who had robbed several banks in the area, and they had a reputation for violence. We decided not to surveille them for long because they were very cautious and their paranoia caused them to move often. We decided an early morning arrest at their rental house was best to get them back in jail as soon as possible. Because of the risk involved in forced entry of armed criminals, we notified the local police who met with us at the parking lot briefing.

The plan was to have a show of force which would overwhelm them into surrendering. We planned to completely surround the house. Marked Sheriff and City cars would park in the street in front of the house. Other officers would be in the back of the building on foot. When all were in place, a supervisor back in the Portland FBI office would telephone the residence, tell the suspects they were surrounded, and to come out the front door with their hands in the air. When everyone was clear about their assignment we proceeded to the rental house located on the corner intersection of two residential streets. My friend Paul was the swat team commander wearing his black swat uniform, but for some reason was wearing an unusually bright yellow hat. He took a position directly in front of the house with a clear view of the front step where the robber was going to be directed to appear. Paul and other officers were crouched behind their cars, heads and guns slightly above the engine hoods.

Because I was usually the number one performer in the physical fitness test runs, I was routinely assigned to cover the rear of the house in case anyone bolted and ran out the back door. I had several catches to my credit.

The radio signal was given, the telephone call was made. "This is the FBI; we have your house surrounded. Come out the front door with your hands over your head. Exit one person immediately behind the other. Leave the phone off the hook."

I waited at the edge of the yard, crouched beside a rhododendron bush. From out in the street on the other side of the building I heard, "Keep your hands up." Then it sounded like World War III broke out. Several shots were fired, and I could see what appeared to be someone in the house moving the curtains of the back windows. I was ready for someone to jump out one of the back windows when I realized the curtain movement was caused by bullets going through the house and striking the back walls. A few were exiting over my head.

"Crap", one of those could hit me." I had no idea what might come out the back door, but I wasn't going to stand up to greet it. I got down into the roots of the rhododendron and waited, and waited.

The action out front that I couldn't see occurred when the robber came out of the house. He stood on the step with his hands together over his head, but he had a small concealed pistol in his hands. On seeing Paul's yellow hat, he lowered the pistol and began firing at the yellow marker and the protective cars. Every officer ducked initially, and then began firing in return. The brief hesitation allowed the robber to spin around and rush back through the front door, but not before several bullets hit his legs. He crawled back into the house and reached for the phone. He cried to the supervisor, "Your guys just shot the shit out of me. What do I do now?"

The reply he received was, "Well, I am going to tell you one more time, and try to get it right."

Both were taken into custody without further incident. However 23 shots had been fired into the house, neighbors were upset, and being the crisis interventionist and public relations officer, I had to calm down all of the complainers. It was just another thing I didn't have entered on my daily planner. When we critiqued the operation, I told my friend Paul that if he ever wore that damn yellow hat again he may get hit by friendly fire.

• • •

Although ordinary robberies became routine, we had to be constantly alert for surprises. What kind of surprises? Little things that just don't seem to fit in the usual manner, for example on rare occasions, a teller may have been in on the robbery scheme. On more than one occasion, a "cute" innocent looking teller fed inside information to a boyfriend who then robbed her. On these occasions the boyfriend usually cleaned out the entire upper and lower cash drawers, leaving us to conclude that he was an ex-con or (would you believe) a boyfriend. A few additional hints were dropped in our direction when neither the marked money nor dye pack was given out, thus the alarms weren't activated. We were led to believe that the poor victim teller was so emotionally traumatized she forgot her robbery protocol.

One type of robbery that always cleared the squad room was hostage taking. Sometimes the "big boys" who had been educated in the nation's progressive prisons adapted styles more upscale than their competition. Their thinking was that if they took a bank employee with them during their exit from the bank (the escape) they would be better assured of fewer immediate alarms and would also avoid a hot pursuit. Generally they were wrong because the well trained bank personnel were quick to set off alarms before they were even aware that someone was going to be taken hostage. None the less, the convicts would single out a bank manager or one of the more attractive ladies, and at gunpoint force them into the getaway car. It was our policy, as well as that of uniformed police, to never pursue a car containing a hostage, so they were correct in that assumption, however the hunt thereafter was certainly more intense. In all of the situations within my experience, the employees were always freed relatively unharmed, other than their emotional state.

• • •

Schemes against banks were endless. They were where the money was, and someone was always attempting to get into it. A memorable attempt began with a phone call from a young man associated with two friends developing bad plans. They intended to capture a banker's wife and child, and demand $150,000 for their safe return. Once again the squad room was vacated.

The intended victim was a bank manager of a National Bank in a neighboring town within the megalopolis of Portland. The informant and two others planned to kidnap the banker's family, (wife and child), and keep them mobile in a van, until their demands were met. Prior to capturing the mother and child, they planned to put a demand note in a phone booth next to the bank. They would then call the Banker advising him to go to the phone booth for important information. The note in the booth told him to get $150,000 and take it to his car, where there would be additional instructions.

I saved a copy of the note that was put into the phone booth and used it for several years as a teaching tool in police academy classes. Except for redacting the Bankers name and the phone numbers, the original note was as it appears on the following page.

Bank 357-

Phone
Booth   357-_____

Mr._____

We've Got your wife and
Kid. Listen.
Do what They Say

ok no mistakes or you will
never see your Wife again

We want 150 Thousand dollars
in small unmarked, Used Bills.
Don't Try alarm any one you are
Being Watched Take money to
your car There Will Be Written
inst on Were to take it to

This note was found in the phone booth outside of the
bank.

Conspiracy cases are difficult to prove. We had to allow the
perpetrators to actively begin their planned act. The banker
and his family were informed of the planned crime. With his

permission we allowed the group to continue their action, with the informant co-operating within the group. He was equipped with the ability to communicate with our on the scene command post. However the group leader cleverly did not share all of his plans with his associates. We were unable to assure that no one was watching the house or family. We didn't know for sure how many "bad guys" were participating in the extortion. Any unusual alteration of the family's daily routine risked a change of plans by the bad guys, and exposed the family to new and dangerous risks. We had to allow the family to remain at home, but provided protection.

The banker went to work as usual. Agents were secreted within the bank as well as at strategic locations to view the perimeter. At first light of day, I and two other agents entered the home with the mother and child. A female agent was to take the pair into the basement which was accessible only from one stairway leading to the kitchen. There they would be protected from any gunfire from within or without the house. I and the other agent, John, remained upstairs behind locked doors waiting and watching. But because of the house location, it was a single unit in clear view from all directions; no backup agents could be placed closer than a full city block away. In the house….we were it.

Knowing that even the most ambitious criminals often rise at the crack of noon, we waited, paced, and waited. At about 11:00 AM my radio crackled with the "Go" signal. The words were, "The friend says the note has been delivered, one remains in the van, three more are heading in your direction." I will never forget the words of the mother. With an unexpected benignant smile and simulated gleeful voice, she shouted, "Whoopee we're ready to play for real." With outward confidence she grabbed her child and rushed down into the basement. Our female agent with less than two years of experience rolled her eyes out loud, turned pale and followed close behind.

Within just seconds I saw three agile guys in ski masks skulking along the side of the house toward the front door. Our plan was to enclose them in the house entry step area, but at the very least get on two sides of them, allowing our backup to arrive from the third side. Personnel on the sides, if necessary, were to direct fire toward the house entry to avoid being injured in a friendly cross fire. The house would provide a barrier to the 4th direction.

As soon as the front doorbell rang I drew my magnum and sped out the back door with an infusion of adrenalin roaring through my veins. John was close behind. I ran around the house toward the front door, but ran beyond the corner of the building, allowing me to get at the back side of the culprits at the front door. It worked, and by catching them by surprise I had them pinned to the house. John was drawing down on them from the side, but backup was not yet near. There were still three of them, we knew at least one had a revolver.

John was to my left. I was closest to the kidnappers, face to face. "FBI, get your hands in the air and Freeze!" Crap, with the ski masks, I couldn't tell which one was the good guy informant. I thought, "Just shoot the first one that pulls a gun." All but one raised their hands. The informant pulled up his mask. The one wearing blue coveralls still had his hand in his front pocket. I could clearly see the outline of a gun in his pocket. The hand was slowly edging upward, and the gun was moving with it.

"Let go of the gun or you're dead." He stopped his movement, but just looked at me. I tightened my grip on the magnum being held dead center in my best shooting position. My gun was out where I could see the tension in my hand causing the hammer to begin moving back near the firing position. He started to draw his gun from the coveralls again, and I yelled, "Don't do it!" He stopped as if trying to decide what to do. Good Heavens, I could see his eyes and he looked so young; I did NOT want to shoot him. "Open your hand and take it slowly from your pocket." I saw his chest shake, and then exhale as the elbow relaxed. The hand came slowly out of the pocket and met the second one at the top of his head. Just then all sorts of back up arrived from the open side of the lot. The rest was routine.

At the after incident critique the agents who interviewed the gunman group leader, said he admitted considering pulling out the gun and shooting himself in the head. During the evaluation it was considered that I might have been putting myself and the others in danger by not firing my weapon when he began to draw his from his coveralls. I countered with my shooting record which demonstrated I could accurately fire sooner than he could draw. I concluded with conviction that if he had attempted to destroy himself, I would have fired before he was able to raise his gun. No further criticism was directed at me; however the reward came a few weeks later.

The informant of course went free. Two of the other subjects plead guilty claiming that the leader planned and directed the entire operation. A trial was held for the young leader, age 19, after which he was found guilty. I testified concerning his actions outside the house, and described the incident much the same as I wrote it above. After the trial, the boy's mother came to me with tears running down her face. She thanked me. Usually mothers are quite angry, and I was a bit unnerved by her attitude. Then she explained, "I thank you for not killing my son. I know he did an awful thing, but you spared him, and I will be forever grateful." I spoke to her with all the kindness I could produce, and departed deeply impressed. I resolved to keep this day diligently in my remembrance. No mother wants to view bullet holes in her son.

WITH NO REGARD

At his best, man is the noblest of all animals;
separated from law and justice he is the worst.

ARISTOTLE.

I mentioned that some crimes cleared out the entire squad, meaning that all agents assigned to that group assembled and worked as a team on just the one case until the initial work began to show some resolution. Extremely serious investigations cleared out the entire office.

Few investigations received that kind of attention. One type always did. When a kidnapping occurred, an emergency briefing was held and every agent, clerk, stenographer, radioman and mechanic made themselves available and participated to the fullest extent of their ability. It was an expression of individual pride, a reflection of their loyalty, a statement of their integrity, a demonstration of their bravery, an outpouring of their unselfishness, their compassion, and an event from which no one even considered not being a participant. Hours worked were only limited by physical exhaustion. Personal hygiene, appearance and nutrition were overlooked until the crisis slowed. Family and friends were put aside for hours or days until the creators of the immediate social cancer were identified, neutralized, or swept to the dustbin of history. These were the times when I was most proud, and variously the most saddened.

The professional indoctrination at the FBI academy included a detailed sermon concerning the pitfalls of becoming personally or emotionally involved in an investigation. We were admonished to remain efficient by always being professional, unbiased and detached from the personal trauma experienced by the civilian population; to be attentive to our obligation to duty and un-phased by feelings and sensibility. It was a professional rule, with merit, because transgressions were contagious. Never deliberate, but any breakdown was immediately felt by associates and only increased the shared burdens. Insensitivity was a requirement, but if it would have been a moral law, we in private were all sinners, walking through hell. All who walked with me could not deny they too felt the pain.

My first passage into this abhorrence began in Tucson on May 29th, 1973. I began my assignment in Tucson, in February 1971, and by 1973 was established and bonded with my FBI co-workers. One senior agent, Jim, a man of good humor and extensive experience had recently become a grandfather. His daughter, Lisa whose husband was serving overseas in the Air Force, had been temporarily residing with her father, for the purpose of having the baby in America, and in a competent Tucson hospital. During that short period, she became known to all of us, and had personally graced my family by serving as a baby sitter on occasion. The joy of the new child was shared by all of our close knit Tucson organization.

May 29th, 1973, was the day of the happily anticipated arrival of Lisa's husband. He was to arrive on a commercial flight from the South Pacific. In the late afternoon Lisa drove to the Tucson Airport, parked her car in the Airport lot, and was never seen alive again.

A search was initiated immediately that night. Circumstances were convincing that she had been abducted from the airport, but with little evidence from which to direct the investigation. The search and investigation consumed our lives for the entire summer. The husband was never a suspect and was quite distraught. Her father was inconsolable. She was found in September at Fort Huachuca, 90 miles from Tucson, by a hiking soldier. He was traversing a desert dry creek (wash) and first only saw her blond hair. But under the hair was a skull, and then more.

I and the rest of our FBI family exhumed the body. I was tasked with helping perform the autopsy, taking photographs and preserving evidence. I salvaged her wedding rings from the residue and gave them to her father and husband, confirming her identification. Don't get personally involved the FBI Academy said. But they didn't tell me about this part.

The investigation remained open for years, long after I was reassigned to Portland. The investigative file consists of thousands of pages detailing the effort. The un-fatigable persistence of Larry Bagley kept the investigation alive until the killer was finally arrested and a jury found him guilty. I testified at the trial during the summer of 2013, forty years from the date she disappeared, and twenty years after I retired. Her father, Jim, a friend of us all, died several years earlier, still searching for the killer. In May 1973, I began my career of so called "Noninvolvement."

• • •

I n Portland, Tommy, a nine year old boy picked up his school books, said goodbye to his mother, and skipped out the back door, across the yard and into the alley. His school was only about four blocks from the house. It was a simple and pleasant walk, down the alley, a "short cut" along a little drainage ditch, through a small field and onto the school play-ground. They lived in a middle class neighborhood, although his father owned more than one hundred rental residences and apartments. He and his parents, along with his other brothers led a low key life in a normal neighborhood.

School started at 7:45 AM. Tommy's mother received a call from the school administrative office at approximately 8:50. It was early morning and she was still at home to take the call.

"Hello Mrs. Rockman, this is Alice from the school admin office. I am calling to verify that Tommy is ill and to confirm an excused absence."

"What? No, are you sure he is not in school? He left more than an hour ago."

"No Mrs. Rockman, I don't think he is here today, but I will check again with his teacher and the class to see if anyone has seen him this morning."

A few minutes later the school confirmed that Tommy was missing.

Mrs. Rockman called the police, and the school confirmed the absence. Twenty minutes later, Mrs. Rockman received another phone call.

"Mrs. Rockman....Mary, we have your son Tommy. Listen to what I say, and do as you are told, and he will be OK. Get two hundred thousand (dollars) in unmarked small bills. Have it by tonight. Don't call the cops or you won't see Tommy again. We will call you with instructions later. When I call, you answer the phone. I won't deal with anyone else."

Mary called her husband who was just arriving in San Francisco for a business meeting. Since she had already called the Police, they agreed to immediately inform the police of the call. The Portland Detective Bureau followed with a call to our reactive squad.

We sent two detectives dressed in City Water Department coveralls into the alley to search the route Tommy walked to school. Half way to the school, on the ditch bank of the short-cut, they found his books, scattered as if he dropped them in a struggle. Kidnappings were rare, but this was obviously real.

During the past couple of years I had established myself on the reactive squad and by that time was on a first name basis with most of the Detectives in the Portland Police Bureau. As a group they were confident, efficient, brave and a pleasure to work with. Most FBI agents avoided the tension of working closely with the victims in trauma cases, and would rather be "on the outside" actively cornering the perpetrators. The inside assignments also usually involved some technical work setting up recording equipment on telephones along with planning and preparing the ransom delivery method. I volunteered for the inside job on a couple of occasions, and thereafter was the "default" inside man.

I met Portland Police Detective "Bud" at a "friendly" service station where we had our cars serviced and where we trusted the proprietor. Mrs. Rockman had been directed to drive her car to the station and appear as if she needed something repaired. The station attendant put the car into the stall and closed the garage door. After introductions and a few minutes lapsed (appearing to fix the car), Bud and I climbed into the trunk. Yes, it was crowded, but car trunks were bigger back in the 80's. The purpose was to get ourselves and our equipment into the Rockman's house without being seen by anyone. We did not know if the kidnappers would be watching the residence, or have the ability to look into her car at some point on the route back to her home. Months later, reminiscing at a tavern, Bud and I laughed at that ride, but there was no humor that morning.

Mrs. Rockman drove the car into her home garage and closed the door. We unfolded ourselves from the trunk, and began our work. The first task for me was to wire a recorder into the house phone line. It was accomplished so that the recorder started automatically as soon as the phone rang. I also installed a cutoff switch to prevent recording innocent friendly calls. In case of failure or a glitch, a backup system was installed, but out of reach of the primary recorder to avoid confusion. As soon as the recording equipment was working I began preparing Mrs. Rockman for the anticipated call; a real life application for all that crisis training. Sensitivity and understanding was required to prepare a mother to talk with the potential killer of her son. She had to have confidence in me, Bud, and herself. She had to know what to say, how to say it, and how to think on her feet if the caller departed from the expected scenario. I would be listening in on the conversation, but her answers had to sound sincere and the delivery had to appear un-coached. I prepared flash cards to guide the conversation in case she panicked and needed prompting. It was still only late morning and we didn't expect the call until early evening. A long day was ahead. We had to keep her strong and confident.

After a couple of early rehearsals with Mrs. Rockman, I began preparing her car for the ransom delivery. We assumed either she or her husband, (he was flying back from San Francisco with the money) would be told to deliver the cash to some directed location. They would probably be told to use their own car. It would likely be dark at the time of delivery. We needed to be able to follow the car at night. That meant it had to be visually identifiable from both the ground and from our surveillance aircraft. For backup to the visual observation I would place a radio locator beeper on the car's frame. The doors had to be modified so that the interior light did not illuminate when they were opened because we intended for at least one officer to accompany the driver for protection, and surreptitiously exit the car at the ransom delivery site.

In my tool kit I had a roll of duct tape. (Never be without it.) I taped the door switch buttons into their closed positions. I also put tape over the headliner light lens. With a small screwdriver I punched a hole in the top of the left tail light. That allowed a small white light to shine upward from the rear of the car, making it distinct and easily visible from the aircraft. We put a dark colored blanket on the floor of the rear seat to cover the secluded passenger. I installed and tested the locator beacon transmitter. During all of this preparation my police partner Bud was busy questioning Mrs. Rockman concerning possible suspects, recent activity, getting photographs and developing any information to give us a lead on who would know the family well enough to plan this type of crime. A radio communication network was established with the outside to coordinate all activities. Arrangements were made so that a UPS truck with a uniformed driver stopped at the house to make a fake, empty box delivery, and pick up photos and other information concerning Tommy.

Outside activity was also briskly becoming organized, so that discrete surveillance of the residence was established. Mr. Rockman was located in San Francisco and his return to Portland was expedited. It was his choice whether he would use real money in the ransom payment, although we recommended that real twenty dollar bills be used with known sequential serial numbers. He followed the recommendation, and the correct amount of money was placed in a specially crafted brief case that was also equipped with a locator transmitter.

By mid-afternoon all systems were "go". Then it was time to wait. It's during that down time, the long wait, that one begins to question the plan with all the "what ifs." Mr. Rockman was intentionally made very visible during his arrival back to the house. He laboriously carried the prepared brief case of money in through the front door, advertising to any observing conspirator that the family was cooperating.

Of course Bud and I were quite aware of the possibility that the kidnappers might plan to storm the house and steal the money without calling beforehand. They could just visit the house and demand that the money be taken out to them. Or, they could have some bizarre plan or demands to put additional family members in danger. We had to be ready….for the unexpected.

Our armed backup coworkers were secreted in nearby buildings and friendly neighborhood houses. Surveillance agents were picketed throughout the area. (The word picket refers to a surveillance that is extended around an area or along a street similar to a picket fence of sharp sticks. The human fence of secluded law enforcement observers provides a continuous surveillance without the observers having to change their location.)

Tommy's older brothers were removed from school and placed under protection at a private location. They were questioned concerning any activity that could be related to the kidnapping. The aircraft, our pilot and observer were put on standby at the airport. Clearance from the air traffic controller was obtained in advance for our air coverage at low levels anywhere within the metropolitan area. Telephone company officials were alerted to attempt to trace any calls to the Rockman residence, however in the 1980's the technique was very difficult unless the call was several minutes in duration. There were no cell phones at that time, and to trace a call, telephone employees had to be posted within the large buildings that housed thousands of wires and switches. Messages were prepared so that every working law enforcement officer in the city, county and state systems was aware of the active kidnap situation, with orders to keep the progressing activity secret.

A major concern with life threatening hostage or kidnapping crimes is that in the initial stages the kidnappers not know that police are aware and working the crime. Knowledge of police involvement greatly increases the danger to the victim, especially if the kidnappers panic and feel the need to dispose of the victim and all evidence. Radio communications were kept to a minimum using coded language, and extended conversations were confined to telephones.

A special team was assembled to be immediately dispatched to the location of the proposed money exchange, but with the need to remain secreted. It was paramount to remain unexposed until after Tommy was released. And of course aggressive activity was planned if he was not released as promised.

Mrs. Rockman was an intelligent lady, in her early 40's. She was an experienced mother and active in the community, small in stature, attractive and well liked. But in this situation, she was terrified. According to the original instructions, the burden of entering the night, to an unknown place and delivering two hundred thousand in cash to people who captured her son rested on her shoulders. She needed help, but our participation had to be discrete and thus limited. We could risk putting a police woman in the car impersonating her as the mother, but only if it was dark. Additional risk would come from the possibility the kidnapper would cause a face to face confrontation. Even worse, if the delivery was not face to face, she would have to exit the car and probably be observed by the suspects. We prepared with several plans, but some of these decisions would be made at the last moment, depending on the instructions of the kidnappers and the strength of Mrs. Rockman. The prompting flash cards that were prepared for the phone call were kept simple. We tried to anticipate any condition that might be a stumbling block. The cards consisted of "Yes", "No", "Why", "When", "How", and a couple of phrases to convince the caller she was acting alone without the police, such as "Please don't harm Tommy", and "How do I know that Tommy is safe." I also had a pad on which to quickly write other prompts if necessary. Probabilities were that the conversation would be very direct and brief.

I was running out of things to worry about when I realized that it was only midafternoon with the probability of a long night ahead. It was time for both Bud and me to rest our bodies if at all possible, with adrenaline surges disrupting normal functions. It was a mild spring day, but we had all curtains and blinds closed. I opened the living room window allowing a fresh breeze to wash our pensive minds. It was quiet, and I felt the anxiety in the house growing with each passing minute, growing until it was not only visible on all occupants, but growing until it began restricting normality, like a huge beast in the room. Nothing within our reach was normal. I knew I must find a cure.

"Mrs. Rockman, do you have any peanut butter?" I asked.

"What?"

"I said, do you have any peanut butter. My coffee and roll of early this morning has long departed, and I thought if you had something like peanut butter, I could make a quick sandwich."

She returned to me from where she was in thought and humbly replied, "Oh, of course, let me make you a sandwich."

"No, I can make it, but on second thought, why don't we make two, I think you could benefit from something to eat. Bud, how about you, maybe she also has some milk." I knew Bud would catch on to my purpose and demand something to occupy her attention."

Bud looked at me as if to say, "Milk, what the hell makes you think I would like milk in the middle of the afternoon?" He politely accepted a glass of water and a couple of cookies.

The activity filled two needs. I truly was hungry, but more importantly guided us into a more relaxed conversation.

Tension was not quite as elevated as I returned to the couch next to the window. The mild breeze was blowing the thick drapery past the edge of the couch to where it was touching my leg. As I leaned back into the couch, with one hand I held the peanut butter sandwich; with the other I checked the readiness of my .357 revolver for the one hundredth time that day. After two bites of the peanut butter I underwent a mental change and was ready for anything.

Fromp! Yeowell, Pfssst, "Jesus what the hell is that?"

The family cat jumped from the outside, through the window into the house. It landed in the drapery and got tangled up in the cloth and my pant leg. Unable to see the monster among us, I instinctively reach for my gun, but with the sandwich in one hand, the gun hand was also needed to repel whatever was scratching the skin off my leg. Bud, a six foot 200 pounder, leaped for the bottom of the air filled drapery to tackle the monster but grasped only the breeze as the cat squirted behind the couch and spun his way into the kitchen. It was funny then, it's funny now. I don't know what I could have done to bind us together as a team, better than the efforts of that cat.

It had been decided that Mrs. Rockman would drive her car, (she said she wanted to), and that either Bud or I would hide on the floor of the back seat. If it was in any manner possible, the passenger would exit the back door as Mrs. Rockman stopped the car wherever she was directed to deliver the money. Bud and I had not yet discussed who would be the passenger because we knew each had the same thoughts and intentions. I believed and thought I should be the passenger, and he thought he should. I knew the matter should be settled before the last minute.

"Bud, I saw a dark colored jacket in the hall closet. I'm going to wear that when Mary and I take out the money."

"Forget the jacket Schreuder. You won't need it. I'll go in the back seat, and I have a jacket of my own." "Hey friend, I know that we are in this together, but there is only room for one of us on this trip, and I'm just a little smaller and quicker than you, and we will be on the FBI radio frequency, so I should go."

"What the hell has radio frequency got to do with it, we have plenty of radios to go around, and I plan on grabbing some freak, not running away from him, that's why I'm going."

"OK Bud, I didn't want to bring this up, and I'm not trying to pull rank, but the FBI has primary jurisdiction in this case, and that means I should be in the back seat."

"Well now, since you bring up rank, I'll tell you what's really on my mind. I'm up for promotion next month. It will be tough because there are more detectives applying for sergeant than they have positions for. If I take a prominent role in this case, which will receive national recognition; I will have a much better chance of getting bumped up. Dory, I need this chance."

" OK Bud, is your jacket dark enough to conceal you at night?"

It was settled. He cleverly delivered a low blow, but he had me cornered. Bud was inexorably certain he could perform the feat of providing security for Mrs. Rockman, and at the same time obtain lead information at the drop site. I did not even faintly doubt him, and was willing to support his chance at promotion, whereas if I were to insist on going, I would gain nothing more than a handshake from my peers. It was an easy decision. We were both surprised that our superiors let us make the decision ourselves, but most likely they too were avoiding the same ego/jurisdictional argument. I let the special operations team on the outside know that Bud would be hiding in the back seat protecting the driver.

That being decided we returned to analyzing our plan. We realized that until we received the directional phone call, the planned reaction was so multifarious; detailing it was a waste of time and adrenaline. The organizations on the outside agreed. Our best immediate reaction would be to stall the delivery a reasonable time to allow our forces to strategically locate prior to the drop.

All that we could do now was wait. It was early spring, too early for daylight savings time. Darkness began sliding in shortly after 5 PM. We watched darkness happen as if it were a rare event. I stared at the phone until I could see its outline, even with my eyes closed. It rested there silently. Personnel on the outside demonstrated their anxiety with nervous unnecessary radio transmissions which were as usual squelched by experienced agents. We avoided all distractions, with no commercial radio, no TV, and limited home lighting. Any attempt to ease the stress was so thinly veiled it was useless. We waited in clumsy silence. Six O'clock, then six thirty; at seven fear began to knot my stomach from thoughts of "What went wrong." Have they discovered our intervention? Have they harmed him? Have they changed their plan for their own security? "All speculation", I thought, "Be patient." At "seven dark thirty" the phone rang.

"Ring", I jumped up and checked the recorder, it had activated. A second "Ring," Bud sprang to the monitor to listen. "Ring", number three and I turned to see why Mrs. Rockman was not picking up the receiver. I saw her standing near the phone, frozen, literally unable to move. "Ring", number four, still no movement. I stepped to the phone, picked up the receiver and at the same time, put my arm around her, squeezing her with a little shoulder hug. "It'll be OK", I whispered. I handed her the phone: she said, "Hello."

"*Mary?*"

"Yes."

"*Do you have the money?*"

"My husband does." It was a coached answer, thinking it might allow us to substitute him or an Agent for the driver, but it was more of a way to stall the delivery for strategic reasons.

"That's no good! I told you we would only deal directly with you. If you don't show up with the money, by yourself the kid is dead."

"I can bring it to you."

"How much have you got?"

"Two hundred thousand."

"Good, now listen close. Come alone with the money. Take highway 26 toward Mount Hood. Turn off on highway 224 to Estacada. At Estacada cross over the river near McIver State Park. Drive into the first parking lot on the left. Drive up to the outhouse and point your car with your lights shining on the outhouse. Leave the money at the side of the outhouse. When we have the money counted in our hands, we will leave Tommy where you can find him. Now repeat it back to me."

Mrs. Rockman did an excellent job of repeating her instructions back to the caller and as soon as she finished, he said, "Be there in an hour" and hung up.

I began to breathe again, and realized we had a real time problem. Our units would be hard stretched to make it to the location in an hour. Bud was already on the phone advising the outside of the location. It would take Bud and Mrs. Rockman a little more than an hour to make the journey, however we reasoned the kidnappers knew it may take longer, but were unwilling to allow time for any other activity. It didn't matter; we had to begin the action.

I helped Bud and Mrs. Rockman into the car with the money, rechecked the marker tail light, and duct tape. Mrs. Rockman seemed to be gathering strength as we progressed. She was performing admirably. As she started the car, Bud slid into the back seat. I put my hand on the back of his neck and gave him a sincere, "Good luck Partner."

By the time they hit the street, I was on the radio broadcasting their progress. The surveillance plane had already been airborne for half an hour, and quickly picked up their location. The ground units trailed comfortably behind, following the dialogue of the aircraft. My job was done for a while, barring anything unexpected.

In spite of all our efforts, we didn't know an important crucial detail. What was the layout of the McIver parking lot, and when would the kidnappers arrive there, or are they already there watching for a possible police presence?

A single undercover car made a slow U-turn in the darkened, heavily wooded area of McIver State Park, then retreated toward Estacada. The driver appeared to be lost, searching for a clue as to where he erred. His conclusion: there was no way of knowing what lurked in the woods, and inserting our operations team in close would be too dangerous. The briefcase was only money; the victim was still a little boy. Bud, with a radio earpiece keeping his blood pressure elevated, comprehended the situation. He was on his own. The arrest team would be stationed at the entrance of the park to; after the money drop detain any passing vehicles. But they would be unable to provide any close cover for Bud. It was decided that he should stay with Mrs. Rockman until after she departed the immediate drop site, and left it to his discretion whether to roll out onto the road leaving the area.

Again I waited. Within almost exactly an hour, I heard a faint radio transmission from Bud, indicating they were crossing the river toward the Park. The next transmission was more of a whisper, "She's out of the car"; then "Package delivered, no subjects observed."

Bud told Mrs. Rockman to slow down about 100 yards from the drop site so he could roll out onto the road. She slowed, but in her anxious state, she was still going way faster than Bud would have preferred. He slid out onto the road landing roughly and rolled into the side ditch. It was dark, a darkness that can only be found in the deep woods. He thought he heard footsteps jog across the road back toward the outhouse, but couldn't see anything. He radioed his position, told all other units to remain in place until he could check the location. He crept back to the outhouse and checked its perimeter. The briefcase was gone. Our people monitoring the radio locater signal already knew. The beeper began transmitting indicating movement only seconds after delivery. We presumed the kidnapper was hiding in the dark side behind the outhouse during the delivery. We were still receiving a signal from the locating beeper but we couldn't openly pursue the money or the villain until we found Tommy. Now Bud waited alone in the dark hoping for good news.

Once again, everyone waited. An eternity of 45 minutes passed when the radio dispatcher broke the silence. "The Police Department has received a call from a citizen who was approached by a young boy who says he has been kidnapped. The citizen is calling from a phone booth (location given) on the east side of Portland. The boy says he was dumped out onto the street by his kidnappers."

Our picket of the delivery route had been strung out for miles between Portland and Estacada. A newer Agent had been assigned on the East end of Portland, and to his joy, was only a few blocks from the reported call. He made what was to be one of the most thrilling transmissions of his career. "I have Tommy safely in my custody."

The celebration was emotional, but short. The locater beacon indicated that the package became stationary only a few minutes after its removal from the parking lot. Who knew why? We could only speculate that the culprit hid or buried the money in the park, or was hiding at a location nearby. Either way, it was not prudent to venture into the dark forest seeking prey that had the advantage of knowing the terrain.

At first light, agents began searching the wooded area of McIver Park. The forest trees there are massive. The search began on a trail leading from the parking lot outhouse. The briefcase beeper was still transmitting a message indicating it was stationary. The signal was strongest in a stand of trees only a few yards off the trail. First thoughts were that it had been buried, but there were no signs of disturbed earth. Then someone looked up. High up in a fir tree hung our briefcase, empty. These jerks weren't totally stupid.

In town, interviews began as soon as employees of the Rockman's company arrived at work. Neighbors were questioned, Tommy was asked to repeat his story several times and the telephone recording was painstakingly analyzed.

Tommy reported he was taken off his pathway to the school by two men in ski masks. They blindfolded him and placed him into a truck like van. He never saw their faces, and they spoke very little. He was kept in the van most of the day and driven around to various places, all the while blind folded. They didn't abuse him and told him he would be released after dark. He had no idea who they were.

Personal crimes like this are usually investigated from the inside out. When a wife disappears the first to be questioned is the husband. An extortion or kidnapping begins with prior friends, neighbors, company employees and expands outward. In this case members of the family and company were very cooperative and progress was quick.

Another family member and an employee of the company listened to the tape recording. The family member was certain he recognized the voice but couldn't immediately identify it. After an hour of thought, he came up with a name. He believed it was a former employee whom they had fired about a month previously. Agents went to work on the name.

The search of the park disclosed the pathway taken by the money carrier led to another open area, this one containing a phone booth. The person directing the outside investigation, Stan, was a veteran agent, with an instinct that allowed him to think like criminals. On a hunch, he contacted the telephone company to determine if they could print out a number for all the calls made from that phone booth within the last few days. Within a day the phone company came back with ten numbers, and the time of day when the calls were made. Three calls were made the evening of the kidnap payoff; two calls to the same number, one before the money drop, and one after. The name associated with the number was the same as the fired Rockman company employee. Well how 'bout that!

The details fell into place. Two friends, one a former Rockman employee had performed the kidnapping. The friend received a small percentage of the money. He was arrested in Portland, but the other had fled to Seattle. The Seattle FBI quickly found where the kidnapper was living. Stan and I flew to Seattle with a Federal search and arrest warrant to assist in his arrest. We wanted to be present to locate the remainder of the money and to interrogate the kidnapper. It all went as planned. After the arrest we had a little discussion wherein he confessed and we recovered most of the money. The court found them both guilty.

I had the pleasure of appearing as a guest speaker several times at corporate functions with the Rockman family. They told an interesting and relevant crime prevention story. Several years later I again met Tommy, then a grown man. We were both proud to be there.

Diary note: Years ago the operational details of this investigation would not have been mentioned because it would have disclosed too many investigative techniques. Now, more than 35 years later, the techniques used then have been so improved they are irrelevant and have been replaced.

• • •

There were others. I remember working another unusual kidnapping as inside man with my friend and fellow agent Paul. The victim's house was south of Eugene Oregon, out of town in a remote area next to a Forest. There was no place to park automobiles where agents could watch the house. They had to hide themselves in unusual country places uncomfortably distant from where Paul and I were in the home. We were shorthanded considering the size of the victim's house, and the large area to be secured.

The house was huge possibly because the owner was a lumber baron. It was a multi storied structure with seven different doors through which an intruder could enter. Our responsibilities were to secure the money, protect the family and to guide the investigation after the return ransom call was made. We waited throughout the long night.

Fortunately I learned at an early age, that darkness can be an ally. I was a kid who played in the darkness, hid from my preconceived adversaries, triumphed in late night games of hide and seek, and even sometimes worked on the farm in the dark. With the right attitude, darkness became a comfort. I was not afraid of the dark. I did say usually not, didn't I?

The wait was stressful. It was autumn. Leaves were blowing across the yard, skittering past the doors and tapping at the windows. Paul was defending the upstairs while I covered the lower daylight basement. We were the shepherds of two other people and one million dollars in cash. The night was long and silent, but we could hear every deer and varmint that crossed the yard. It was indeed not a situation for someone who was uncomfortable in the dark. Godzilla would have been frightened out in those woods. We were forced to stay awake all night, as were our cohorts outside, because it was the perfect place for a kidnapper or extortionist to charge into and demand their ransom. Presently we call that a zero tolerance situation. There was no room for screw-ups.

The call never came that evening. We were preparing for another long session the next day when we received a call from the FBI office in Sacramento. The couple had actually been kidnapped but they were taken to Northern California, where they were chained to a tree in a forest. They were left there overnight and escaped their chains. After walking to a road they flagged down a Deputy Sheriff. The case was quickly solved. Paul and I viewed the entire exercise as a dress rehearsal for something bigger.

Adam J. Schreuder

*All say "How hard it is that we have to
die" – a strange complaint to come from the
mouths of people who have had to live.*

Mark Twain

Oregon is beautiful in the spring…when it quits raining. The countryside south of Portland boasts of small farms, vineyards, horticultural nurseries, orchards and berry fields. Rows of strawberries stretch from one country road to the next. A hundred shades of green fold over the rolling hills under puffy white clouds suspended in dark blue.

Folks living there seem to absorb their character from the land. Families accustomed to work, live in perky little farm houses skirted with white fences. Sleek horses reach their necks through the whitewashed boards to nip the roadside wildflowers. Families, whose roots are not in the hillside history, have come there to work, and because "It is a good place to raise a family."

In that picturesque countryside, it was one of those grand days. Charla and Pauline, neighborhood friends young in their teens, still looking for a place for life to happen, ambled on the road between their homes. Two beautiful young girls on a harmless stroll down a country road seldom traveled; what form of life could prey on that?

A car appeared slowly over the hill. The girls stepped to the side expecting the car to pass. But it slowed and stopped in their presence. Expecting the two passengers to be an acquaintance, the girls hesitated briefly, and were surprised to see two young male strangers.

Almost immediately both men scrambled from the car and grabbed the girls. A struggle ensued while both girls attempted to escape. Pauline broke free from her would be captor, tried to help Charla but was beaten away. In fear she ran from the rear of the car. Charla was overpowered by the larger male, now assisted by his partner and was dragged into the car. Pauline screamed after her friend as she was carried off into the horizon.

Pauline ran to the nearest home and hysterically reported the horrible event.

As always the county Sheriff's Office, (I'll leave it un-named) was quick responding to a forceful abduction. Our office and others were notified, and because it could resolve into a kidnapping, we responded in full force.

I responded to the call at midday. As I sped through the docile countryside, I pondered how something as grave as this abduction could have happened in such a setting. My initial thoughts were that whoever did this didn't live out here. Arriving at the girls address, I saw a home that was typical and belonged. A modest white house with an unattached garage, rested humbly on a well-groomed lawn. An early season garden planted out past the garage was beginning its seasonal promise. This was a place that proud ambitious people called home. I hadn't even seen the parents yet, but I already began to empathize.

The primary county officer assigned was Tony. Many officers that I worked with were great, but Tony was special. People all over the county, both good and bad, respected Tony. He was of average height, but what he lacked in altitude, he made up in strength. Tony could hurt you just shaking hands. His razor gaze met you straight in the eyes and his speech delivered no vagaries. A first impression of Tony was lasting, because he appeared to be ice veined, intelligent, and all business. But I had grown to know him through past associations. He had a sensitive and caring sole. As "inside man", I was grateful to see Tony.

When I arrived, Tony escorted me into the living room. The scene was less chaotic than usual. Tony had settled the parents into a fact finding discussion. I met both of Charla's parents. Her father worked in a nearby town, and her mother Anna ran a business out of the home.

Pauline, the girl who escaped had already been interviewed in detail, and would again be questioned by agents from my office. While Tony and I both began gathering descriptions and facts from the parents I went to work installing recording devices on their telephone. I noticed that the house was exceptionally neat and clean. Kneeling on the porch floor to attached equipment left not a trace of dust on my suit pants. The fresh kitchen aromas smelled as if it belonged to a mother who cooked. Family photos were respectably placed in conspicuous locations. My eyes fell on one frame of an attractive young girl, resembling Anna. When it was appropriate I asked, "Is that Charla?" The answer came in tears. Tony apparently had not gotten to that part yet.

Anna seemed to be the nerve center of the family. Even in her distraught state, she held on to reason, and provided intelligent assistance. Ever struggling with emotion she was articulate and softly expressive. She was attractive in her mid-thirties. An athletic petite form with shiny brown hair and liquid brown beautiful eyes; eyes who's gift was the privilege of receiving their glance. She appeared as a time advanced image of her missing daughter.

Tony needed to put in motion county wide and state wide efforts to locate the abduction vehicle as well as posting descriptions of Charla and her abductors. The FBI would wait until a ransom demand was made, or until the federally required 24 hours before launching nationwide efforts. Regardless of the federal statute delaying jurisdiction we always participated immediately, helping wherever we could.

Tony left shortly after I arrived. He had photos to distribute initiating a search and other descriptive details. Charla's father went with him to pick up the remaining member of the family. Charla's younger brother would be kept at a friend's home, for the evening or until any danger had passed. Agents and officers were discretely posted outside.

I was left alone with a mother who was realizing her beautiful young daughter had been captured by two undefined monsters. It was my job to provide hope and support, to intervene in a crisis, to make things happen in logical order. I was puzzled and in doubt about how to console a mother under these circumstances. For a few moments I felt like a valueless fossilized ham sandwich, anticipating I would soon fail my own lecture.

Remedy must come with truth. Truth in heart rendering losses is better revealed slowly. It was a time to discover individual personalities, uncover hidden consciousness and craft sentences with sensitive words. But Anna quickly processed the information I passed on. The truth was this abduction appeared to be unplanned, unrehearsed and had no outward financial motivation. All other motivations bore far more dire consequences. Predictive discussions of physical and sexual abuse were avoided, and the hopes of release and escape were sustained. But those dark fears were the direction toward which the truth was progressing.

Anna needed to talk. She told me about Charla's life. She told me about her first steps, her childhood sicknesses, her favorite toys, her school work, her love for animals, her favorite deserts, her love of friends and country life. She held Charla's picture in her lap, and retrieved several other photographs from her family collection. She fingered through each one slowly, blinking tears from her vision. She spoke of Charla's favorite wardrobe items, how she liked to laugh and remembered the times when she cried. Anna lovingly brought out a sweater resembling the one Charla was wearing earlier in the day.

And then she said, "When you find her, she will be wearing a sweater that looks like this."

What I felt then, was indescribable; an incommunicable experience. In her absence, Charla still had a sad almost unbearable presence. Anna sobbed, took my hand and said, "I know you are only human. But please find her, and help us through this."

It was a day in which I was reminded what I was, or should be on the other 364.

We sat waiting hopefully for the call, the confirmation of life. I had already reviewed what should be her response to a demand call, so we passed the tense hours in conversation. We talked and I took my turn. I had a son her daughter's age, and another the same as her son. It was impossible to separate my inner personality and thoughts from the real world in which I was now conversing. It comforted her when I eased away from my professional façade; a good thing because by then it would have been unprofessional to coldly maintain it.

At dusk, she realized how long we had been waiting. She asked, "How long does it usually take before a kidnapper will call to ask for ransom?"

I answered honestly, "They usually call within two or three hours of the abduction." Then to ease the pain I added, "But sometimes they don't trust telephones and mail a note."

She wasn't buying it. "It's already been to long hasn't it."

"Not yet", I said. "Sometimes they have to travel awhile to get to what they consider a safe place."

Considering my answer, she asked, "How long can you stay with us?"

"I'll stay here through the night." And quickly added, "This couch looks better than a lot of others I have slept on."

Her expression changed as if she had just arrived from some far-away place and said, "My goodness, you haven't eaten all day, and we both need to maintain our strength."

"Let me make you something. What would you like?"

"Well, when I impose on people like this, I am not accustomed to ordering my preferences."

"Don't be vain. Would you like a sandwich?"

"Sure, I'll bet anything you make will be good."

I got up stiff legged, checked the recorder and asked if I could help. Her husband was just arriving and had been made aware of the same information I was monitoring in my ear piece. The news basically was no news. The vehicle in question was only described as a dark mid-sized sedan, containing two males, late teens to early twenties. That narrowed it down to thirty percent of all cars on the road. The direction in which they fled led to the coastal highway, and they could have gone any direction from there. The father reported that their son was safely with another family to shield him from much of the trauma.

We ate in near silence, endured small talk for another hour until I announced I was going to rest for a while, but would be awake there in the living room for most of the night. I explained if the phone were to ring, they were to answer it on the bedroom extension and I would monitor it from my post in the living room. Anna gave me a blanket and disappeared teary eyed and contemplative.

It is in the long hours of darkness while allegedly resting that I sort out my thoughts. With full awareness that there were many minds, brighter and more alert than mine, actively working to find Charla, I repeatedly examined the events of the day. Plaguing questions persisted, like "What have I forgotten." "Did my associates get everything from the friend who escaped?" "What are the odds that they will call?" "What can we ask to verify they are keeping her safe?" "If they abuse her, where will they leave her- - how will they leave her?" "Where should we place our immediate emphasis and how soon should we change?"

Rambling thoughts bruised my mind for hours, and were interrupted occasionally by semi-conscious jolts thinking the phone was going to ring, or had rung. Bouts of anger helped keep me awake. I wondered why nature seems to have a conflict with man, wherein we destroy the good and the trophies of the world yet allow and preserve the bad. We shoot the prize elk, and doctor the lame, feed the weak and slaughter the fat, continually observe the extinction of the relic and sustain the vile. These bastards undoubtedly will destroy a young girl just because she is beautiful, and when we find them, we'll store and preserve their miserable asses for the next 70 years. Why should an innocent young girl be tortured by two degenerates? It was enough to make one become independent of the human race. It was futile, but I lay there consciously listening for the ring of a telephone contemplating how I might defeat the darkest parts of humankind.

The night passed slowly, like darkness without time. With anxiety accelerating my heart, I began to set erect longing for the fading of the North Star or the first rays of light, as if it would sweep this all out of existence. Physical movement was always followed by a relapse into thinking about how I was going to tell Anna if Charla was not found alive.

Morning came early with an awareness of the soft padding of dainty feet. A faint whispered inquiry followed, "Did you sleep at all?"

"I don't remember. Did you?" "I tried. I know it's foolish to ask, our phones never rang, but have you learned anything new?"

"No I haven't but I am going to have a conference with the leaders outside as soon as they are apprised of everything recent."

During the night, I found a way to explain what is true, but neither of us was ready for it yet.

"Will you be leaving then?"

"It depends on what happens this morning. We'll give them some time to call this morning, but if we don't hear anything soon, I will join the others and be of more use working outside."

"What will you do?"

"I'm sure we will start an organized search. Then I will go where ever it leads us."

"I see", she said disappointedly. "Can I get you some toast and coffee?"

She walked forlornly back into the kitchen. I understood that my leaving was tantamount to ripping out her last strand of hope and security. But Tony had also been thinking. He learned that the family regularly attended a local church. Tony contacted the minister and arranged for his arrival at about the same time as my anticipated departure.

I entered the kitchen, looking like I had slept in my clothes....precisely. Charla's father appeared, sighed and sat, silently brooding at the table. He appeared quiet by nature and because he had been with Tony, I didn't have an insight into him. But I could tell, he was not handling the events well. OK, perhaps I wasn't either, but we had to regain some strength.

Anna broke the silence with a knowing question. "Hasn't it been too long, to expect a call now?"

It was an entry into the discussion that I had been dreading. I had to honestly prepare them for the truth.

I began with my thought out introduction. "As these things go, the absence of any communication is not at all promising."

Before I could finish my comments Anna interrupted with, "What's that mean?"

It was time that I demonstrate some professionalism. I spoke slowly and contemplatively, pausing to be sensitive and to let it sink in.

"The activities here follow a certain profile. It does not appear that Charla was taken for monetary reasons. It appears to be more in the line with what we call a crime of opportunity. Considering the age of her captors, the next logical reason would be that she was taken because she was a young pretty girl."

I was unnerved by the iceberg stare from Anna. She clearly knew what my oblique approach meant.

"With that motivation in mind, we will expand our search to encompass all the possibilities involved investigating sex offenders."

It was a brutal spear that they both knew was coming. Anna sobbed and stepped over to me. She put her head on my shoulder and shook with grief. Her husband slumped pale in his chair.

"Will she suffer?" "What will they do to her?"

She sobbed so violently that I put my arm around her to keep her from falling. It was a natural gesture. I was on the edge of losing it to my own emotions, and knew it was time to suppress my empathy and inject some "Tough Love."

"Now listen to me! I told you I would help you through this. This is going to work both ways, because we need your help too. There are dozens of people out there who have worked all night looking for Charla and the guys who took her. They have not given up hope, will not give up hope, and neither can you. You need to be strong with the rest of us and see this through. Your son needs strong parents to help him with his loss too. Now look at me, and tell me you are going to hang on."

Then I wished I hadn't made that last statement. I will never outlive the memory of that look.

I finished my toast with a dry mouth shoveling it into an upset stomach. My radio informed me through the earpiece that Tony was only a few minutes away. I checked the phones and departed.

I walked to my car thinking of myself, "What a Jerk! I know how this will probably turn out…even worse than I alluded. I've been through this before." Meanwhile the entire state was desperately searching on a mother's hopes.

After a shower, fresh clothes and black coffee, I joined a convoy of seven agents. It was our mission to contact every motel on the Oregon coast from Astoria to Newport. All law enforcement had been provided a description of the abduction car, and a description of the two young men, but they were so vague no valuable leads had been developed. Our best chance was to contact motel owners with a photograph of Charla, knock on doors and ask questions. Community awareness was paramount.

There are an astounding number of motels dotting the coastline. Each agent covered a specific area, and we met later to divide and assign outlying possibilities. By eight that evening we had exhausted all hope they had retreated to a coastal motel. The next day we would meet to cover restaurants, medical clinics and hospitals.

Within a couple days of our search, Tony got a break. They received a call from a young man who said a friend confided he was with another associate, and together they had abducted a girl on a country road.

Events happened quickly from that point. I am not certain of the details and sequence but Tony located the suspect named by the informant. An interrogation resulted in a complete confession. Information was provided to locate Charla.

Details are inappropriate here, but I must provide enough for you to understand....the deep everlasting emotional affect that seared us all. The confessor said they drove toward the Oregon coast, each taking turns assaulting and abusing their victim. After many such assaults she became a liability. The confessor was delegated to take Charla into the roadside ditch and stab her to death. He attempted to do so, and returned to the car. The driver asked if she was dead. He replied that he wasn't sure. The driver then took the knife, went to her body, and cut her throat. She was left nude in the roadside blackberry bushes.

I received the last bit of information as coastal authorities confirmed they had found Charla, in the bushes as described. I knew I must be available to bare the awful news to her parents. They needed to hear it from us before the story hit the news. I couldn't contact Tony and he wasn't answering his radio, so I drove directly to the family's home. I was too late. Tony and the minister were already there.

I waited silently on the porch while they went through it. They were sensitive, but untimely businesslike with things like identifying the body and the other associated horrors. The minister offered his seminary teachings consoling that Charla was now in a better place. I waited, hiding my own pain.

Charla's father left with the minister to inform her little brother. Tony retreated to his car to recover. Tony and I, in this case were no different. I was probably the only person who understood his anguish, and the feeling was mutual. His self-consoling action was to follow through on an arrest warrant for the second abductor.

Anna was quietly crying in a kitchen chair when I entered. She stood and walked to me and I held her. I wept with her. For the first time in years, I was able to let out the pent up sorrow for so many victims, but more than any, I grieved for Anna. I held her and we sobbed together.

I was one of several in the group that arrested the apparent leader of the duo. We found him at his parent's home, a modest place in a town south of Portland. I truly feared, given the attitude, anger, and disposition of the local law officers making the arrest that they might shoot him in the process. It may have happened, but he did not offer them the chance.

An old adage declares that time heals all wounds. But they don't specify how much time it takes. The usual legal process took its course. The newspapers put the story to rest. I went about my other duties, but could not release my concerns for

Anna and her family. Some weeks later, other work took me too close to the home and place where it all began. My conscience nagged me that I owed Anna one more conciliatory visit. But as I walked up to the door I wasn't sure how it should happen.

OK, what about all that stuff in the lecture about how we weren't supposed to get personally involved? If you need an explanation, then you don't understand. My brief association with Anna gave me an understanding and appreciation of things that I otherwise would not have known. It's not love one feels for a person of such misfortune. But the word admire, sometimes gets a loose misapplication as does the word love. There are things that I may admire; a painting, a trapeze artist, or a song that embeds itself into my mind. One wouldn't say he is in love with these things, but they still persist in great favor. They are things that you wouldn't change. Please don't! Admire them as they are.

Call it situational admiration, compassion, empathy, or whatever you want. But with another person in the midst of fear and uncertainty a certain bond develops. It is a bond that I cannot express within the ordinary conventions of composition. Thus I returned once more.

Anna was honestly glad to see me, relieving my fears that I would be an unwelcome reminder of the ugliness within our past. I could see a lingering sadness in her eyes. Conversation was awkward. She had busied herself with her business. She hired another person to help her. Her son was having trouble adjusting to the loss of his sister. I said I had a new boss. But it all fell, as if it were a scripted making of a final farewell. Words were of no use at all. We seemed to be isolated by a power unwanted, unable to ever again reach the sole of the other. It was as it should be.

As I walked back to my car, the gravel beneath my feet was blurred, but my weary eyes had shed their last. The words of an old Chris Christopherson country song kept running through my mind.

There's no use in asking
How this story ends.
It's over.
Nobody wins.

A Two Way Ladder

O ur organization seldom kept an SAC, (Special Agent in Charge, who is the regional boss) in place longer than two years. Some of them didn't stay around that long. In my 15 years at Portland, we had eight different SACs, and average of less than two years each. The reason was, almost all of them were advancing their career, if not to Washington D.C., then on to a larger office. After each change of management a resulting shuffle of personnel followed. The new boss would exercise his preference on whom he picked for his closest personal assistants; or as we called it, the "Palace Guard." The frequent changes validated the popular occupational philosophy, "Be careful who you step on going up the ladder, because you will meet them again on your way back down."

By its nature, it was a problematic policy. If a new boss picked a person for a certain position within the office, that person may have not wanted to serve in that job. However it was supposed to be a compliment to fill a Palace Guard position, and it was an insult to the boss to refuse the "opportunity". In the process, hard feelings arose from others who wanted to rise to that position, not to mention the poor soul who was demoted. Few were those who ascended to the top of the ladder and stayed there. In my years of service, I made the trip in both directions several times.

Washington D.C.'s (Headquarters) promotion of SAC's was even more complicated. To become an SAC one had to move repeatedly, for most of a 30 year career. The hardships of moving negated any extra salary obtained through promotion, especially if considering the family trauma. The majority of agents preferred to advance to a senior grade field agent, invest in a good location and remain there. That left only a few volunteers for management promotion, and unfortunately most were motivated by ego and potential fame. Whoa, now I don't want to paint with a broad brush, all of management as being ego motivated. But as the saying goes, 95% of them gave the other 5% a bad name. I shall illustrate.

First of all, I plead guilty. I will not pretend I didn't offend anyone, didn't exercise personal favors to get into or out of a position, but never did I ever intend to harm anyone in the process. My personal assignments (not to be confused with individual case assignments) were most often against my wishes, and thereafter were for self-preservation. Anyone harmed brought it on himself. I will explain later.

At earlier duty stations, San Diego, Phoenix, Tucson, I never worked directly for a SAC, so I have no reference to any of them until arriving at Portland. The first two top level bosses in Portland were still a couple levels above me, and my interaction with them was minimal. I thought their performance was admirable and satisfactory. I interested the second one in the Police and Firefighters Olympics, and ended up traveling with him on several occasions to compete in track meets.

I first began to be noticed by management when I began to be effective on the reactive squad. I obtained a Master's Degree in behavioral science and police administration, and had worked successfully with several bank security officers training bank personnel regarding kidnappings and robberies. Agents who represented the FBI as public speakers were required to attend a week of specialized public speaking training at the FBI Academy. After receiving that course, number three SAC, we'll call him Bob, willingly granted me an occasional leave of absence to address bank conferences and I was often requested by name because my program was entertaining. That led to additional requests for luncheon and banquet appearances, and eventually I was a regular twice a week performer.

The first bad rays of sunshine broke over me by chance. The agent whose job was to represent the Oregon FBI as news media representative was testifying in court when a portion of the ransom money from the D. B. Cooper case, (a famous airline hijacking case which has never been solved) was found at the edge of the Columbia River north of Portland. News reporters descended on the location in swarms. Although I was organizing the excavation of the river bank, I was told, because of the absence of the regular media representative, to control and speak with the media. That media coverage was broadcast nation-wide, and clips of that coverage are still aired each year near Thanksgiving, the anniversary of the original crime. It went well, and within a few weeks our new boss, John promoted me to news media representative. I objected, but the former representative had served for several years and wanted out. I was it. I think it was then that I coined the phrase, "No good job goes unpunished."

I did not view it as a promotion. Frankly, I got no joy out of telling about exciting investigations, I wanted to be conducting them. Sure, it was good for my ego to be seen on television, and have my comments on local radio stations. But the thrill of that was short lived. Within a few months my fellow agents began to opine that those who can't....talk and teach, and those who can....do. Although I tried to give extensive credit to individual agents for their efforts, the news stations often credited me; or in one way or another mentioned me ahead of the others who were doing all the difficult and good work. Of course that created resentment. The harder they worked the more credit I got. But on the other hand, I worked well with the reporters, developed trust, and was increasingly sought for sound bites and filmed interviews. That created another problem.

Remember I said we had an ego problem within management. To illustrate, it was specific policy that all written news releases begin with: Mr. _____, Special Agent in Charge of the _____ office advised today that.....then the subject of the release. I took a course in newspaper writing in undergraduate school, and even if I didn't I would have known that any good news story leads with a summarizing sentence of the event. The lead sentence would not under any normal circumstances be that Mr. ___ is the Special Agent in Charge of the FBI. Whenever a news release was distributed in that format, the press always changed it and often left out the name of the SAC entirely. To the wrath of those sensitive SAC egos, somewhere down in the middle of the article reporters usually quoted me. Why were we mandated to that format? Simple; the people making the policy suffered under the egocentric idea that they were so important they needed to be mentioned at the top of the article.

The first two SACs I worked for in that position were no exception, but they were also intelligent decent people. They recognized the problem and accepted my explanation, but were only satisfied if I occasionally got them before the cameras and featured in radio talk shows. That was normal; after all they were the boss. I could keep that balance and eventually became friends with them to the extent that I became suspect of being an informant or confident to the boss. It was a natural progression of street agent suspicion, and I was warned by the outgoing media agent that it would happen. I have several scrap books full of news articles quoting me, I became well known, but I was not happy.

The next SAC, Art, was a normal good natured man. I continued as news media person, but was allowed to work other worthwhile cases on the reactive squad, and participated in public affairs. Life was good for almost two years. Art moved on like the others, but came back to Portland to retire. In retirement he became a good friend. He did accounting for his church and lived a short distance down the hill from me. We were in an investment club together, where he was treasurer. I was president, and began to notice that Art was making errors in our financial statement. It was uncharacteristic of him. I'll shorten the narrative by skipping to his medical diagnosis. He developed a brain tumor and died suddenly. We worked within the FBI family to help his wife through the hard times.

The next change of command, Bill, appreciated my work, and demonstrated it by giving me much more. Admittedly I was not over assigned with my duties, and had been working extra conducting police training. Oh yes, I forgot to mention that while working for Art, I attended the FBI Academy for several weeks of training to become a Police Instructor, and also to become a hostage negotiator. I enjoyed the duty, and organized several appreciated courses in crisis intervention and hostage negotiations. Alas, Bill combined the job of news media and chief training officer into one job and gave it to me. Again I resisted, requesting regular street agent duty. The boss declined, and ordered me to submit a memo requesting re-assignment to the position known as the "Police Coordinator". I objected to administratively asking for something that I really did not want. At least he had a sense of humor, so in one last desperate act of protest, I composed the memo in which I wrote:

"I have been requested to assume the position of Police Coordinator." I am apprehensive about assuming such a position because I tried it once and couldn't walk for a week."

I over estimated his sense of humor. I soon submitted a proper memo and assumed the position. During my time in that position we tripled the number of police schools conducted and maintained a high profile in local news outlets. I had a personal secretary, and another helping part time. The poor lady was so overworked she was very near a nervous breakdown, and I too was feeling the stress. However Bill did not want to spare any more agent time for training. I began to turn down requests for training because we were spread way too thin. Bill resented the cutback.

I was burned out. I wanted out of Headquarters politics, so I asked a couple of times to be transferred to the resident agency in Bend Oregon. Bill declined each time saying, "Your career path does not include Bend."

Regardless of a few minor riffs, Bill and I got along well, and he performed well in his own right. He was soon summoned to Headquarters to be an assistant director, thus skipping several rungs of the ladder. He told me that as soon as he got established there, he had a position in his division he wanted me to fill. That was another ray of misfortune. I told him I was not interested. I insulted him by declining his opportunity offer to advance to Washington, and my star began to lose its glitter. I made it worse by asking him to remove me from news media representative before he left Oregon. He refused saying "That will be up to the next guy." He left town and I never heard from him again.

So let's talk about the next guy. To make things simple, I shall just refer to him as Ego. Ego had gotten into trouble with the National Director of the FBI. Ego had been the SAC of a large eastern office, and according to inside information began to think he was more important than the Director. After several national media appearances, embarrassing to the Director, Ego was demoted and sent to Portland. Marvelous!

Ego was bitter upon arrival and with his introductory remarks referred to Portland as a "Bush", (as in the outback or small time) culture. He cared not if he said so in the company of other public officials. He often reminded Oregon counterparts how important he had been in Washington. As the office public representative, it left me in a position needing to apologize for his attitude and constantly trying to calm the offended former friends of our office.

At my first opportunity I tried to resign from the news media job and asked to be sent to an investigative squad. He of course was offended and declined my request.

Ego soon became a public relations disaster. He was a man so concerned about his self-importance and image; he carried it around as if it would break. Few among my age and cloth were impressed by the grandeur he thought evolved from the accident of his birth. He expected to be featured on TV on any insignificant matter, even when TV reporters had neither the time nor the desire to interview him.

After his performance in a particularly boring TV interview held in his office I was summoned to his throne. Enswathed in self-adulation, he asked my opinion of his performance. My behavior at this point will appear stupid by most critics, but it must be understood that I was no fan of this coxcomb and wanted reassignment. In addition my farm boy attitude was still hinged on honesty. My work ethic dictated that "If you are going to work for a person then for God's sake do work for him." If conscience was my moral medicine chest, it also contained a bit of poison.

Ego's articulation in front of the TV camera had been bad. It was frequently punctuated with "You know" and "I mean" and more "ahs" than needed. So I told him. I mentioned as discreetly as possible that his performance would be better if he in the future concentrated on eliminating those excess pausing words. I doubt that anyone had been so bold before him, especially an underling such as me. His Washington D.C. backdrop was a firewall so bloated with like-minded egocentricity, unwilling to admit weakness among their ranks combined to, in his mind, make his gonads so big and mine so small; how dare I assault with such blasphemy! I might as well have launched a nuke at my star.

But the old bloat wouldn't re-assign me. It was if he wanted to hover over me and punish me until I was a defeated wimp. He pursued me like a disease. But often combat makes bad men worse and good men better. I worked harder than ever to maintain our agency image among our peers. Ego jealously recognized my personal success, and established a new public relations policy. Neither I, nor either of my assistants was to attend National Academy or other associated law enforcement functions. He dictated that only he, the head of the field office, should attend. Similarly we were prohibited from interacting with any of the senior law enforcement command officers within our state. It was an incredibly bad PR move. For several years I and other agents had been fishing with leaders all over the state. My assistants were both attractive, popular women, who had been representing us at events for years. They were missed immediately. While he persisted in his arrogance he destroyed the real face of our office.

I was not alone in my struggle. Office moral deteriorated while a cadre of employees was provoked by the appearance of his pulpy face embodied in self-adoration and conceit. Still, others sucked up to narcissistic incompetence hoping to approach the ladder.

I finally realized that as long as I wanted out of the detestable assignment, I would continue to be diminished there. I set my sights on working in the low key Counterintelligence Squad, supervised by a real gentleman. I caused an associate to leak information to Ego, that my worst nightmare would be an assignment to the Counterintelligence Squad. Bingo! It worked.

I began working for Gentleman John who was also not in good graces with Ego because of John's good manners, sensibility, and disdain for "almighty's" posturing. Note that Gentleman John is a different person than the SAC John referred to earlier. Shortly after my reassignment to new work, Ego acquired a new second in command, whom we will just call Snake. Ego downloaded all of his derogative information onto Snake and left on re-assignment to a larger office. On the evening of Ego's departure, John and I sponsored a "wheels up" party at my house. It was to be a one keg quiet, discreet, celebration of Ego's migration to the south. Not so surprisingly, 70 plus people showed up to join in the revelry.

After that party, I was firmly off the ladder, happily grounded in reality and real work. But the news of the party and my reputation was passed on to the new boss whom we will refer to as Sluggo. Sluggo was another ego, this time a small man with a small man complex.

I avoided Sluggo as much as possible, devoting my energy to my new found profession....spy catcher. My first closed door encounter with Sluggo came after I received a fat letter of commendation from another division wherein I had been assigned temporarily (for three months) undercover, posing as a contractor. My mission there had been quite successful and the letter said so.

Sluggo summoned me into his office and said in words to the effect, "How could you have done this? I'm surprised because I have been told you were unworthy of difficult assignments."

I looked him square in the eye and replied, "Maybe somebody was wrong."

He gave me the letter, without congratulatory remarks and I went back to work.

I vowed to never approach the ladder again, but was determined to show the bastards what an "unworthy" agent could do.

OK, enough of office politics for now. All of this will have greater meaning later including more about Snake and Sluggo, but there are other pertinent events that must first be told.

At the Lower Rung

By the time I secured my desk in the Counterintelligence squad, I was known as a senior agent. I had been promoted as far as possible without going to Washington D.C. I was again happy after several years of frustration and stress. I was still a member of the emergency reactive team, the hostage negotiator, and occasional police instructor in schools and academies that I preferred. In many respects I was very lucky. I seemed to have a guardian angel that placed me in just the right place at the right time. For example, most agents work for years, hoping to find and arrest a criminal on the FBI's most wanted list. I was lucky enough to arrest three of them, (always with the help of co-workers.) One we had to work for, the other two nearly fell in my lap. I was fortunate to be the sole negotiator that negotiated three airline hijackings, which are the prize event for a negotiator. Several other hostage situations presented several memorable experiences. These are all stories for another time, but a few can be captured within short summaries.

The first airline hijacking became less tense after I convinced the hijacker to release all passengers and crew. However the Captain (pilot) began sympathizing with his captor, a young man about the age of his son. The Captain took over the microphone and became the spokesman for the hijacker;

mainly because he thought we would harm the young man in the final moments of the ordeal. With only the Captain and the hijacker on the plane, I told the Captain to tell the Hijacker to walk off the plane alone, and leave the pilot in the cockpit. The Captain replied, "Well, no! What's he got to gain by that?"

A second incident found me and another negotiator huddled in a mechanical building at the end of the Portland Airport Runway, talking to a hijacker through the ground to airline attendant telephone. The hijacker was very verbally abusive to the passengers and crew, threatening to explode a bomb he claimed to have in a shoebox. I kept him on the phone while my friend Paul and another agent entered the cockpit through the forward windows. I knew they had the "green light" to forcefully intervene if they had the chance. I was pressing the hijacker to give me the details of his bomb. When he said, "I am shielded", I knew that he was not too bright and was faking the explosive. I felt triumphant and asked him to repeat his statement for clarity and assurance. Just as he spoke I heard a "bang"! It was one fatal shot from the agent with Paul.

The third incident occurred at the Hillsboro Oregon airport. An alcoholic hijacked a commuter plane in southern Oregon, mostly for sympathy and possibly hoping we would end his life. I began negotiating with him about 9:00 PM and worked until after 3:00AM before he surrendered. His alcohol rendered him ineffective and all the passengers and crew eventually ran down the ramp to safety. As they were running away from him he shouted, "Come back you #$%&s, damn you are in trouble with me now." Of course they continued to flee leaving him in solitude.

I continued to talk with him, reducing his anxieties and gaining his confidence by saying we would not harm him and would seek help for his problems. However Ego (remember the boss previously mentioned) grew impatient. He wanted to conclude the operation and go home. The SWAT team was outside surrounding the plane. Ego ordered the SWAT commander to bang on the sides of the plane with their rifle butts to frighten the hijacker out. Of course the loud assault on the plane fuselage brought the adrenaline back into the exhausted hijacker, destroyed the trust I had established and prolonged the episode for another two hours. The hijacker eventually ran out of the plane, straight toward some of the SWAT team. He had been telling us he had a weapon, but the team exercised great restraint. Instead of firing at his charge they just grabbed him and threw him to the ground. We then saw that he had broken his vodka bottle and faintly attempted to cut his wrists.

One of the other more remarkable hostage problems occurred when two robbers attempted to rob the Ringside restaurant and lounge in Gresham Oregon. They attempted the robbery near closing time, at midnight on a Sunday. However they didn't do their homework and failed to notice that the County Sheriff's substation was only about two blocks away. The officers responded to a silent alarm and caught the robbers still inside the restaurant.

A standoff developed with the heavily armed robbers inside with the patrons, holding them captive unless they were allowed to escape. The negotiation took 17 hours. I alternated with a county deputy negotiator who did most of the talking. His attitude was they were his fish and he wasn't going to let go of them. During a brief conversation I had, the robbers let me speak to one of the hostages. It was an important breakthrough because through the captive we could determine how many robbers were inside, what kind of weapons they had, if any injuries occurred and other significant information. I could tell by the background sounds a raucous party was in progress. The captive paused and said in a slurred thick voice, "Look buddy, right now I'm drinking an eighty dollar bottle of wine. Could you call me later?"

People do strange things under those circumstances. One guy broke out of the bar and ran to safety, leaving his wife inside to fend for herself.

It all ended with no one being injured. That's what hostage negotiators are for.

Between those brief interludes, I was learning the counterintelligence (CI) trade. For the uninitiated, CI is a self-descriptive word labeling activities that counter or oppose the intelligence gathering efforts of another, usually hostile, nation. Lumped in with that responsibility, we also investigated terrorism, both domestic (from inside the country) and from abroad.

Although it was not considered glamorous and macho, as was much of the reactive work, it was a nice change. The work was much more cerebral with less fence jumping, alley running and fugitive wrestling. The nature of the secret work was low key causing those not involved to often think we were doing very little that was of value.

For example, an investigation might indicate that a certain foreign student was acting as an intelligence agent for his home country. Arresting him would be of little value. He would be deported and his home country would send back another. It was far more valuable to befriend the student, or compromise him in some way to gain his cooperation. In counterintelligence language, the process would be called "doubling" him so that he would be a double agent or in essence switch to working for us providing information about his home country. It was a slow process, requiring hours of clandestine meetings and psychological development. It was quite rewarding to "open up" a foreign agent to the point where he would identify all of his contacts and other agents on his team. While it was personally fulfilling, there were no arrests, no announcements, and no in house recognition. We told no one of our accomplishments and kept a low profile.

If an active intelligence agent were identified, we again seldom arrested him. We countered his activities. We watched to see who he was contacting, determined where his contact worked, and learned what kind of information was being provided. In that effort the information flow could be stopped, or modified to be false, inaccurate or in some case downright damaging. (Sorry, I can't provide specific examples of that, but you get the idea.) If a person were providing an intelligence agent with the engineering details of a wing on a new fighter jet, the data could be secretly modified to the point it would leave the foreign engineers scratching their heads, wondering how the Americans ever got the darn thing to fly.

In Portland, we spent hours determining the location of dead drops, meeting houses and clandestine signals. Much of it sounds as boring as it was in real life. But a great time was had by all during active surveillance of foreign intelligence officers. The experiences would fill a book, but I'll share some of the best here.

• • •

R ussian ships routinely cruised off the west coast. They were configured as fishing vessels, but we knew that several were intelligence gathering ships, monitoring radio transmissions, military activity, and generally soaking up whatever they could.

Portland had a large shipyard for the building and repair of oceangoing vessels. The Russian ships could get permission to enter the Port for repairs and emergency supplies. Whenever a foreign ship, from certain listed countries entered the port, we were notified, especially when one of the surveillance/fishing ships entered. We were interested in the configuration of the ship, checking the length of the antennas and watching where the crew went. At times they were regulated and confined to the ship.

I contemplated the uniqueness of the job. I was tasked to gather intelligence on those who were gathering intelligence. For years we had been watching these people and taking photos of their ships from a distance, and learned not much more than arrival and departure time of certain named vessels. I began to think of it as a kid's game during a school recess. I resolved that, "If I am going to do this, then I am going to go all in and get some results."

When I received the next Russian ship notification I had a plan. I had been in the military long enough to understand service men, and especially sailors who had been on long sea duty.

We had several women in our typing pool who were outright beautiful. They were also good sports and eager to get away from their word processor to work real intelligence cases. I picked three of the best and gave them a quick training briefing.

"Tomorrow, wear something tastefully provocative, and look your prettiest…not cheap, just pretty. We will travel to the shipyard at about noon. We'll approach the vessel we are interested in, a Russian trawler, and I will introduce myself as a container broker and all three of you as my secretaries, saying that you have never been aboard a foreign ship before and would like to experience boarding a real deep sea trawler. My prediction is the captain will welcome you lustfully, as will the sailors. Have them show you as much of the ship as possible, but for God's sake, stay together and don't get separated. I will be right behind you with my camera. We'll start out by my taking a few photos of you ladies on the ship or possibly with the sailors. Then your job is to distract them while I photograph as much of the ship as possible. I particularly want to photograph the bridge, all the controls and any written material in view. I'll have two cameras on me, as you know; the second one won't be visible. So ladies, I know you can get their attention. Just keep them entertained long enough for me to do my job."

They giggled with excitement, and probably spent the rest of the day discussing what they were going to wear.

Tomorrow became today, and the young ladies were eager to play the game. They looked perfect for the job. I cautioned them again about staying together, and to keep me within screaming distance. They gasped at the comment, but were all willing volunteers.

I approached the trawler, noticing that part of the crew was already staring over the rail at my companions. The Captain was a middle aged, round faced Russian who spoke very broken English, but had an understanding vocabulary. He didn't even wait for me to complete my rehearsed introduction before he welcomed the ladies aboard. The scheme worked perfectly. The crew swarmed around the girls, who smiled and flirted with them like butterflies flitting from flower to flower. They batted their young eyes, asked questions and rewarded the lonesome sailors with fake admiration. From the very beginning I did not receive the attention of a single crewman. My camera became full of photographs that included the radio bridge, ocean charts, the wheel house, several documents written in Cyrillic and English. The crew was about to break out the vodka when I reminded the ladies that "We have a business to run and must get back." It was a fun day, even for the Russians. We learned more from that day's photographs than we had in the last several years.

We repeated that performance several times. I alternated the ladies in the typing pool giving other volunteers their chance on the counterintelligence stage. It was disappointing to all when we noticed some of the previous names were again on the trawler roster. It was fun while it lasted.

• • •

Investigations in Counterintelligence (CI) operations were very diverse. We worked closely with several companies in the technology manufacturing business. Foreign countries were constantly attempting to steal proprietary information. We helped foil plots involving economic and product espionage because it damaged our own economy.

I developed a training program for technology workers and enjoyed working with security officers of national companies. Intel Company constantly worked to keep the designs of their new computer chips secret. Even the Nike Shoe Company struggled to keep their new designs secret. It was not uncommon for a firm like Nike to host a trade show, putting on view their new styles of merchandise; and then discover that one of the samples had been stolen. Other countries would steal the sample, take it to their overseas factories and counterfeit the product. Then they sold it worldwide as if it were the original true Nike. The counterfeiters often had their copied product ready for market about the same time as the original.

I worked another similar program involving classified contracts. Throughout our area, various companies manufactured parts for defense material. For instance, a little company out in the woods might make lenses for rifle scopes and perhaps for satellite cameras, along with ordinary eyeglasses and wine bottles. The lense part of their operation would have to remain secret, and our program involved visiting these companies to assure the confidentiality was maintained. It involved frequent trips all over the northwest, through which I met many good people. It was a welcome switch from searching filthy houses for robbery loot.

One related matter had an interesting conclusion. I became aware of a German National, suspected of spying on United States defense industries. I tracked him through sensitive methods that need not be disclosed here; however it also took many hours of plain old foot work. We watched the guy for days. Finally I watched him enter an airplane charter office at the airport. I happened to know personnel within the office, so after the suspect left I made an inquiry. The purpose of the suspects' visit was to charter one and maybe two flights over several unspecified locations in Oregon and Washington for the purpose of "Photography."

First we must realize that there was no such thing as Google Earth back then. Undeveloped nations did not have effective satellite image capability. The only way of obtaining aerial photographs was to fly over the target.

The pilot was briefed so he would notice and record every location photographed. He subsequently reported that the suspect had him fly over several defense manufacturing and military buildings while he repeatedly photographed them with various lenses.

During the investigation, European intelligence agencies friendly with the US were contacted and it was determined that the suspect was a known intelligence agent of a hostile country. Better yet, Germany was attempting to put together a case wherein they could arrest and prosecute the suspect for acts of espionage in their country.

Encouraged by the European interest, I tracked and logged the activities of the suspect until he left the US a month later. I sent a report to Germany, and as usual, never learned the results.

Months later I received a teletype through FBI headquarters from Germany. The suspect had been arrested and a trial was planned in Germany. The message requested my presence as a witness for the trial. However they politely advised that although my presence would be helpful, it was not essential for successful prosecution. It was a long distance reward for the work I had done. I was thrilled.

But remember Snake? He had labeled certain people in the office unsupportive of his cause which was attaining promotion through self-aggrandizement. To maintain his weed garden, he strove to keep critics unseen, unrewarded, and at the bottom of the ladder. I as well as my boss, John, was one of those benighted people. To Snake, the thought that I could receive a subpoena to Germany, the equivalent of an expense paid vacation, was unthinkable. Through whatever contacts he had, the Germany trip was cancelled. I knew not, who could be so poor to be his friend when his true character was exposed. I accepted the rebuff, still happy to be "unworthy" and at the bottom of the ladder. I knew what I had accomplished and ignored his obloquy. Score one for Snake. The mainspring of his nature was selfishness, but "what goes around comes around."

Snake and Sluggo had zeroed in on John, because they could remove him from the supervisory position if they could get him failing at anything. However our entire squad got behind John and supported him in every way. It was easy because John was quite likeable. However he did not fit into Snake and Sluggo's mold. John was a mild mannered person who at one time had been in a seminary intending to become a priest. He changed his vocation, but not his character. Thus John did not swagger to the rhythm of Sluggo, and at times fatefully rolled his eyes out loud in disapproval. So as we worked, we collectively watched our backs: more on that later.

• • •

U nder John's supervision, and with the help of several senior agents who were competently at the bottom of the ladder, the CI program was active, inventive, and visionary. Our work was being noticed by Washington headquarters, and assistant directors appreciated being able to take credit for our work. Headquarters also had ideas of their own. A classified defense program was developed that needed to be implemented in a small number of field officers. This program fell within the "need to know" category, sometimes called "compartmental" classification. In other words, unless you were directly involved, you were to know nothing about it. John was told by Washington to assign one and only one agent to the program, and Washington would take care of the rest. Neither John nor any of the other management in Portland were briefed on the nature of the program. I met with a Washington assistant director, was schooled in the program, and was told that once a year, someone would come to Portland from FBIHQ to test me with a polygraph to determine if I had told anyone about the nature or details of the program. Just the thought of that is enough to scare a normal person, even if you don't talk in your sleep.

The work was complicated, but actually took very little of my time, so that I looked upon it as just another extra duty. However the fun of it was that Snake and Sluggo had no idea what I might be doing when I left town. It figuratively drove them nuts. Knowing their frustration I made a big deal out of it every time I disappeared for a couple of days to work on the project. Their frustration was so evident that just for fun on one occasion I honestly took personal leave (vacation time) for an entire week, but caused them to think I was out of town on the special project. They never thought to check the vacation roster. John was in my camp and went along with it.

We also broke new ground countering foreign agents.

First, let me explain in general terms, that whenever an official from a non-friendly country obtains a visa to travel in our country, they must obtain a permit through the State Department. Usually known intelligence agents are clearly marked as such, but are allowed to travel freely, except when they are at the time not on vacation and are working for their government. Then they must stay in hotels designated by our government. (The FBI) They must also submit a travel itinerary, reporting the names of the people and businesses they plan on contacting. Certain parts of our country are off limits to all foreign agents, known as restricted locations.

Ok, those were the rules, but most foreign intelligence agents cheated anywhere and every time they could. The only regulation they could not sidestep was the official notification of their presence in the country. In absence of proper notification we had the authority to arrest a foreign agent working in our country. At best we knew ahead of time, their travel plans, and had access to their lodging locations. At the worst, we had to figure it out as we traveled secluded in their midst.

Traditional practice was for us to surveille foreign agents the entire time they were in our territory. However it became a burdensome activity, in which we learned almost nothing while burning hundreds of hours and money in the process. Seattle was full of foreign agents because of Seattle's level of foreign commerce. Portland was an area approved for travel, so many ventured to Portland as a R&R side trip, or to escape Seattle's close surveillance. We decided to make some changes.

First, we changed the approved location of their lodging. We knew they were all on a budget, so we designated the most expensive hotel in town as the only approved site. For a reason we cited it as being closer to downtown business and shopping as well as being safer.

Second we changed our surveillance process. We began watching them discretely, and in the absence of any suspicious activity (the nature of which I will describe later) we began open observation resulting in personal contact. It was a radical departure from international convention. Worldwide, intelligence agents were never confronted by other opposing intelligence agents and in the beginning doing so really freaked them out. It was expected that we would lurk in the shadows, denying our existence and theorize about their movements. Not in Portland, not any more.

Two Russian agents, one from the KGB, and another from the GRU (military) came to Portland for a two day visit. They stayed in their Hotel most of the morning, only departing apparently to purchase gifts of beauty products and clothing. By mid-afternoon they began walking the streets together. The only effective way of staying with people of foot, is to also go out on your feet. They walked in a grid pattern for over an hour, with no obvious purpose. We had been exposed enough times that we certainly were "made" so we arrived at a landmark decision.

I walked up to them. By now they surmised who we were. I asked, "Are you guys lost? Where do you want to go?"

The older quickly breathed a sigh of relief and said, "Jakes."

Jakes was a well know restaurant in Portland. It was nearing the dinner hour, and we were all tired. I beckoned to my surveillance team and said, "Follow us, we'll take you there."

We walked to Jakes in a group; two of them, and four of us. Once inside we sat at separate tables, but I bought them their first drink. Our waiter was badged and told to be sure our table was served before theirs, and that we had our check; ready to go before our new friends.

It worked fine. If they intended to contact anyone at Jakes, they had a problem. We continued with a close surveillance. Did I say close? As they say out West, "Boy and Howdy."

After their first drink and another one, the KGB officer rose and headed for the men's room.

I said, "I'm not going to let him go in there alone, this could be the place of a "brush" contact. (Meaning a quick exchange of physically prepared intelligence by bumping into another person.) I stood and walked into the room behind him. He proceeded to the wall urinals, and alas, there were two hanging on the wall. Unabashed, I strode up beside him, and unzipped.

He looked my way and said, "Isn't this something?" Filtering out his meaning through broken English took a couple of seconds. I wasn't sure he was referring to his anatomy, or to the situation. I speculated on the latter and agreed, with a neutral, "Yah." If I was wrong, this certainly did have the potential of really being something.

He said, "We talk later, Yah?"

I agreed, "We'll walk back with you."

The waiter did a good job, and we all left the restaurant together. Both spies were openly conversational. We talked about travel, our jobs in a benign way, and concluded by comparing our retirement systems. They lamented about the economy in Russia and expressed hope for the future. The friendlier of the two, hesitantly asked how I viewed the relationship between intelligence agencies in Russia and the U.S. I remember my comments.

"We are all playing for a team; different teams of course, usually opposing each other. Sometimes our coaches may be wrong, but we must play according to their policies if we want to stay on the team. As long as we can prevent either side from going to war, we have succeeded."

He looked at me with his round Russian face and smiled a sincere smile. The other scowled suspiciously. The conversation ended in a handshake, and I never saw him again. I have wondered about him. I thought how strange it is, to make friends with one who is supposed to be an enemy. I prefer to think of it in a positive way. Even if we never see each other again, at least we saw each other once. Did he survive to collect his retirement as I did? Would his associate report him for fraternizing with the enemy, to gain favor for himself? If so, would it be a win for my team? I hoped not, but it would depend on the attitude of the coaches: wouldn't it?

. . .

C I work granted a special kind of freedom within a much regulated agency. We had freedom to govern our own movements, to scheme against the enemy, to plot intelligent counter attacks, and to be inventive. Even though we sometimes aggressively ran our adversaries out of our territory, we necessarily spent many hours on the road. On the bright side, fewer hours were spent transcribing interviews and writing investigative reports. Our information was kept on a surveillance log, collected and turned in to a computer analyst. Our surveillance teams varied from four vehicles to eight with an airplane for "top cover." Only the special problems included top cover, but in the latter years the need was frequent.

Most of the travel activity occurred in the summer months. Foreign agents wanted to make their travel to meet submerged contacts appear like summer vacation. Each part of the world had its own format for espionage. Most of the communist countries operated in the old fashioned personal brush, dead drop, or electronic communication methods. The Chinese seldom used electronic methods and preferred personal contact. The

Muslim countries were the least sophisticated. They recruited and maintained with open visible meetings.

Since I will use the above terms randomly in composition I'll again explain their meaning. A foreign intelligence agent, will have undercover spies working for him. Information must be exchanged between the two. Assume a spy working for a missile design company steals fuel composition data used in the latest ICBM. He must provide that data to his handler, who is the foreign intelligence agent. Sometimes he also expects to be paid. Instructions must also be passed from the intelligence agent to the undercover spy concerning targets and future operations. The contacts are limited and secret so that the operation is not compromised. Again note that anything I mention here is outdated and unclassified. Methods used in the 1980's and 1990's are so obsolete an explanation and definition of each can be found on the internet or in Wikipedia. However the intelligence collection operations continue under modern methods, with occasional fallbacks onto the older simple techniques, glamorized in fiction spy novels.

A personal *brush* occurs when an agent exchanges information usually in written form by casually meeting his contact of provider in a crowd or on the street. The exchange occurs when the two brush by each other passing the material unnoticed. When done well, it is very hard to detect, thus participants must be closely watched in close quarters.

A dead drop is a location used to secretly deposit written messages. The location is used by both the spy and his handler, the agent.

Electronic communication was constantly being improved; however it was often used by communist countries in a standard format. We called it Short Range Accelerated Communication or SRAC for short. The equipment used for SRAC was usually a high frequency transmitter aimed at a compatible receiver. The high frequency of the electronic signal made it difficult to intercept by the opposition, but had the disadvantage of being line of sight transmission within a short range. To effectively direct a message, the transmitter was placed in a (now old fashioned) video camera, and pointed in the direction of the receiver. Video cameras at that time were often the size of a small box of cereal. Lenses were large making the assembled apparatus bulky. However its presence and use gave the sender an appearance of harmlessly taking scenic photographs while transmitting a message. The transmission was electronically accelerated to the extent that long messages were sent and received within only a burst of a few seconds. Again, it was difficult to detect. The use of a video camera fit nicely into the façade of touring the US on vacation.

The Asian countries often communicated with dead drops accompanied with physical signs in the area to indicate if the planned drop or perhaps personal meeting would be used. For instance, an undercover agent might place a small pyramid of rocks on the shoulder of the road in a designated geographic area to indicate a dead drop had been filled, or that he was prepared to meet his handler. Simple natural signs were used to avoid attracting attention. A myriad of signs were used; an object as plain as a stick in the road, or a bicycle with a certain type of luggage rack parked at the supermarket, or a chalk mark on a power pole. Again, it was hard for us to find and interpret the signal. How did we do it? I can only disclose some of the old ways.

First and foremost, it was important to know and anticipate the route of the intelligence agent. I will discuss how we did that later on, but first let's relive one of the typical operations.

We were notified that one of the communist bloc countries had a known intelligence agent "on vacation" who would be travelling through Oregon. His vacation route included an overnight stay and a tour of Crater Lake.

The first "Bingo" occurs with the mention of Crater Lake. Many intelligence operations that used SRAC preferred transmitting at Crater Lake. Any lake has a wide open space, across which radio signals can be transmitted. A receiving person on the opposite side can easily seclude himself and pick up the transmission. Crater Lake was particularly suitable because it had a paved road completely around its circumference to accommodate the receiver, who only needed to sit in his vehicle at a scenic turnout and accomplish his mission. We were quite familiar with the geography of Crater Lake. It was a favorite hangout of intelligence agents, causing us to be frequent visitors.

Crater Lake was a full day's travel south of Portland, so the agent's first night with us began at a motel in Beaverton, a suburb of Portland. We observed the agent and his family at the motel pool. The family consisted of two grade school aged children, and his wife. They were a normal looking European family....except! While lounging at the pool, mom carried a small point and click camera. She took several family snapshots. Dad carried a full sized video camera, which he never used. However he kept the camera by his side, never letting it out of his sight. It appeared that none the rest of the family were allowed to touch the camera. It appeared to be his most important possession, one which he did not trust to leave in the motel room, or the trunk of his car, but was never used. His inexperience betrayed him, our experience allowed us to prepare for what kind of an operation his mission would be.

Our mission would be to allow him to complete his transmission, where ever it occurred. Our accomplishment must be to observe and identify the receiver. We readied the best of our assets for another trip to Crater Lake.

Our surveillance the next morning began early. A couple of inexperienced young agents were on our surveillance crew. My early morning briefing emphasized that we would be watching a trained agent, who would exercise his trade craft, and work as hard to analyze our presence and movements as we would attempt to understand and detect his. My favorite explanation was used to emphasize the importance of this being competition between two teams, and our team had to "be on its game." Final instructions were to stay "loose" (not too close) and let him get out in front of us without us being exposed. (Made)

We disbursed around the motel, picketed so as not to leave any exit unwatched. The agent (target) loaded his family and his precious camera into his car and began his journey. His first move was to circle the parking lot, attempting to notice anyone prepared to follow him. We dodged that detection effort. He then went out the side of the motel lot onto a side street that did not necessarily lead directly to the freeway. The young lady on our team quickly dropped in behind him. The experienced guys stayed put realizing that the target was not finished "cleaning" himself. Sure enough, the target lead our lady straight into the stem of a cul-de-sac turn around. He made the U-turn and met her face to face on his way back out. He had intelligently studied a street map and burned her within the first two minutes of our journey. Frustrated by her over aggressive error, I suppressed my anger, and suggested she meet me at the motel lot.

The conversation went something like this. "Do you realize what happened?"

"Yes, I got burned."

"Exactly, and now that means he knows were are going to be with him his entire journey. We might as well climb into his trunk."

She was a tough smart agent, but tears were beginning to glisten in her eyes.

She said, "I'm sorry, I should have studied the map more."

"Look, let's just get over it. I made a mistake once. But we have to fix this and fix it quick. You don't live far from here, so go get a quick change of clothes. Wear a hat this time. Hurry back to the office and get another car. You should be able to catch us somewhere near Eugene. Have the office tell the State Police you will be running code three until you join up with our group. That way you won't be stopped for speeding. When you catch us, stay near the rear. We don't want the target to see you anywhere again today. Maybe by tomorrow, he won't recognize you. So get to it, and we'll see you in a couple hours."

I felt sorry for her. It was a hard way to learn, but like any other team; you don't win the game making mistakes. To her credit, she soon joined us, and played very well from there on.

The trip was uneventful for the rest of the way. The target booked his crew into the resort. Our team left one set of eyes on the target, while the rest of us occupied small cabins on the periphery.

The next morning the target was up early, walking round the lodge and parking lot. He glanced at his watch several times within the first hour. Bingo again! The inexperienced and anxious begin to look frequently at their watch when the time to "go operational" nears. Even with the very experienced, many of them become very nervous when it becomes time for them to go to their planned location and transmit. They pace around and keep looking at their watch, because the person receiving has been told to be at a specific location, and receive at an exact time. The other indicator was that he separated from his family. Mom had taken the kids, hiking in another direction, while the target paced around the lodge.

One of our team commented, "He looks like he is extremely frightened and apprehensive."

It was true. I thought about how he must feel. It was probably his first assignment of such magnitude. He was in a strange country. He had an important mission, to the extent he was accompanied by his wife and family, all of which was expensed by his sponsoring country. He was being closely monitored by an agency with a reputation of being among the best counter-intelligence agencies in the world. He could be arrested. If he was arrested, what would become of his wife and children? Could they apply for asylum or would they be sent home? If they were sent home without him, would they suffer for his incompetence? How would he be treated if he returned in disgrace?

I almost felt sorry for him; almost, but not quite. This was competition and I don't ever remember suiting up, or settling into the starting blocks with the intent of letting the other guy win just because he needed a ribbon. This guy's job was to do harm to, or steal from the United States of America. I intended to have a little fun with him at the expense of his obvious fear. If he had a cardiac arrest from fright, I might feel sorry enough to call 911...if I could remember the number.

We knew the time for transmission was nearing. We picketed our agents around the lake to observe any and all cars in the area at whatever time our target started "taking pictures."

At twenty minutes to nine, our target exited the lodge carrying his camera, entered his car, and drove half way around the lake to a trail head leading down to the lake shore. It was still early enough that there were few cars on the lake perimeter road. He saw me behind him, but knowing it was time for his connection, he had to decide to transmit, or to fail.

He walked, descending the trail to the lake. I made a decision of my own. All of our team was in place. We were going to identify every person who was around the lake at the specific time in question whether the target transmitted or not. So did I care whether he transmitted, or chickened out? No! This was our chance to have some fun with this obviously new kid to the business? I was free to make this a trip he would remember.

I parked my car near his, got out and began walking down the trail, about 50 yards behind him. He reached the bottom of the path, stood alone next to the lake, and checked the time on his watch. I am sure that in his intelligence school he was told that we might watch him from a distance, but we never physically approached one of them during an operation. Well not this time.

It was sandy at the bottom of the trail. I walked quietly up behind him, and within about ten feet of his back, I said quite forcefully, "Good morning." The poor guy nearly jumped out of his shoes, grabbing his precious camera just before it hit the water.

He looked palely up at me and choked out a similar greeting. Then he stood there seemingly paralyzed, unable to decide what to do next. I could almost read his mind. He had to be thinking, "How the hell am I going to be able to go back home after coming all this way, and tell them I failed." To do so would surely be the end of his career.

With an evil grin, I spoke to him one more time, slowly so that he was sure to understand. "It's almost nine o'clock. You better transmit because you are really going to look bad going home a failure." Then I turned around and walked back up the path. In the trees, forty yards or so away, I watched as he checked his watch once more, and "photographed" an area directly in front of a distant roadside view point. My team mate nearby caught the movement, used his radio and we zeroed in. We had three solid possibilities. With a quick call back to Portland, we had all three under the microscope. We'll leave our story there, other than to say the cooperating person was identified. During the late 80's we experienced at least four to five of these experiences at various locations each summer.

• • •

Another frequent operational location was along Interstate 84 where it follows the Columbia River from Umatilla all the way to Portland. Observing a road map, you will notice that the Columbia separates the states of Washington and Oregon at that location. Across the river from Oregon and Interstate 84 is Washington State Highway #14, which runs parallel to I-84 on the other side of the river. While I-84 is a 4 lane freeway, capable of being traveled at speeds of 80 to 85 miles per hour, Washington State 14 is a two lane, windy narrow string of blacktop. In spite of its inferior condition, it is frequently traveled, both by heavy trucks and tourists looking for a view away from the freeway.

There are very few bridges crossing the river to join the two highways. Once on the Washington side, many miles had to be traversed before it was possible to return to I-84. The geography made it a perfect location for secure SRAC communication. The speeding driver on the Oregon side could outrun our agents on the opposite side of the river. Once he was comfortably ahead of our team on the Washington side, he could suddenly stop and transmit his message to a strategically located receiving operative across the river on the slower traveled side. The receiving operative could get the message and move on before our agents arrived to observe or identify him. The river offered a natural security barrier, separating sender from receiver.

To identify the receiver it was necessary to have our team on both sides of the river and directly opposite of each other. However the targets could travel 80 mph on the freeway while the average speed behind trucks and tourists on the other side was only 55 mph. The speed differential made it impossible to keep up with the Oregon cars while traveling the narrow road on the Washington side. Of course that is exactly what our opponent wanted and expected. But somehow we needed to be on the Washington side with two cars reasonably opposite the targets when they stopped at turnouts on the freeway side. It was a problem, until put to the minds of a couple old farm driving boys.

With air cover, the pilot and his observer could see the entire Washington road for several miles. There were no blind corners from up above. Trucks did not block the aerial view. An astute observer with a radio could tell a driver down below if it was safe to pass. A driver with a lot of nerve could on command pass on a blind curve, around any vehicle, and proceed at high speed. With constant advisement, a steel gutted driver could maintain the same 80 mph the targets on the Oregon side were traveling. It was easy for the air observer to keep us paired up. Oh yes, and all on tires from the lowest bidder.

Here I must stop and offer a prayer for the many people I frightened to near death passing them at 75 mph around a blind corner or going up a blind hill. Many were the jaw dropping looks of complete amazement. Some I imagine are still talking, 30 years later, about some fools on Washington Highway 14, racing each other, passing on totally blind corners and hills. "Why, they could have killed us all." But it worked. The transmitting targets on the Oregon side, never imagined in their wildest dreams that we could put part of our team on the other side and keep up. Sometimes even now, I break into a pensive smile. My observing spouse will inquire, "What's so funny?"

"Oh, nothing much; I was just thinking of something I did a long time ago."

Some other little tricks involved driving at night. In this diary I have mentioned working in the dark, and the positive attitude for darkness that helped others adapt. At the age I was 25 years ago, I could see well in the darkness. We climbed Mount Hood, beginning at midnight many times. I hid in the woods and watched for extortionist payoffs in the dark and could actually see what was happening. But driving in the dark, without headlights took some adjustment. "That's stupid", you say. "Why would anyone do that?" Ahh, another campfire story.

Following another car in darkness was usually easier at night, because one could remain one or two cars behind, and appear as nothing more than another pair of lights. The lights alone bore no identity. In a temporary situation, I would reach into my bag to tricks and bring out a small transparent blue dot that could be adhered to the outside of a tail light lens. The small blue speck was usually unnoticeable in the daytime, but at night, the tail light emitted a soft purple glow. It was easy to keep track of a car with one purple tail light.

We were accustomed to following targets at night in the city. But it really presents a problem on a country road, where there is no traffic. How do you explain two or three sets of tail lights behind a paranoid driver, way out in the country?

A radical Muslim religious leader who had participated in a destructive act of terror in the east, in the company of others, traveled to Seattle, and subsequently to Portland. It was during their religious period of Ramadan, wherein they were fasting and resting in the daytime, then feasting and traveling at night. It was important to know whom the suspect (target) was contacting, and why. He traveled with several others in a seven passenger van. They of course were not required to file a travel itinerary and we had no idea where they were going.

After chasing the target around Portland for a day, they headed south, out of town, on I-5, late in the evening. We anticipated Eugene, or California would be the next stop. However, half way to Eugene, the van turned onto a gravel road to the west. We had a crisis that had to be solved immediately. We could not allow ourselves to be seen. We hoped the detour was only a short emergency bathroom stop, and sent one car tailing behind. But the van kept moving, apparently intending to take the country gravel road all the way to the next town to the west, which was Corvallis, the home of Oregon State University. Our front car dropped back and turned as if into a driveway.

He turned off his lights and soon realized he could see well enough to drive without them. Imitating his lead, the rest of us did the same, and our entire team began following the van, like a blackened out tail on a kite. One of the less experienced drivers kept stepping on her brake when she was unsure of where the road turned on a corner. She drew the wrath of several others in line, because one tap on the brake created a burst of red lights that not only blinded our group of imitation bats, but could potentially expose our presence. The only discrete way to slow down a car quickly without a brake is to downshift. It was hard on transmissions, but we tailed undisclosed in the dark for 18 miles.

In Corvallis the purpose of the trip became obvious. The cleric (target) was the guest of honor and speaker at a large gathering of men. The meeting was within a large building, surrounded by a small parking lot. The lot overflowed with cars, parked bumper to bumper. The closeness of the vehicles made reading their license plates impossible without walking up next to the car within a few inches of the plate. We needed to obtain the cyphers on those plates, all of them, and would have to walk among the cars to capture them. Why did we need to know who was attending the meeting? It was known that the cleric was an organizer of destruction. If the cleric were able to recruit only one person from the audience to his cause, we would have a starting place to sort that person out from the remaining harmless and curious. That's just the way it worked.

We reasoned that if our target and all the attendees went to the trouble of attending a meeting at 3:00 AM, they weren't going to disband soon after assembling. We posted one person near the door of the building and the rest of us went to work with pad and pencil. Meanwhile the person at the door, our sneaky little undercover girl, noticed that the entry to the building was a foyer type of small room, separated from the main part of the structure. The foyer was filled with shoes, apparently removed from the feet of the attendees. She couldn't resist the temptation, when she was struck by an idea to delay the crowd within if they should suddenly disband. She snuck into the foyer and mixed up dozens of pairs of shoes. We were well withdrawn from the building when the chaos of leaving began.

The other obvious difficulty encountered by a surveillance team is fatigue. The target had relief drivers. We did not. That same evening, after observing the group from early morning, through the night, the van and its occupants drove to California. So did we.

• • •

While our team, and others were out having all the fun, our admired supervisor, John, was fighting off the administrative attacks of Snake and Sluggo. We knew from inside information that an inspection team would be coming from Washington Headquarters for a regular operational/administrative inspection, and that John would be targeted for removal from his position. Under those conditions, any small deficiency would be magnified and used against him. We resolved to band together and defend him against all accusations. From within the squad, we formed what would forever be called "The gang of eight."

One evening, shortly before the inspection, the gang of eight, and John met at my house, in sworn secrecy. We planned our counter attack. Standard procedure would be that inspectors would interview every senior agent on the squad. All of the gang of eight were assigned a specific topic to discuss; exposing the bias and incompetence of Snake and Sluggo We equipped ourselves with certain descriptions of outstanding performance by our supervisor.

Throughout the meeting, John remained humbly silent, complacently accepting our strategy. He was too much of a gentleman to wage war. The gang of eight felt differently. We knew that if John fell, the rest of us would also be in jeopardy.

The tactic worked. We successfully defended John. Snake and Sluggo were thwarted in their removal attempt. However, even in our organization, it is difficult to keep a secret among nine people. It was also evident that John had been supported by some sort of organized effort. The word got out about the gang of eight. In most quiet discussions we were admired, but not in the head office.

Sometime after the inspection a large "bust" of a fugitive bank robber was planned in Eugene. The arrest involved the SWAT team, and members of other Eugene Law Enforcement Agencies. Neither I nor any of my squad associates were involved. We did not work the rough and tumble stuff anymore, and were glad of it. The operation was successful, but the reactive squad returned with a unusual disturbing story, that was repeated by many throughout the office.

According to the rumor, after the fugitive was arrested, he was placed leaning forward over the hood of a car to be handcuffed. During the handcuffing which was being done by one of the SWAT team members, (*ALLEGEDLY*), Sluggo walked up and fist punched the prisoner in the side of the head. This was unheard of behavior from an agent, much less from an SAC.

The agents present were even more embarrassed because the act took place in full view of officers of the other agencies. In many circles, this could have been judged as felony assault.

Again, I emphasize, I was not there, and being in disfavor of Sluggo myself, I even declined to participate in related conversations. Based on the temperament of the witnesses, I sensed that something would come of it. The agents in Eugene where the incident occurred were the most embarrassed, and some were quite verbal about it.

The expected happened. Because of the Eugene incident, and other turmoil in the office, a letter of complaint was sent to FBI Headquarters. We learned an inspection team was in route.

Sluggo then made what we thought was an incredible error. He called an all office meeting. In front of all personnel, instead of being humble, he gave a feisty denial.

The prudent action would have been to announce the pending arrival of the inspection staff, and to request the cooperation of the office to resolve the unfortunate misunderstanding. Instead he declared, "We are going to fight this lie anyway possible and clean house when it's over." No one was impressed.

The inspectors came and went. Sluggo was absolved of any wrong doing. The very agents who were so verbal in the beginning, apparently developed amnesia by the time they were interviewed. Comparing their pelted derided speech at the outset, to the encomium presented to the inspectors, a few statements had to be a rat eyed lie. It takes a strong individual to volunteer for a position at the bottom of the ladder.

We'll never know how Headquarters learned of the alleged incident but Sluggo and Snake had irreversible opinions. The blame was cast onto the gang of eight.

Not long after that, Sluggo was reassigned. The replacement SAC appeared to be an honest person, a decorated war hero, who occupied his office like a luke-warm jug of water. He was tepid toward personnel action, became a moral sand pile, and delegated most operational matters to Snake who continued his pestiferous pursuit. Marvelous!

The Last Straw

The last significant case I was assigned was decisive in my career. I was of retirement age. For the most part, I was being left alone to do the agency's work, and was happy to contribute without administrative conflict, although Snake was always prepared to strike. He had eventually been successful in demoting John from supervisor to street agent. John was devastated, and retired a short time afterward. Moral was low, but mine was not bad. I could retire any time I wanted. Snake's never ending quest to retaliate against whoever reported his and Sluggo's transgressions became a witch hunt. I resisted him by supporting the freedom of expression and rights of the individual concept, wherein if an honest person witnesses a perceived wrong, that person has the right, in fact has the duty, to report that wrong so that it may be investigated and corrected, or be proved invalid. The juvenile idea that the "whistle blower" should be punished, and the villains cajoled, was not in my conscience acceptable. I openly stated that of all agencies in America, we should be able to tolerate and understand the need for internal examination, and favorably respond to investigations of alleged wrong doing. My attitude only served to intensify the spotlight from no more than a salaried ass.

A seldom investigated violation in the Portland Division was civil rights. It was unusual to have a civil rights violation alleging anything other than some sort of police brutality or police misconduct. Because of our close relationship with the police department and county sheriff departments, it was necessary to select agents to investigate civil rights violations who did not on a regular basis work closely with local law enforcement personnel. It required personnel who would be immune from accusations of granting personal favors or favoritism. The natural choice was the agents in the CI squad. Local Police did not have jurisdiction in espionage matters, and the CI squad did their thing independently. No one else wanted to work civil rights cases, so the responsibility fell on the CI squad. Marvelous! Reality was that few agents in the division had a better relationship in the area than some of us older agents who had worked with the police for, in my case, almost fifteen years. But what has reason got to do with public administration? I was assigned the most notorious and bizarre civil rights case the division had ever experienced, and which ultimately received national attention.

The squad supervisor asked me to respond to a request from Clackamas County concerning a serious child abuse case, involving a death, and possibly a civil rights violation. The situation that developed was shocking.

A summary of the problem was that a cult leader (Big L) of a religious group, most of them African Americans from Los Angeles, had settled near Clackamas with his followers. Children of the group numbered fifty-three. The group, parents included, had "showcased" the children to earn money and donations. Their claim to fame was that the children, were all supposedly super athletes, and could run marathons in record times, allegedly far superior to their contemporaries. To achieve the expected performance, the children were severely disciplined and tortured. In spite of their required athletic performance, they were poorly fed, and poorly cared for.

The incident that finally drew law enforcement attention occurred when one female child, age 12, stole a piece of zucchini from another, because she was hungry. She was beaten for the offense in front of the others, until she passed out. They draped her out a window so she could "get some air." But hanging head down through the opening, she took her last breath and died. Almost an hour later, cult members took her to the local fire department, requesting that the paramedics revive her. According to the paramedics at the station, her body was barely still warm. She was pronounced dead at the fire station.

Emergency response officials at the fire station notified the Sheriff's Department of the unusual death. Sheriff's detectives were astonished to find secluded in the residence, fifty-three children of various ages from three to fifteen. Many of the children appeared to be abused. The officers were overwhelmed with the responsibility of removing the fifty-three children from the residence. They all had to be transported to protective custody, somewhere.

Connie, the female deputy with whom I subsequently worked with for two years, called a commercial tour bus. The children were shipped to Clackamas County Children's Services, who were in turn overwhelmed.

The county pleaded with me to assist them with the investigation, on the basis that the civil rights of the children were violated. They pointed out they did not have the personnel, or resources to work this case, no matter how egregious. The

Sheriff agreed to commit two people to the case part time, for as long as it took to resolve.

Researching the law, I found that a case could perhaps be made showing that the children were being held in "involuntary servitude", or in simpler language, the children were held and worked as slaves, for the benefit of their captors. But that would have to be proven.

I mentioned I thought this case was bizarre. Well, picture this. My investigation objective was to show that a black minister of a black church, along with many of the parents of the children in his group, held fifty-three kids against their will, virtually in slavery, forcing them to perform strenuous physical acts; and further, while forcing this physical performance inflicted punishment severe enough to cause the death of one child, and injuries to others. In addition to all of that, I had to show that the cult benefited monetarily from the servitude of the children.

The newspapers and TV stations got the story by monitoring police radios, and in a short time the appalling behavior of the group was getting national coverage. Civil rights cases are not prosecuted by local federal authorities, but are handled directly through the Department of Justice (DOJ) in Washington DC. As a result of a couple of phone calls to the DOJ, two of their civil rights attorneys boarded a plane for Oregon.

It took very little for me to convince the two ladies from the DOJ that the case merited prosecution. By then I had interviewed a small number of the children. I invited one of the DOJ attorneys to sit in on a conversation with an eight year old boy who had been punished for breaking some petty rule, such as using more than one square of toilet paper after a bowel movement.

His description was, "They beat me with a belt. It hurt so bad, I couldn't stand up no more. Cause I couldn't stand up, they tied my hands together and hung me up on a door. I guess I passed out, and when I woke up, I was surprised I was alive."

That sort of story coming from a little, loveable, well behaved boy, would certainly make one believe that several people needed prosecuting. But my jurisdiction did not involve simple or even aggravated assault. The county would prosecute those violations. But county laws would result in only punishing the few who held the belts and administered the lashes. In absence of federal involvement, all the other conspirators would go free when in fact they had participated in the overall slavery of the group for at least two years. It was a mountain that needed climbing, but proving involuntary servitude was going to be difficult.

Jean was assigned to work with me. I needed another agent, especially a female to interview the many young girls who were victims. Jean developed a special rapport with the kids, and presented herself as non-threatening to the adults. She worked hard, contributed great ideas for the management of the many witnesses and was a great partner during the entire two years it took to resolve the case. But I am getting ahead of the story.

For all the reasons mentioned above, this type of investigation had never been attempted before. It was clearly going to consume many hours of investigative time, and was not going to be something macho and glamorous to aggrandize Snake. He opined that the case was a waste of time, but was glad to have me out of his way busy with some harmless pursuit. On the other hand, he was greatly concerned that I should so often be in the company of two high level attorneys from the DOJ.

After I had been working on the case for several months, one of Snake's suck up legal advisors chided me with, "You still working with your little kiddies?"

It was presented in a manner to clearly imply that a real live macho agent would spend his time with adult crimes, and leave attending to children for women.

I grunted an unintelligible answer, and he continued with, "You'll never get even one indictment in that case."

I wouldn't let him get under my skin, but answered, "What makes you so sure?"

"It's a shitty case. You should have let the county do their job. Nobody's going to make a case against a black church for disciplining their own black kids."

In my stress reduction lessons to police I use to frequently say, "You are only as big as what you allow to upset you."

I took a deep breath and said, "I guess we'll know in time. But I'm glad it was worthy of your attention."

I walked away not allowing a rebuttal.

The kids were disbursed to foster homes in both Oregon and Los Angeles. Jean, the two county deputies and I interview them all, as well as their parents. Some of the parents were away from the cult commune in Oregon during the time of the incident. A few claimed they thought the commune was a decent church camp where their children could have a fun and athletic summer. It took many months for most of the children to suppress their fear of their former captors and candidly speak with us. Jean and I made many trips from Portland to Los Angeles, slowly making friends with the kids, and getting the truth. We conducted approximately 500 interviews in at least seven states. More than 20 FBI offices were involved with the major portion being handled by the Portland and Los Angeles offices.

How do you know you are getting the truth from an abused child? When ten or more, living in separate towns, not communicating with each other, provide corroborating detailed accounts of events, you know it must be true. Most of the parents were honest religious people, who were just ignorant of the inner workings of the cult.

I could write a book about this investigation but for the sake of decency, I will skip over the sordid behavioral details of the sadistic, adulterous, narcissistic cadre of cult leaders. Instead I will quote an unbiased account. An article in the *"Oregonian"* newspaper dated Sat. Feb. 9, 1991 states in part:

> (Court records) allege: "The children who did not want to perform, who made mistakes and who did not fully comply with the defendants orders were struck with long wooden paddles and whipped with razor straps, braided cords and rubber hoses. The children repeatedly were threatened with physical punishment and frequently were forced to watch other children being whipped and beaten. The children were required to spend large amounts of time standing in line, to remain silent for long periods of time in 'quiet drills,' and were isolated from their parents, other relatives and neighbors. The defendants, in order to exert absolute control over the children and to break the children's will and spirit, subjected them to an inadequate diet and nutrition, inadequate and overcrowded housing, inadequate schooling and systematic beatings."

It will suffice to say that it took two years to throw enough bricks into the relationships to obtain statements from the children, and confessions from the adults. Eventually, the entire cult broke apart.

One of our final interviews was with the Cult leader. He was a six foot six, former basketball player, rejected from the National Basketball Association, turned self-styled preacher. He was articulate, convincing and apparently sexually charismatic. He led a life of royalty and luxury and adulation among a flock of naive followers.

After studying his activities for more than two years, I was certain that during an interview, if left to the momentum of his own ego, he would talk himself into a conviction. However, interview preparation was extremely important. He would be expecting confrontation and conflict. We would instead greet him with respect and dignity. I anticipated he would respond with relief, and allow his own ego to describe in detail his accomplishments, which were ultimately against the law.

We did not summon him into the FBI office like a common criminal. Instead we rented a suite in the Holiday Inn Motel. We arranged for a table and comfortable chairs next to a kitchenette with water, orange juice and cola. The atmosphere was pleasant and dignified. Jean and I would be the only interrogators, with no other officials present.

"Big L" began the interview by posturing himself, including influential name dropping, and then by insulting my female partner. His exact statement was, "I didn't know you were going to bring along Sally Double O Seven." Jean bristled about to machine gun him with a retort, but after a wink from me, she smiled and the condescending statement endured for ever after. Jean had sweatshirts made, with the inscription, "In memory of Sally 007". I still have mine somewhere in my closet.

The interview went as expected. We let him talk, and talk, and talk some more. We had lunch brought in. "Big L" kept talking, and "Sally 007" kept taking notes, mostly out of "L's" view. Finally about mid-afternoon, I summarized all that he had told us; he acknowledged his own statements, not realizing he had confessed to every element of the offense being investigated. We dismissed him and celebrated. We were ready to go to court.

After two plus years, Jean and I went to Federal Grand Jury, and got indictments against the Cult leader, and eight other adults. The little girl died October 14, 1988. On Saturday Feb 9th, 1991, newspapers cheered the arrest of the cult members. Approximately two years and six months of frustrating challenges concluded with the majority of our office participating in the arrest of nine individuals we had been told we would never successfully bring to court. Snake resented our success and was reluctant to furnish assistance from his squad. But he had to; it was an office special. Again the national news outlets wrote: "FBI Director William L. Sessions said Friday in Washington, D.C. that the Portland indictment 'sends a clear message that such a degradation of human freedoms will not be tolerated. This case is particularly disturbing because of the ages of the victims."

Clackamas County successfully prosecuted four members for manslaughter. Federal trial of the others was about to begin, when in September 1991 I received yet another call from Clackamas County. "Big L" was just found dead on the floor of one of the Cult's residences.

The deputies I had been working with for the duration of the Cult case and I responded. We conducted a thorough crime scene investigation surrounding "Big L." We interviewed the cult members who found him, and from the very beginning, I thought the circumstances were very unusual.

According to the witnesses, "Big L" had been living in the house all alone. Two of the female members went to the house that morning to bring him food and found him face down on the dining room floor – dead! However, they did not call authorities until three hours after their discovery. Their excuse... they were confused about what to do.

Inspection of the scene and body failed to disclose any signs of a struggle. The kitchen was clean, except for an empty water glass by the sink. The house and body gave the appearance of the deceased being alone in the house, getting out of bed in the morning, and dying shortly afterwards. Although witnesses said he was living alone, various items of female clothing and possessions were in the house. They were not identified as belonging to anyone in particular, and were explained as items of convenience for various guests.

I would have preferred to do more investigation at the scene, however I had no jurisdiction, other than "Big L" was expected to be a witness in our pending trial. There were unexplored possibilities. Several irascible females had been indicted as a result of his testimony. Why had they not summoned authorities sooner? Why did the house look so well kept; could the women not have cleaned up a crime scene? Several witnesses might tell conflicting stories if questioned separately. Alas, I was told to leave it alone, because any wrong doing would have to be prosecuted in county court...a place where I did not belong.

I attended the autopsy of "Big L". No one wanted to observe the process, and my partner refused to go into the morgue. I had been through many such procedures and found this one quite interesting. I won't describe the event here, but must reveal that in the deceased's stomach was a strange green fluid. I suggested that the medical examiner take a sample for a toxicology report, however I did not see him do it, and wonder if he did. During the process it became clear, that the county had spent a fortune on the overall cult investigation and considered "Big L"s demise a stroke of good luck. I had different thoughts, but again, it was not my investigation, and not my call. The autopsy conclusion was that the cause of death was from "an undiagnosed diabetic condition." Many years later I still wonder about that coroner's decision, but to debate it would have to include a long discussion of "What is justice?" Hmm.

Another display of the county's ambivalence occurred with the burial of "Big L." There are regulations governing where and how persons may be buried. However cult members rented a back hoe, dug a hole in the yard in back of the residence where "Big L" was living, put him in a box and buried him in the yard. County authorities acted as though it never happened. I concluded they were fed up with the entire group.

After "Big L's" death, the cult crumbled. They were so difficult to defend, several attorneys resigned before the trial. The most difficult question I answered on the witness stand was to explain the full meaning of the Involuntary Servitude law. I say that in jest because after two years, I could recite all of its complications in my sleep. Before I began my answer, I asked the defense lawyer if he wanted a summary or "the whole thing." He said, "Give me the whole thing." I spoke several explanatory sentences and paused for a breath. The lawyer interrupted as if to ask another question. His attempt to expose me as an uninformed investigator had failed and he wanted to move on. I said, "Wait a minute; I'm not done yet." The Judge laughed and I finished the long explanation.

Sentences were given to each member, specifically directed to be without parole. Jean and I along with two other hard working prosecuting lawyers had done it.

At the conclusion of the court proceedings I received letters of commendation from officials in Washington D.C., as well as from local agencies. It was strange to be praised by so many outside of my own office, while being ignored by those within.

Stop, Stop, Stop!

Grandpa's diary leaves unmentioned a very important event which I discovered only after looking through several scrapbooks that Grandma Patty meticulously compiled. She saved volumes of news articles, along with a multitude of congratulatory and thank you letters received by Grandpa. One congratulatory letter helps explain the omission. The letter concludes with:

"Dory, wanting to be like guys like you is the reason I came into the FBI. You served capably, proudly, honorably, and always with a terrific sense of humor and self-deprecation. You should be proud of your years and of the fact that you made a difference. I wish you well in retirement."

As the letter implies, Grandpa would rather make fun of himself, than boast of his accomplishments.

In the scrapbooks I made a remarkable discovery. I found documentation confirming that Dorwin Schreuder, on March 20, 1992:

"...is awarded the Criminal Investigator of the Year Award in recognition of the exceptional performance of his duties...", by the United States Department of Justice.

Documentation of this award begins with a letter to Grandpa from FBI Assistant Director, Larry A. Potts, dated Feb 14, 1992. This was simply a congratulatory letter, or as Grandpa would say, "An attaboy."

On March 8, 1992, the Attorney General of the United States, William P. Barr, wrote to the Director of the FBI, William S. Sessions, four full paragraphs praising the work accomplished by Grandpa and his partner Jean, concerning the Civil Rights Investigation.

Another letter dated March 20, 1992 was written by the Director of the FBI, William Sessions, to the Attorney General, thanking him for his recognition and comments about Grandpa and Jean.

The next letter also dated March 20, 1992, was from Assistant Attorney General, John R. Dunne to Mr. Ernest J. Alexander, National President, Federal Investigators' Association,

Washington D.C., nominating, and confirming Grandpa as Criminal Investigator of the Year.

Two additional personal letters were written to Grandpa, one from the Director of the FBI, William Sessions, and one from Mr. Charles H. Turner, United States Attorney for the District of Oregon, both commending him for his outstanding work.

Why was none of this mentioned in the Diary? It's because, Grandpa never received the formal award. According to Grandpa, the award was kept secret from the person he refers to as Snake. However just before travel reservations were made to Washington D.C., the reward information was leaked to Snake. According to sources friendly to Grandpa, Snake was then able to get someone in FBIHQ to disapprove the award which they had already approved. Grandpa was informed by his own contacts within the Justice Department, that the withdrawal caused considerable dissention within the Department of Justice. To demonstrate their support for Grandpa, the DOJ did not nominate a replacement for the award; it was not given to anyone that year.

In Grandpa's opinion, he was not given the award because of his re-occurring conflict with Snake. Such an esteemed award would have given Grandpa Nationally recognized credibility. That level of credibility would then be dangerous to Snake if Grandpa continued his criticism.

In Grandpa's words, "It's the only award that I ever got, that I didn't get. I'm sure there's a lesson in there somewhere, but it's coming out of the wrong school."

In those same scrapbooks are a total of 15 congratulatory letters to Grandpa including praise from every FBI Director from J. E. Hoover through Louis Freeh; two letters from Assistant Directors, and many others from grateful citizens. The commendations vary from negotiating three airline hijackings, capturing three top ten fugitives, several hostage resolutions, kidnappings, and public educational accomplishments, to name a few. From my perspective, in spite of the opposition, Grandpa rose from the bottom rung to finish at the very pinnacle of the American ladder. Best of all, he got there not from the politics of "sucking up", but ascended through his values and the real work he accomplished.

At the conclusion of the almost three year investigation I was not in the mood to return to the trivia of daily survival in a politically charged environment. The witch hunt still persisted, and would as long as SNAKE reigned.

I worked a few more months in FCI and was reassigned to the reactive squad. I was burned out. I no longer saw any value in the tireless repetitions of life. I always said that when I wasn't having fun anymore I would retire. More than one friend had offered me interesting employment away from the FBI, a predilection I could no longer resist. I was struggling with an old Will Rogers saying, "*Don't let yesterday use up too much of Today.*" Yup, it was time.

The chief administrative officer in the office was a good person, and a close friend. I asked her if she could process my retirement papers in confidence, so that I could quit on short notice. She willingly accommodated my wishes. I cleaned out my desk the night before a Thursday, in the last of November 1993. The next afternoon I went to my supervisor and announced that I was retiring.

He gave me a startled look and said, "Oh my gosh, when?"

I said, "Tomorrow's my last day.

Made in the USA
Charleston, SC
02 April 2016